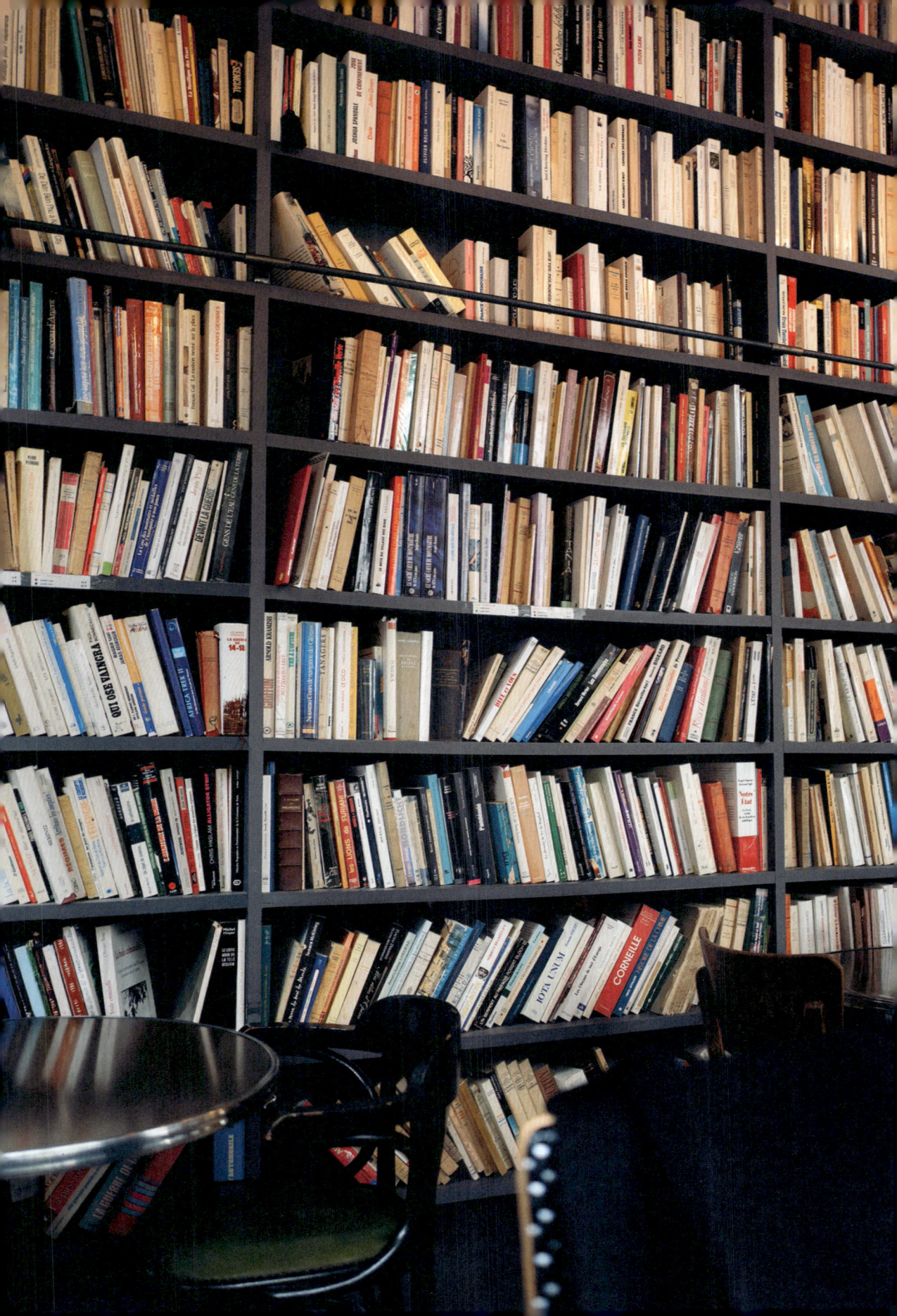

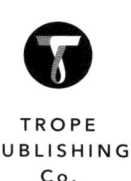

TROPE
PUBLISHING
Co.

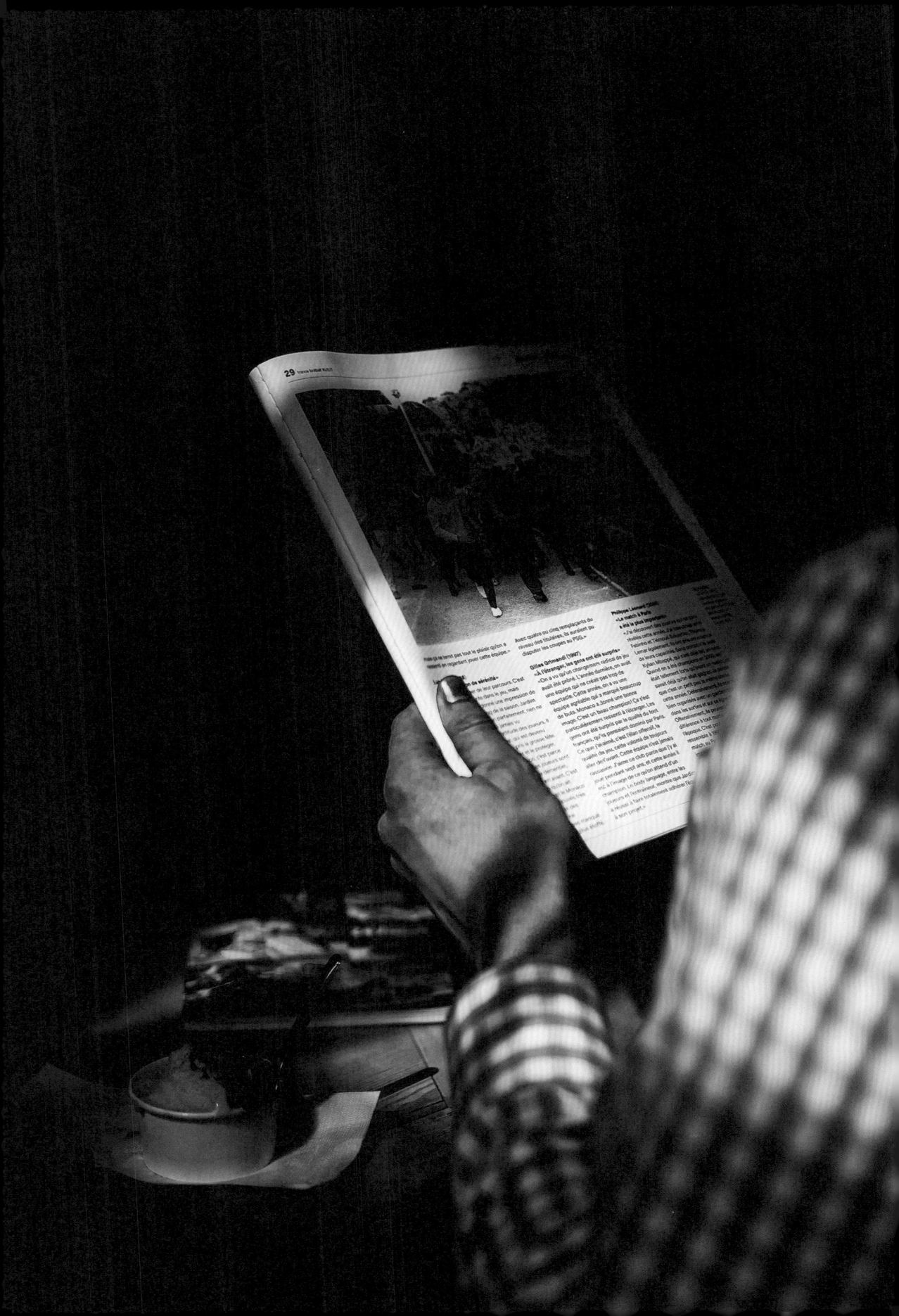

The Reader

Vol. 1

Introduction

We've always been drawn to books.

As people who work in book publishing, that likely does not come as a surprise. Reading is an intimate activity, yet it is one that we so often engage in publicly. On the daily commute via public transportation. Sitting on a park bench during a quick lunch break. Lying on the beach during a lazy day.

The images in *The Reader* share the universal nature of reading, wherever you may be. This collection features images of readers in 19 countries, from 18 talented photographers. Despite the diversity of these locations, each image portrays the deeply personal connection between a reader and the printed word.

Throughout the book you'll find essays from owners of independent bookstores throughout the United States — those important arbiters who help us readers get books into our hands. Their words on the importance of reading and the cultural impact of books continue to stick with us, and we hope they resonate with you, too. *The Reader* invites you to pause and reflect on the quiet beauty of reading, both as a solitary act and a universal human experience.

SAM LANDERS & MICHELLE FITZGERALD

Editors

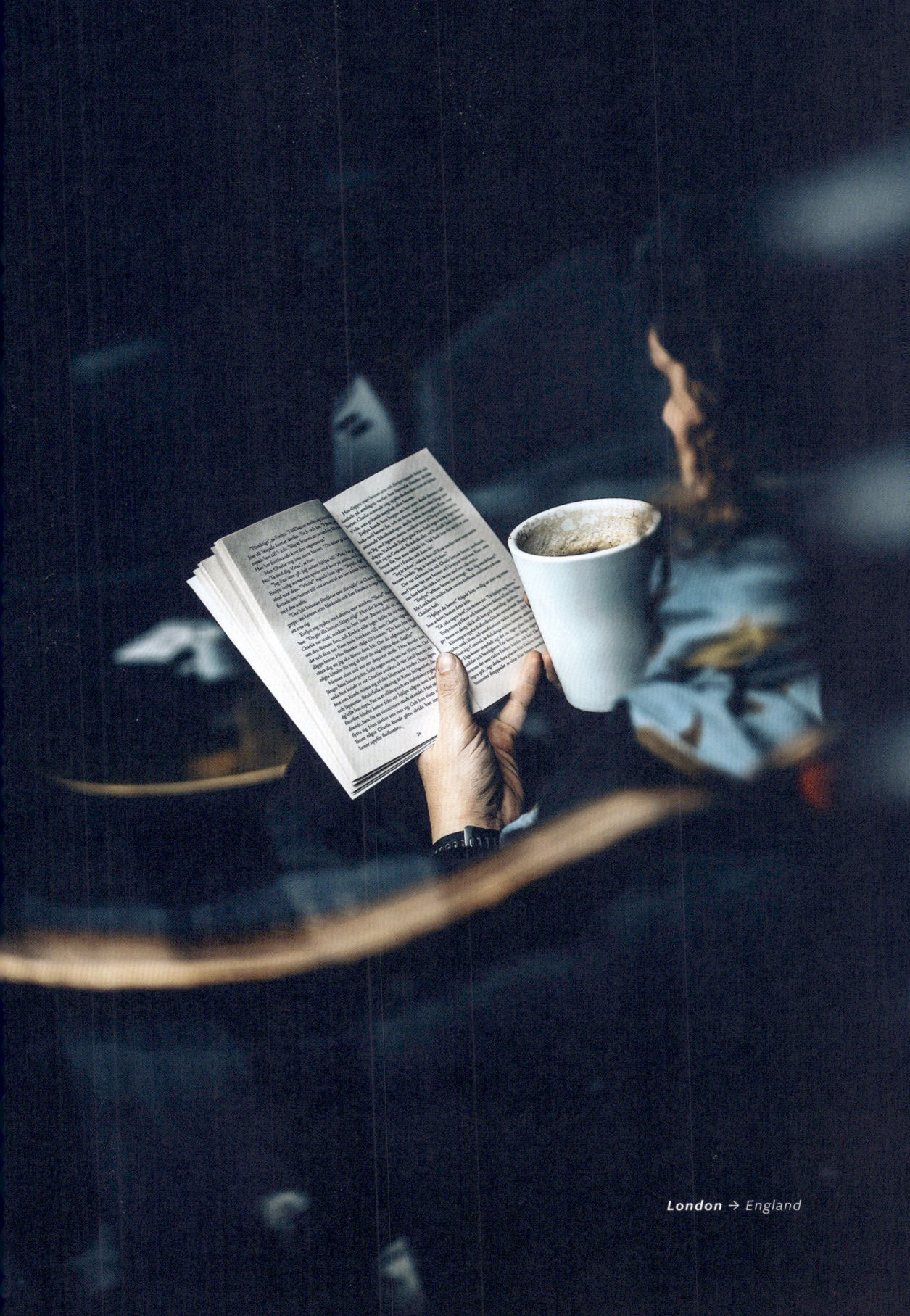

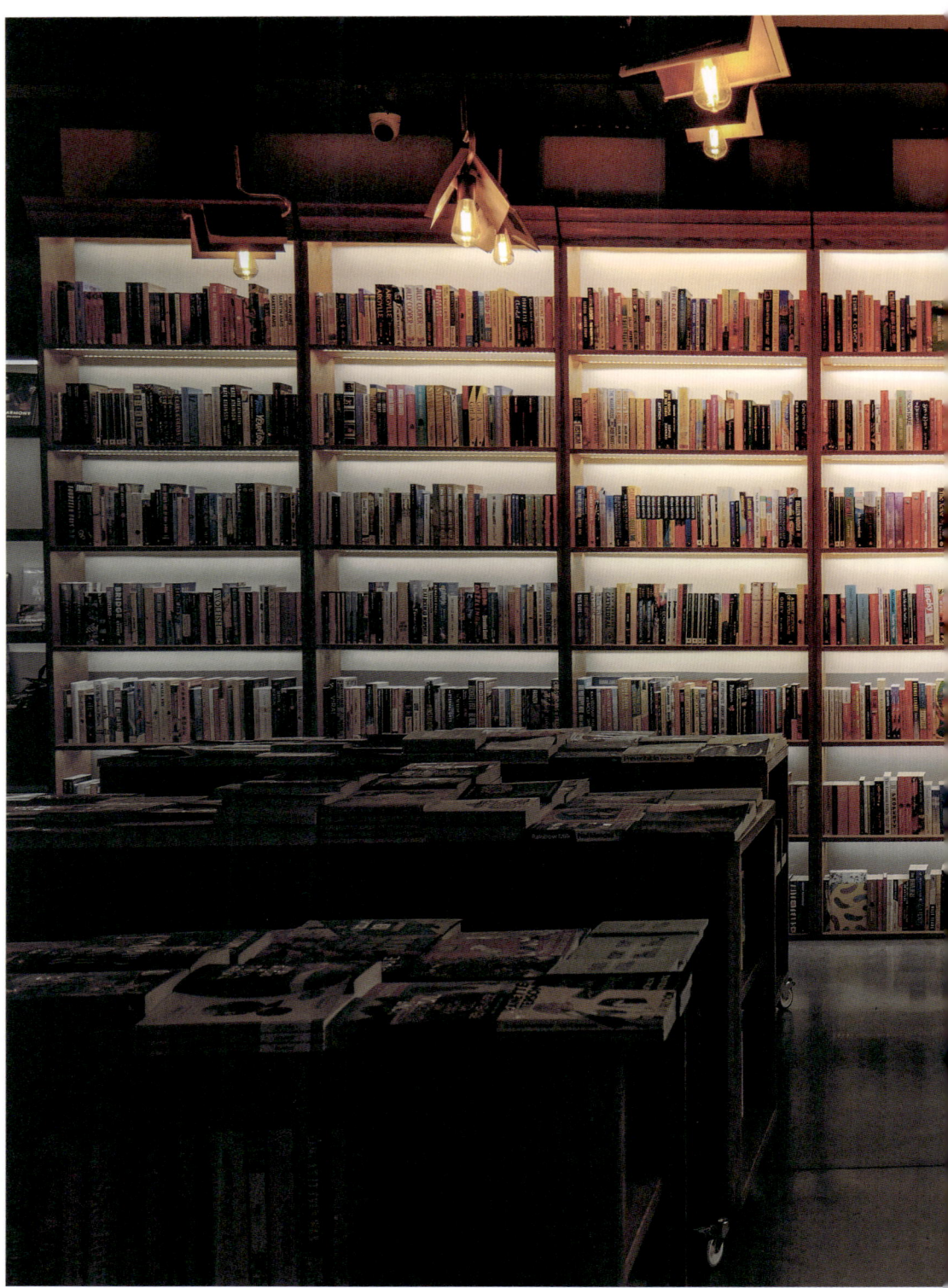

Istanbul → *Turkey*

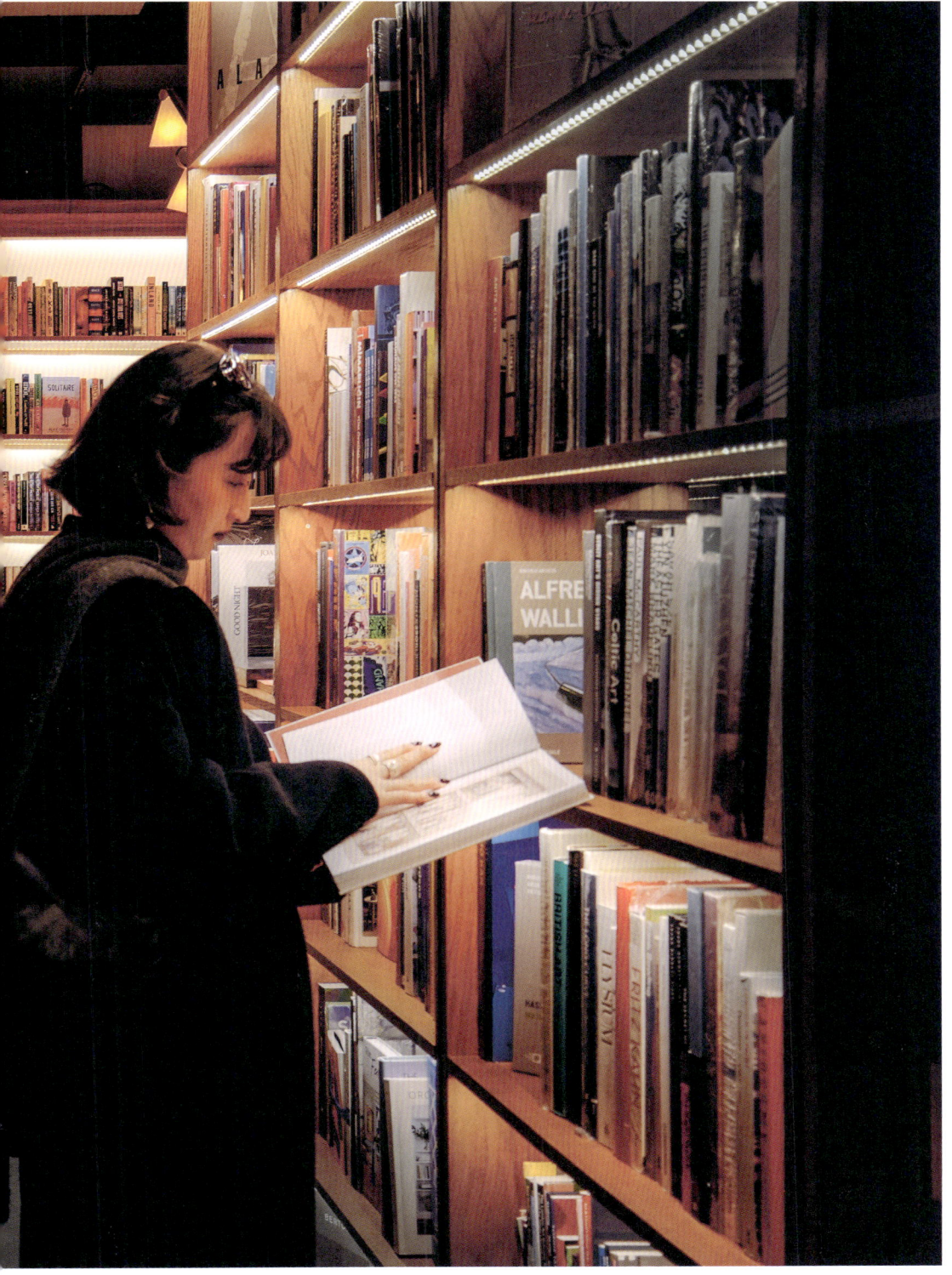

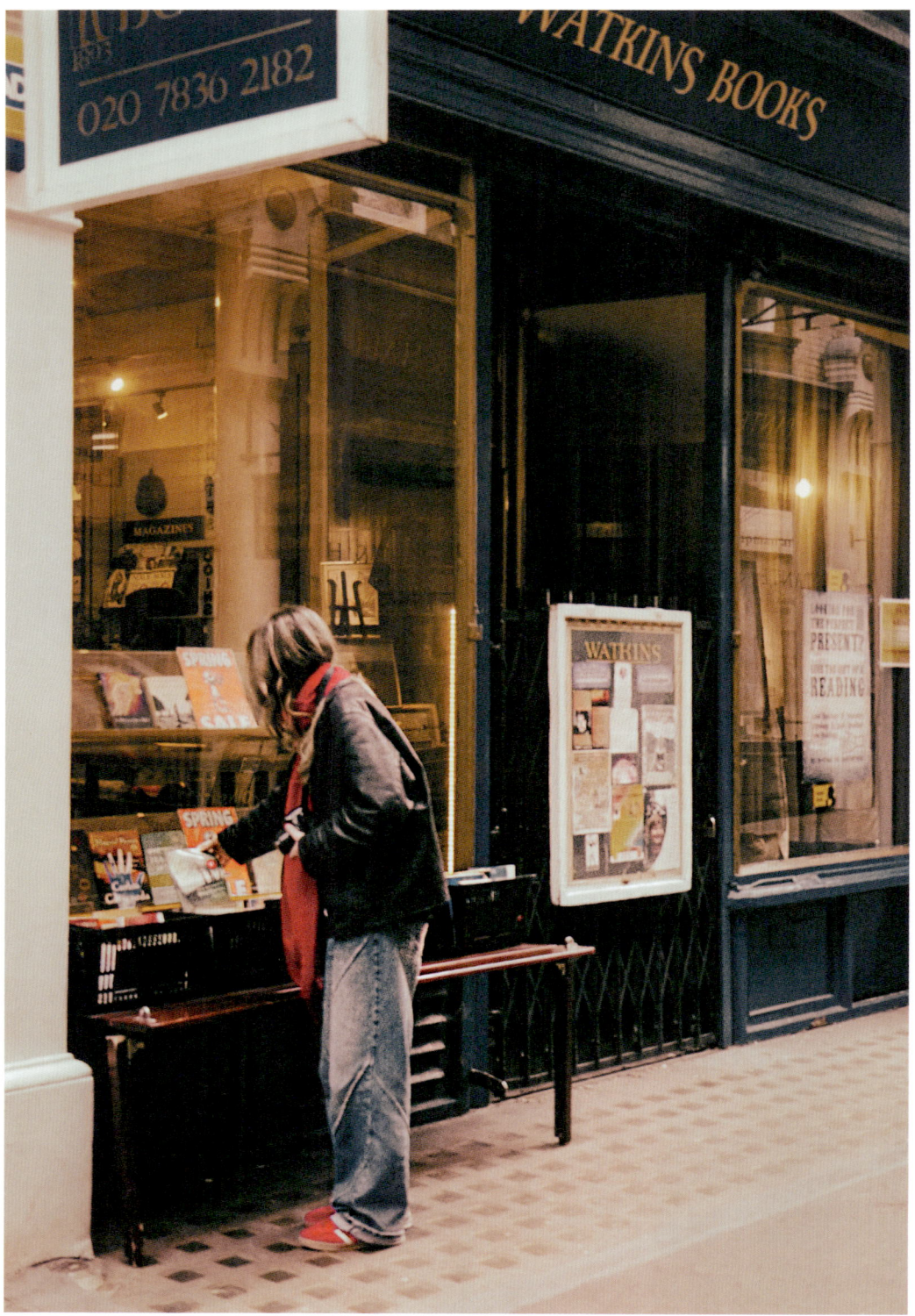

London → England

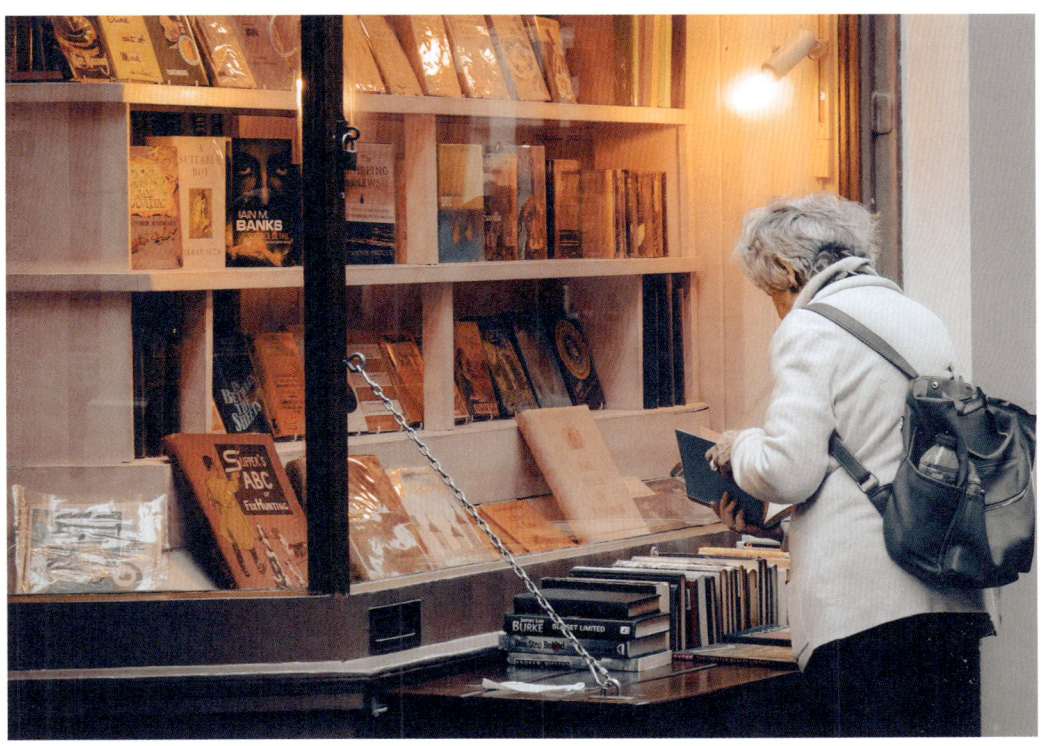

London → *England*

"You will learn most things by looking, but reading gives understanding. Reading will make you free."

PAUL RAND

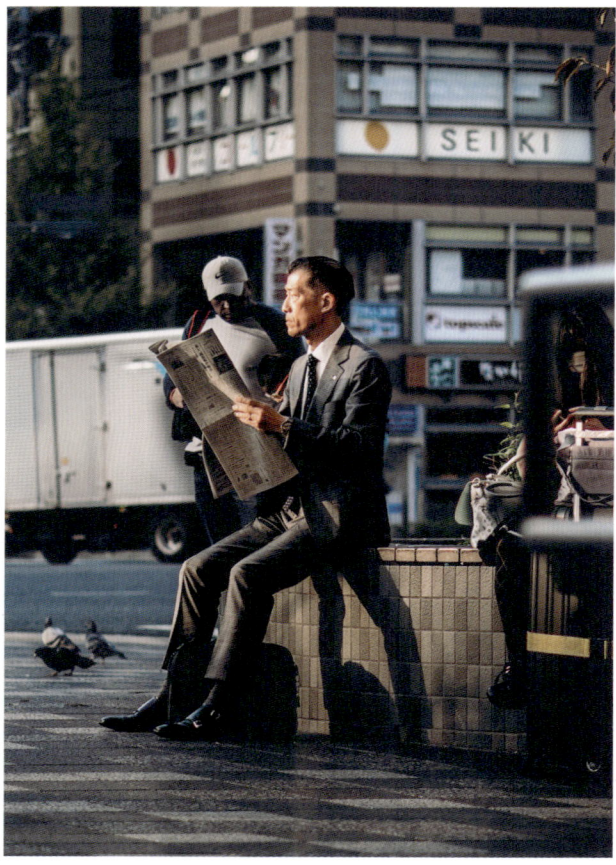

Kyoto → *Japan*

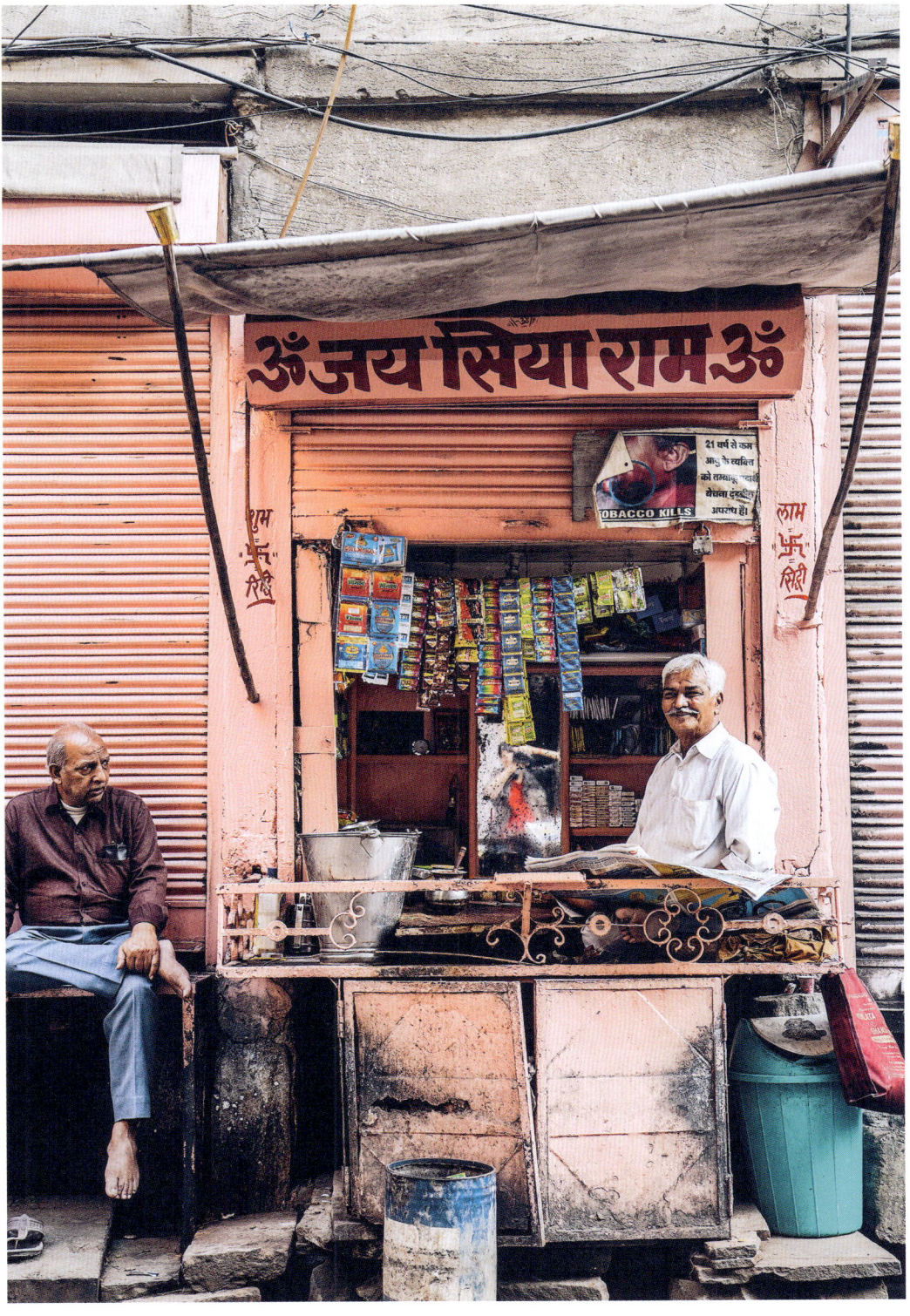

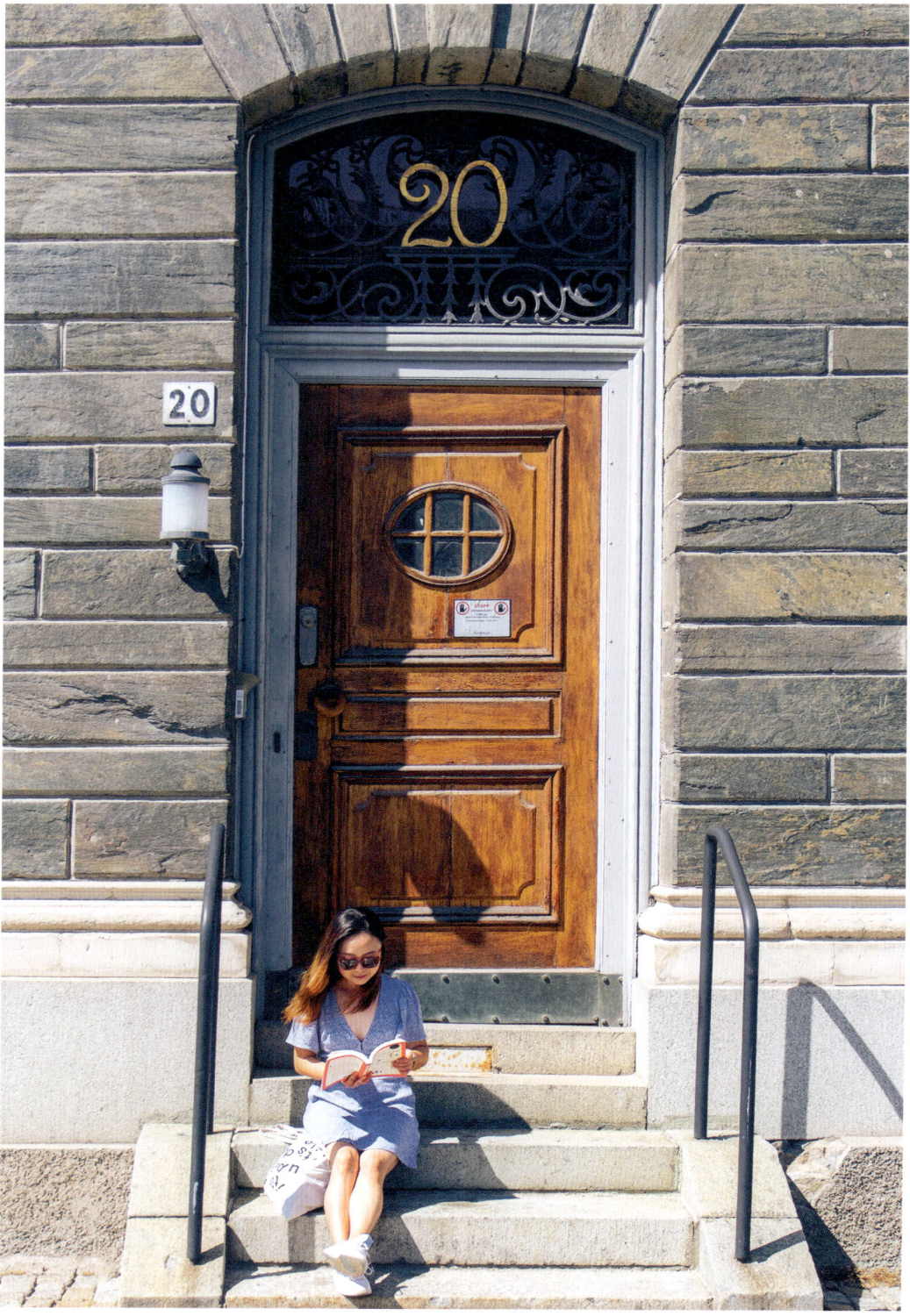

Stockholm → *Sweden*

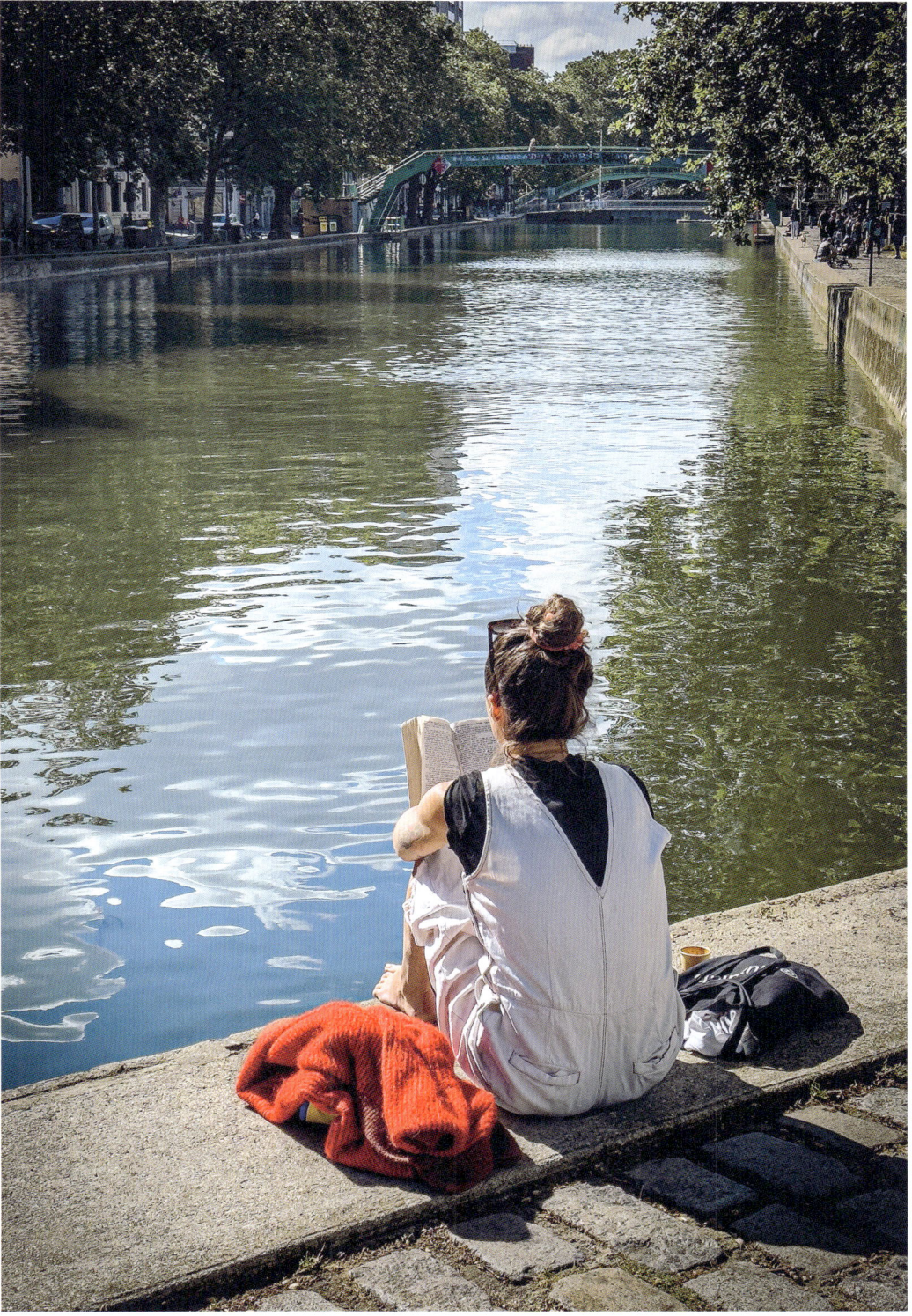

Paris → France

DAVI MARRA, *Co-Owner*
Lofty Pigeon Books → Brooklyn, New York

A book is an undepletable resource

able to cause ideas to grow in any climate, into any form, and never the same form twice. To sit and read a book is to plant a flag in your own imagination, to claim mental sovereignty without borders, and to tap into an ancient chemical reaction that allows us to sit absolutely still and understand one another.

I sat and read today, I traveled and laughed and knocked loose some pebble of memory that had been buried. I turned the pebble around in my mouth, spit it out, and scrambled back up the page to where my attention had lapsed. When I resumed reading, I was aware of some new arrangement, that there was something old now under the sun.

I sat and read. I came to a halt, got inside myself, and rolled the shutter down to close out life's din. All in my mind I animated a stranger's thoughts, using just a few dozen symbols to call from the depths of my experience, in a dance with imagination, the astonishing breadth of the human condition. I discovered a beam of light shining on an old forgotten way of living, so I kicked the door open and let my mind out to wander for a bit, to pull stuff up from the earth and chew on it. I remembered that we were meant to give meaning and assign value to the objects around us, not vice versa. We bring ourselves to books and then allow them in, a meeting rather than a consumption, even if the idea of consumption drives a lot of the publishing industry today.

I sat and read and, enraptured by the voice in my head speaking another's story, the voice coming from a place before thought and judgment, I beheld again the fragile yet unkillable thing connecting us all.

Reading books is an act of astounding intimacy, maybe the ultimate intimacy, and a resounding fuck you to the people and corporations who want to strip-mine your attention, drown your imagination in blue light and toxins, and make you forget the anti-authoritarian, anti-capitalist, world-making and world-re-making power of deep literary communion, broad literary community, and unfettered daydreaming. Please join me, take any book off the shelf that piques your interest, have a seat, and read with me for a while.

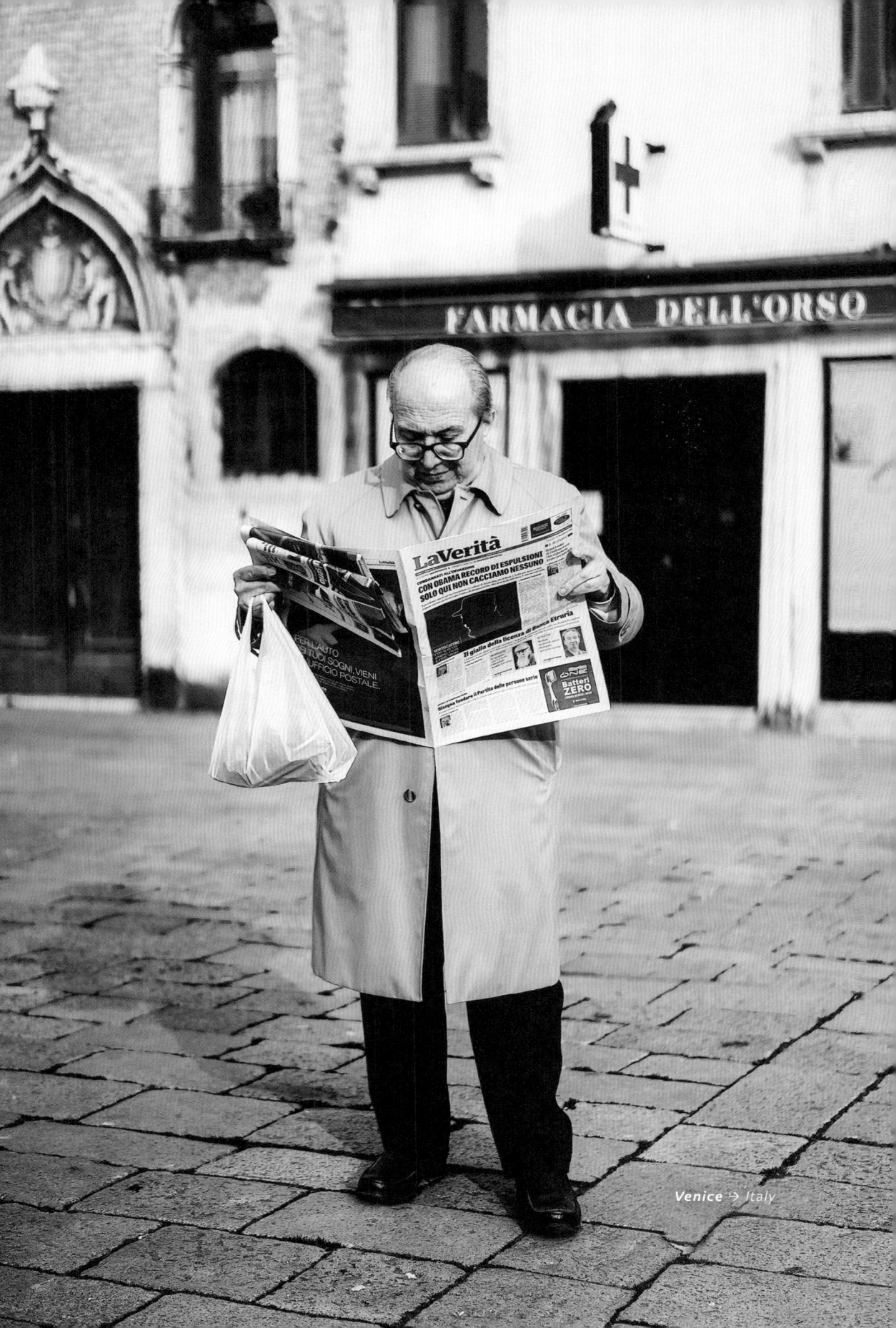

Venice → *Italy*

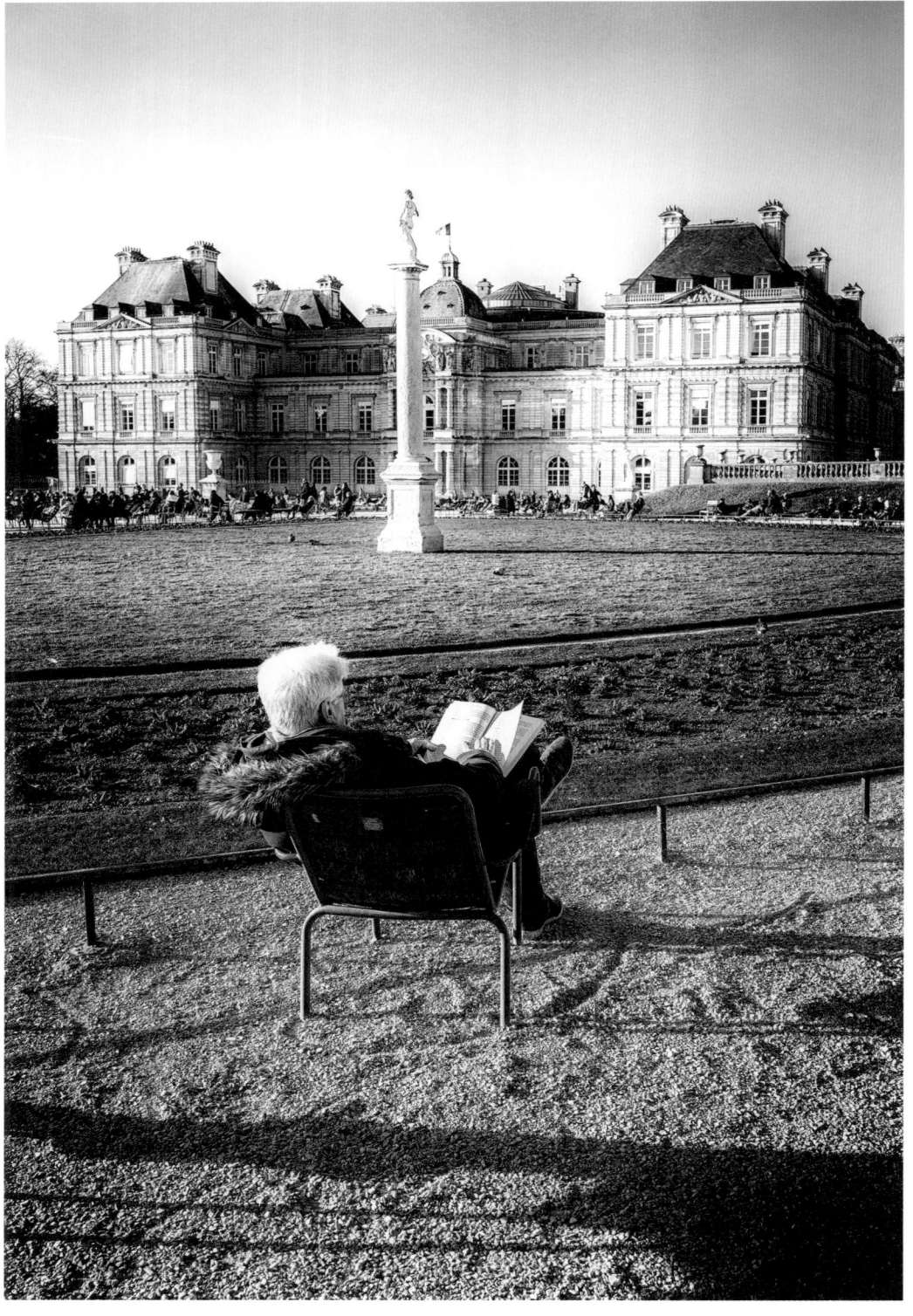

Paris → France

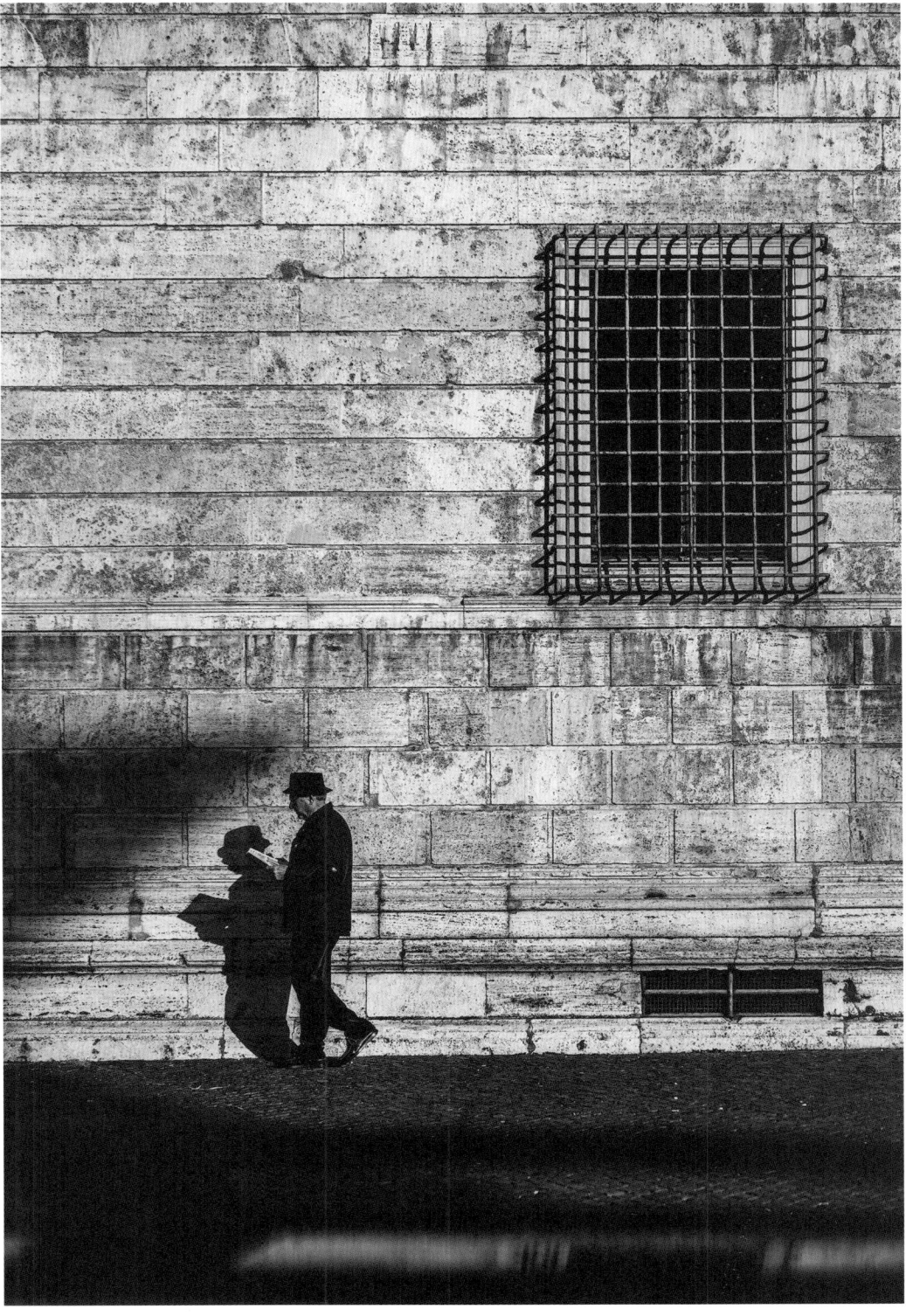

Rome → *Italy*

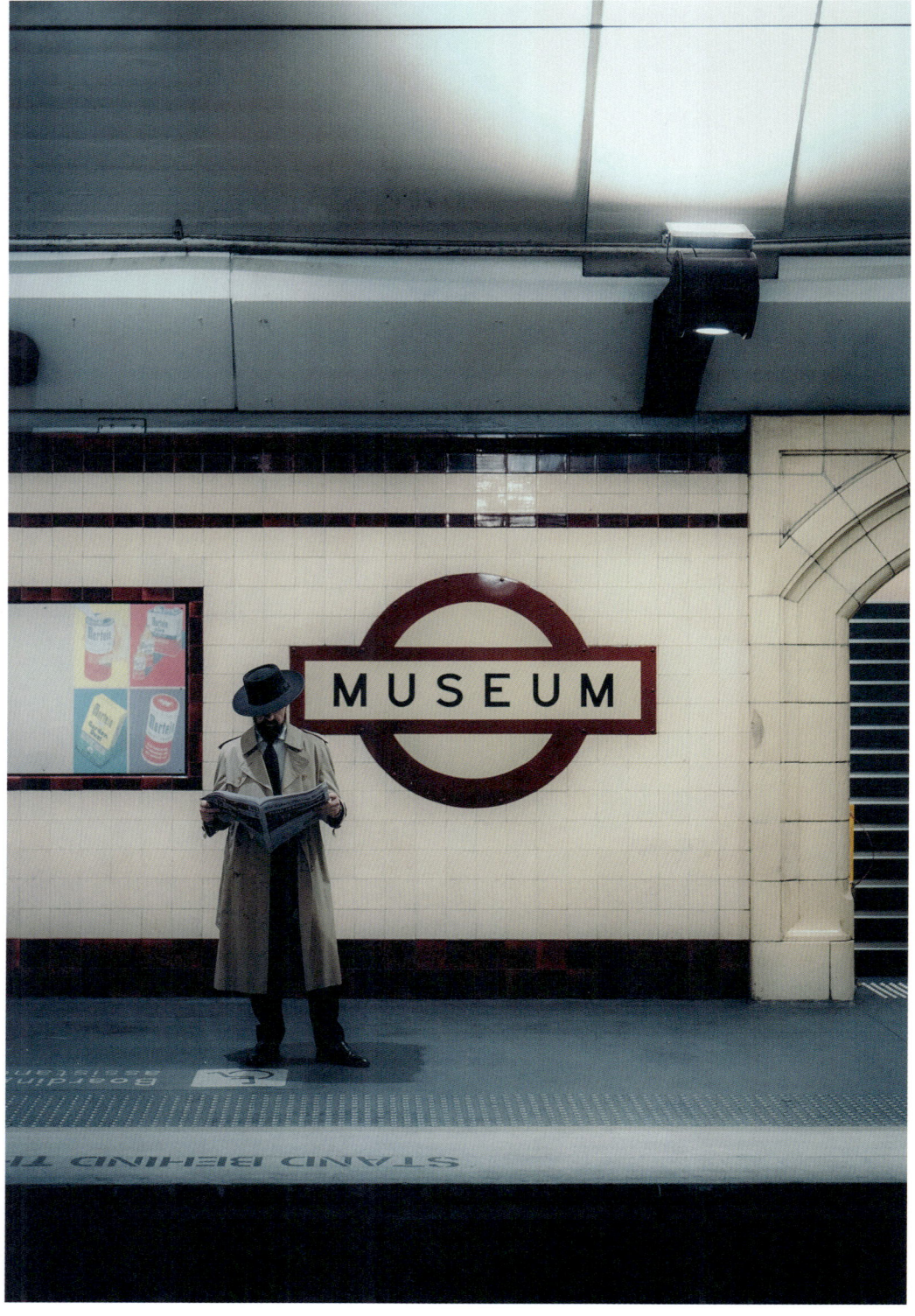

Sydney → *Australia*

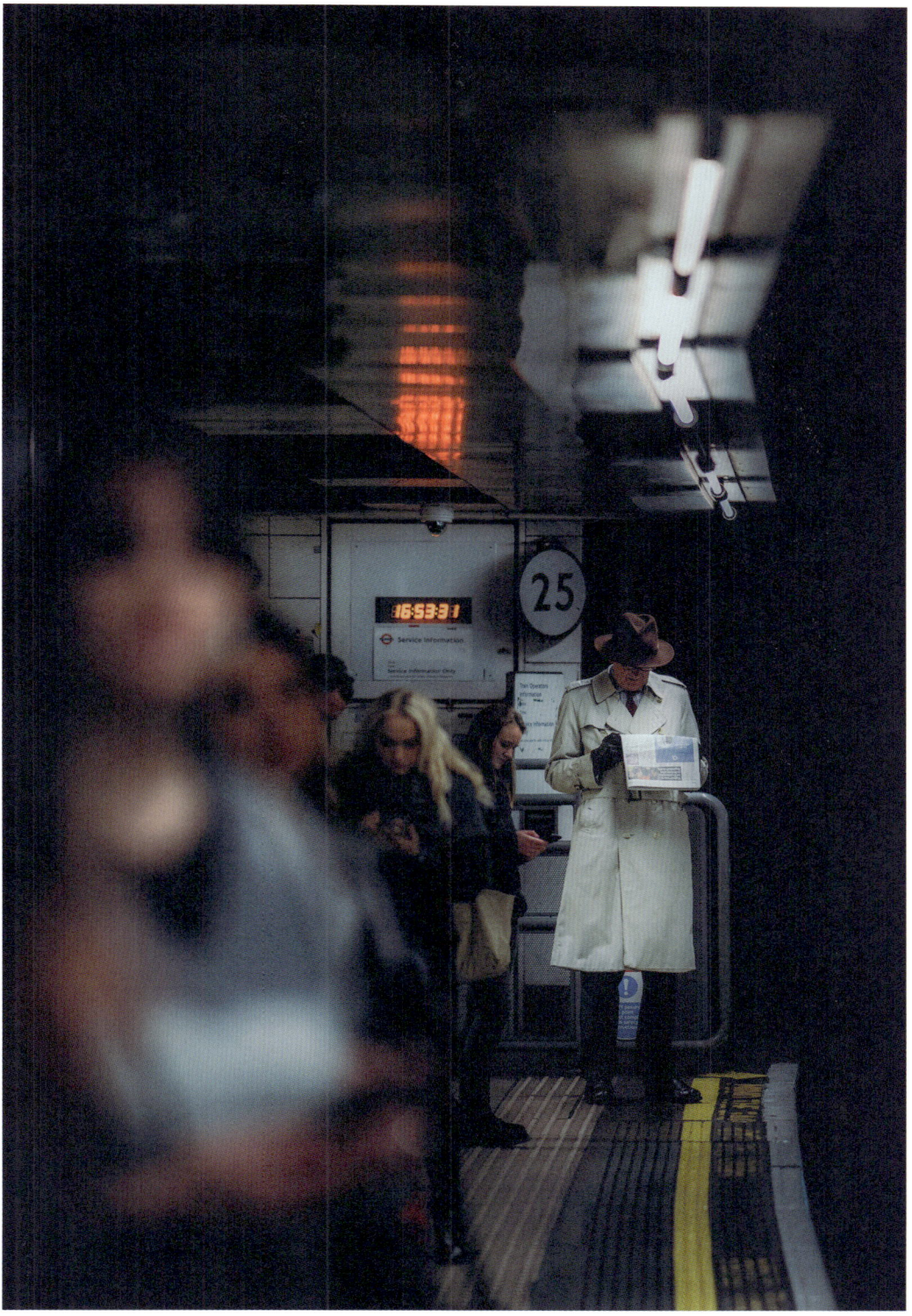

London → England

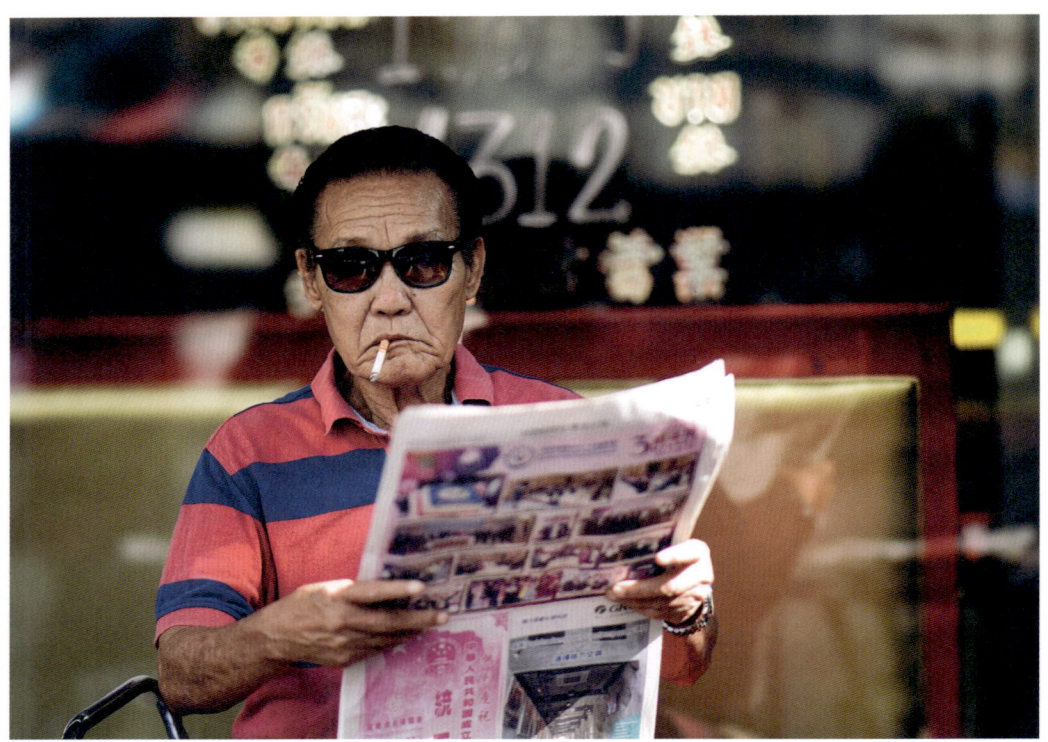

Los Angeles, California → *United States*

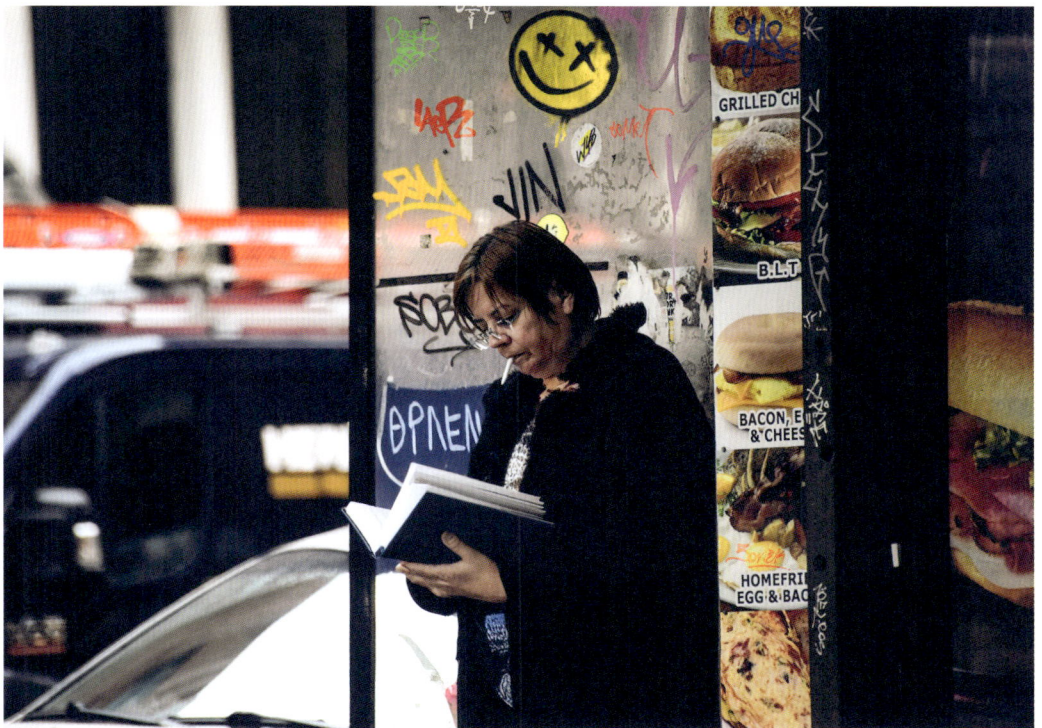

Los Angeles, California → *United States*

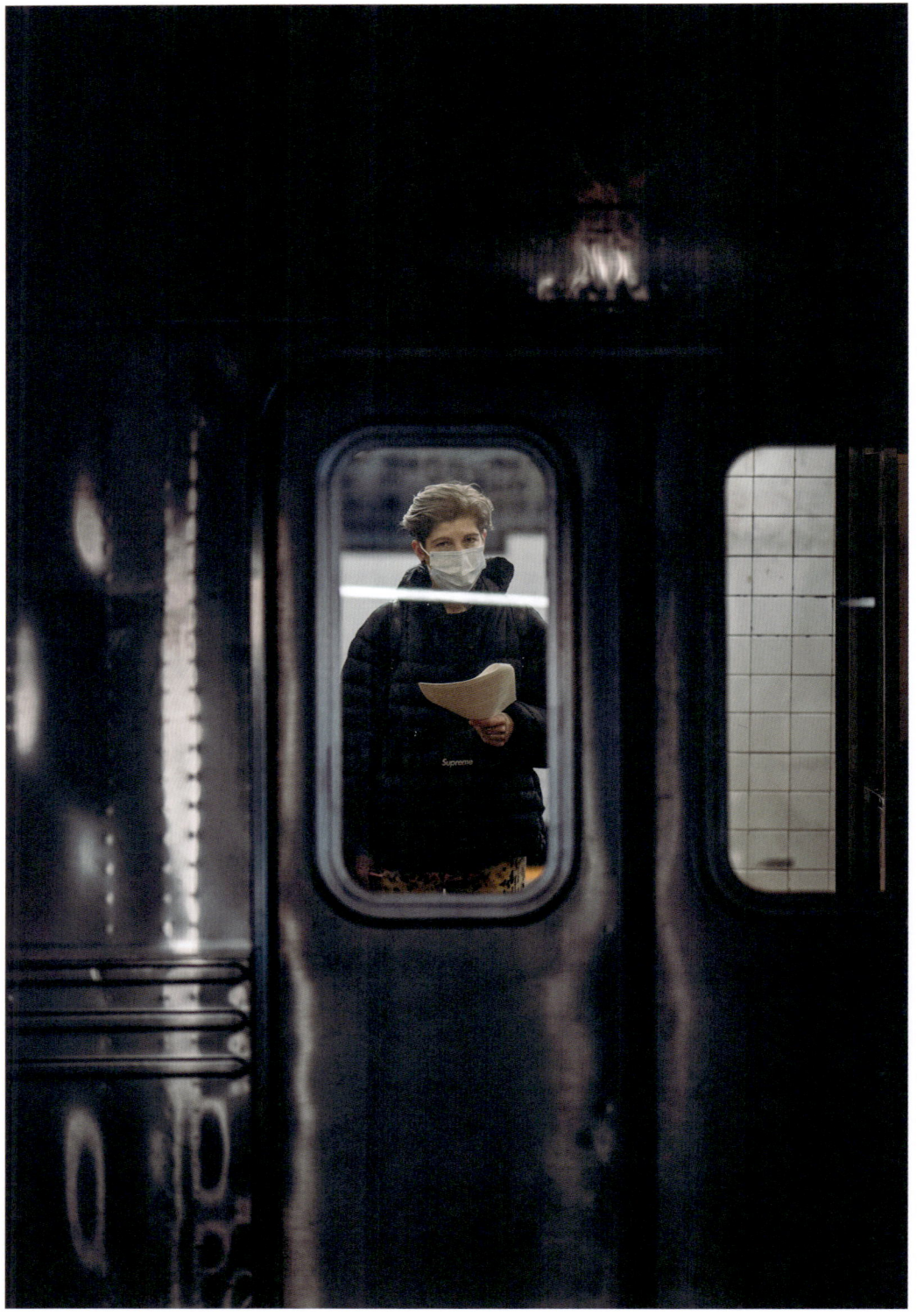

New York, New York → *United States*

"Once you learn to read, you will be forever free."
FREDERICK DOUGLASS

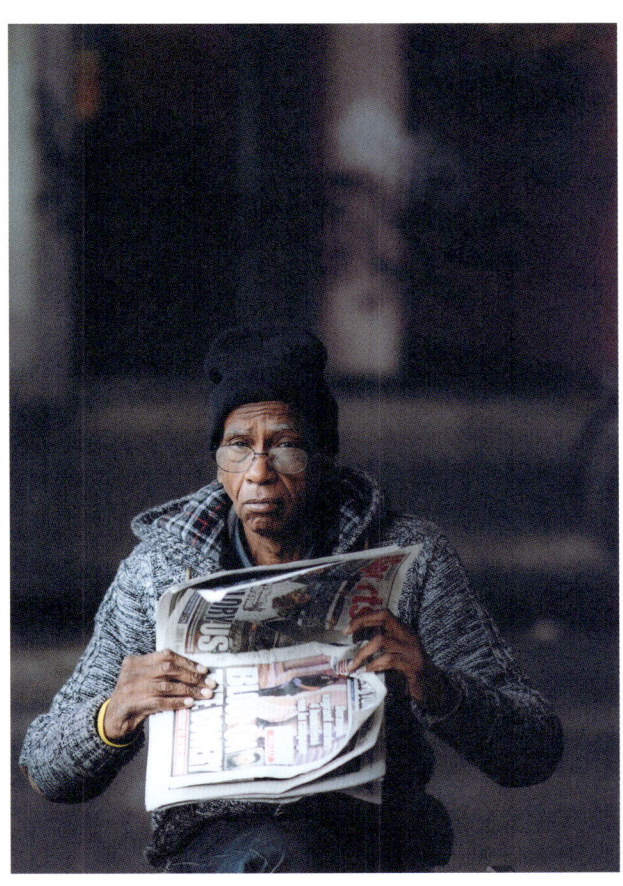

New York, New York → *United States*

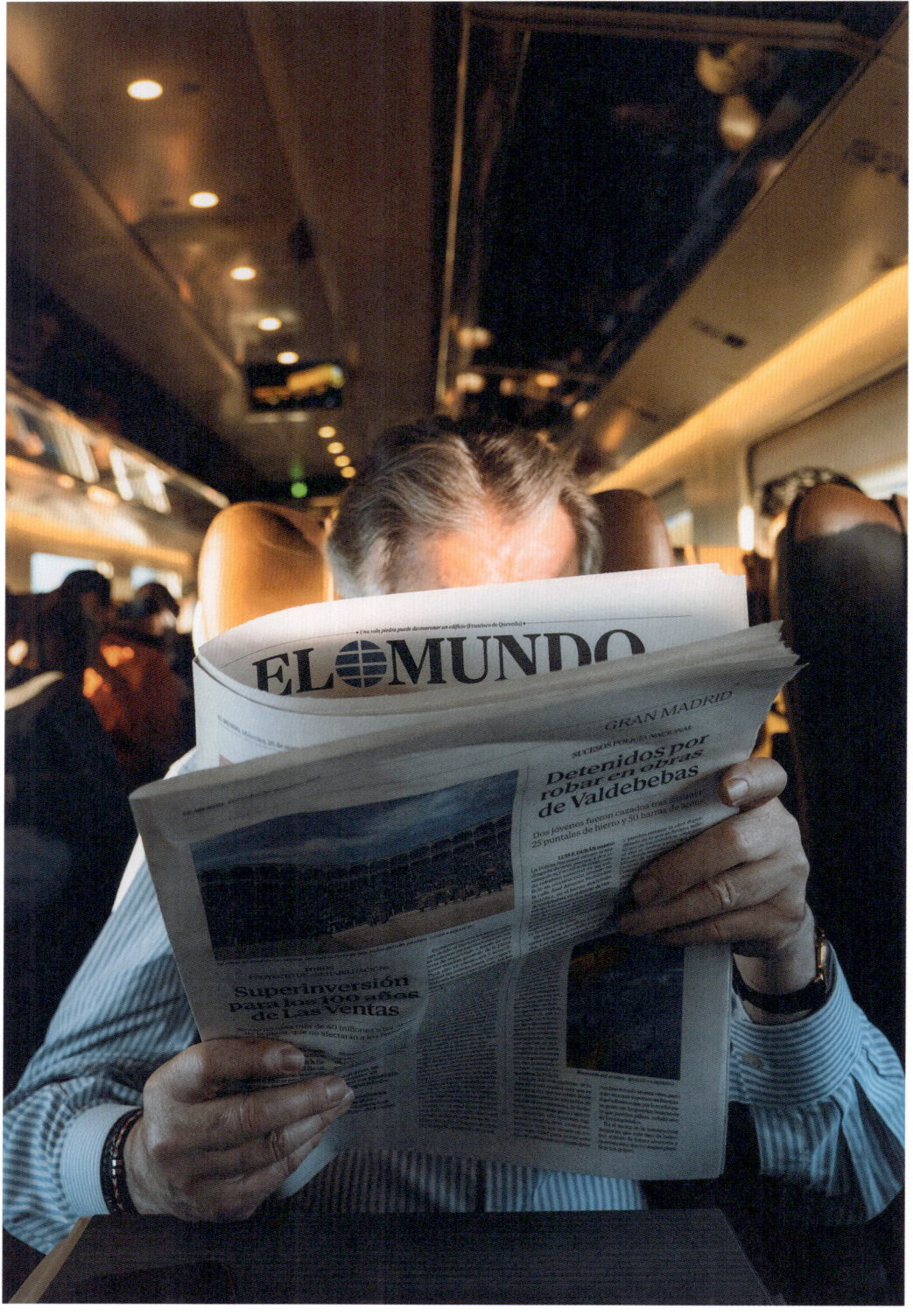

Madrid → *Spain*

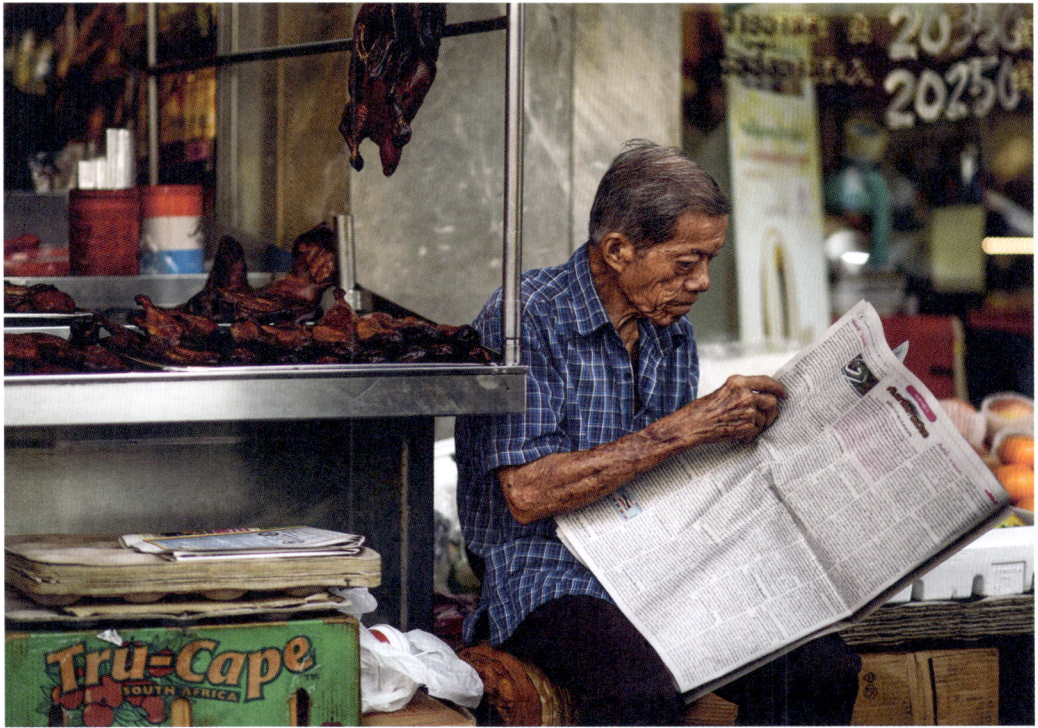

Los Angeles, California → *United States*

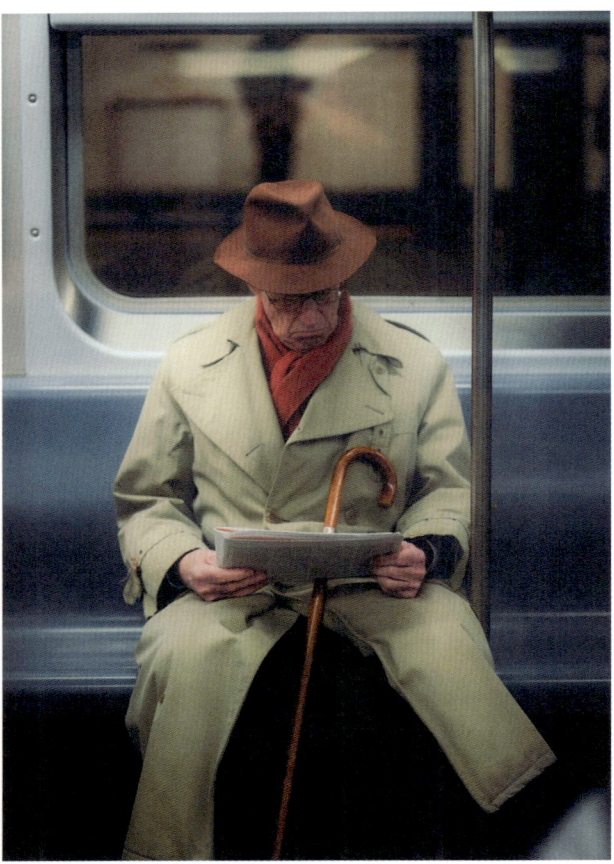

"Literature is the safe and traditional vehicle through which we learn about the world and pass on values from one generation to the next. Books save lives."

LAURIE ANDERSON

New York, New York → *United States*

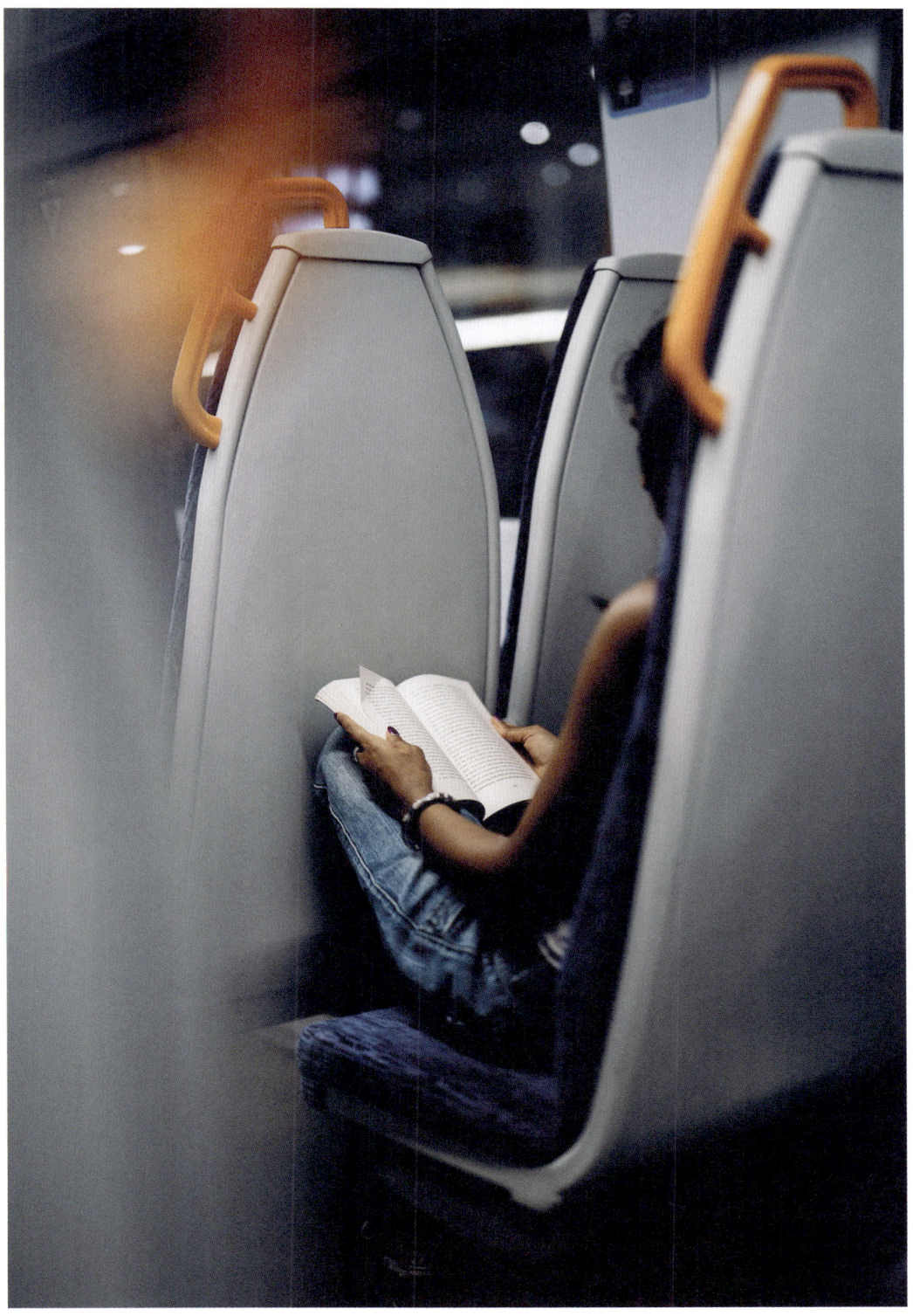

London → *England*

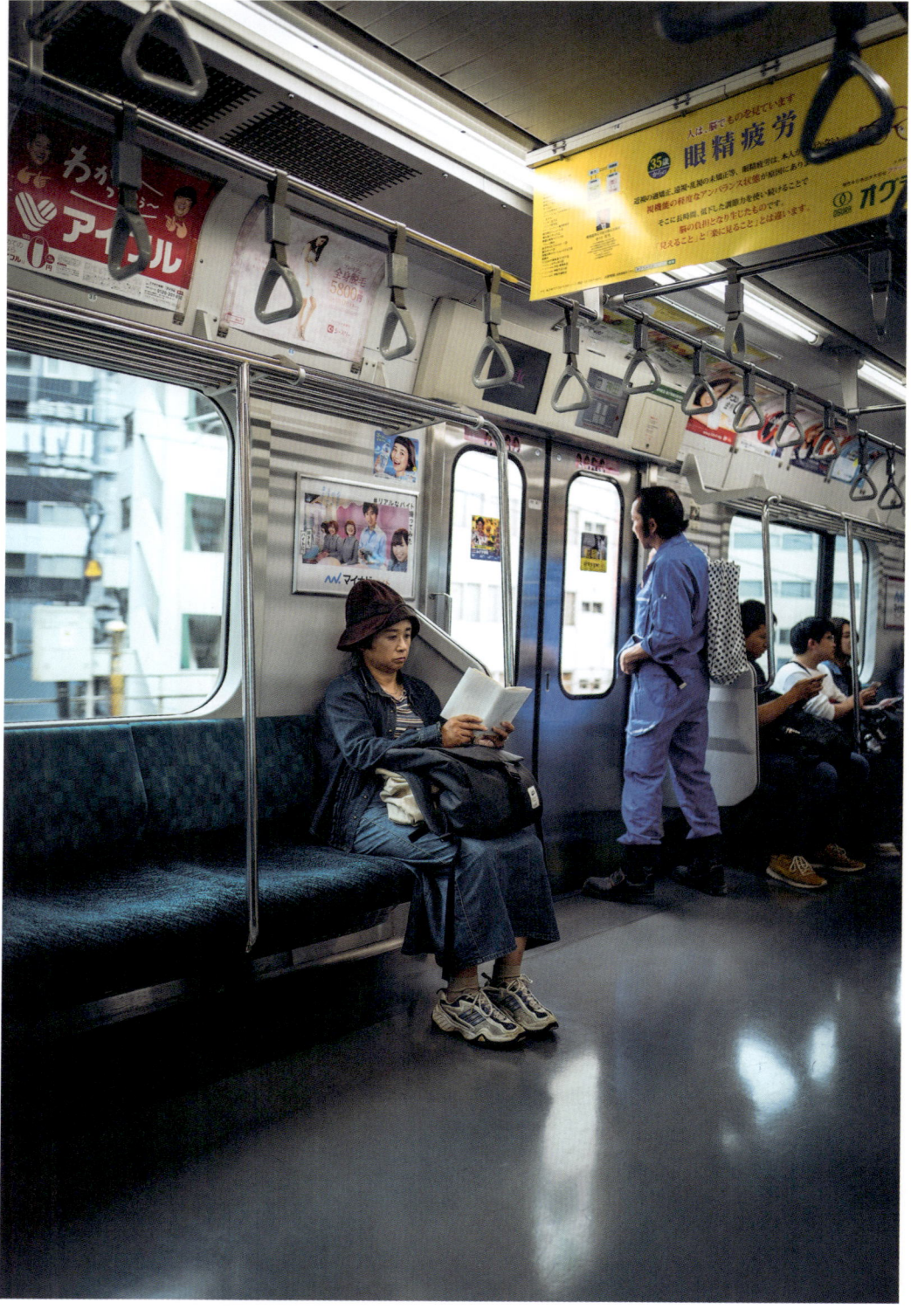

Tokyo → *Japan*

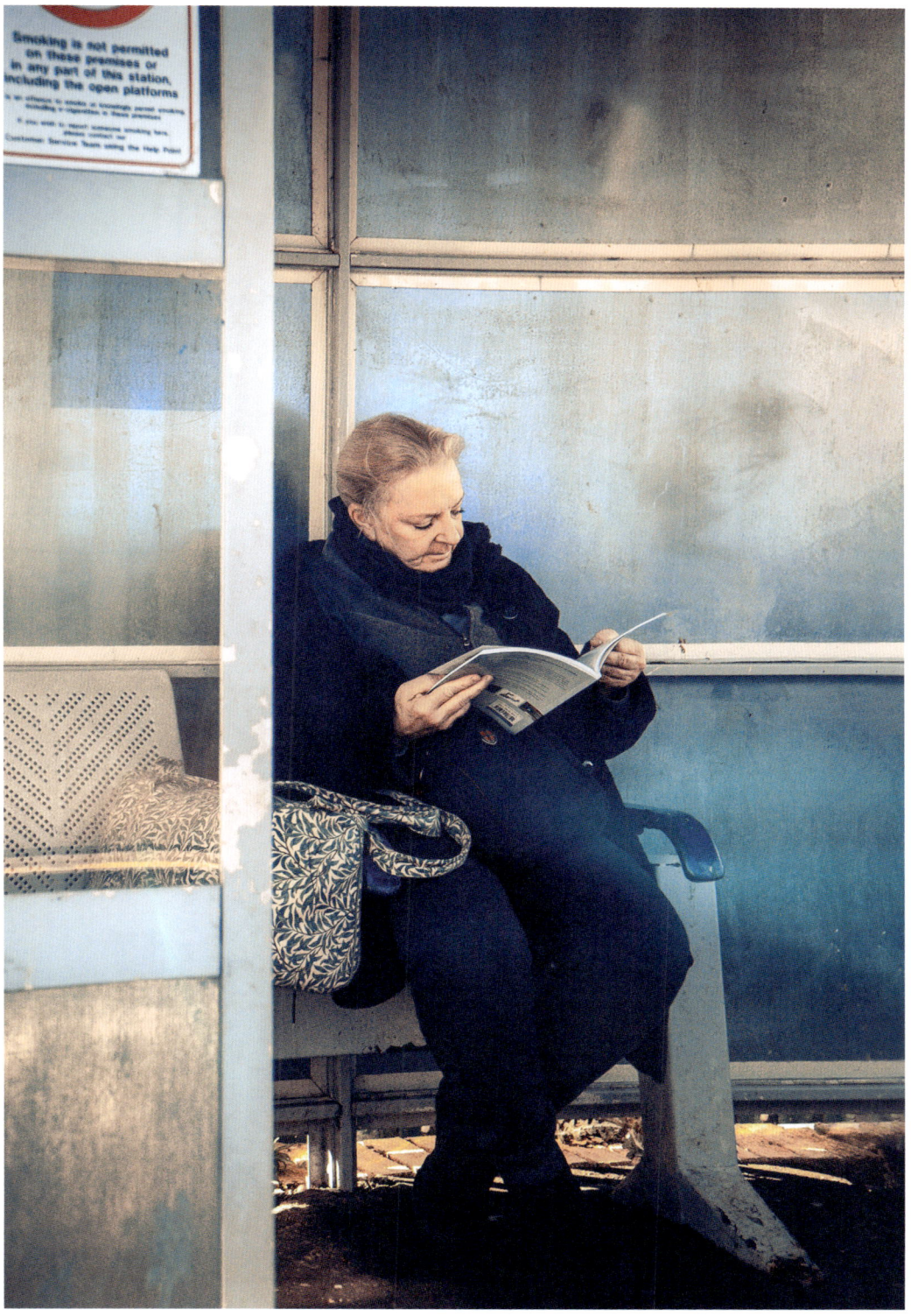

Falkirk → *Scotland*

"A great book should leave you with many experiences, and slightly exhausted at the end. You live several lives while reading."

WILLIAM STYRON

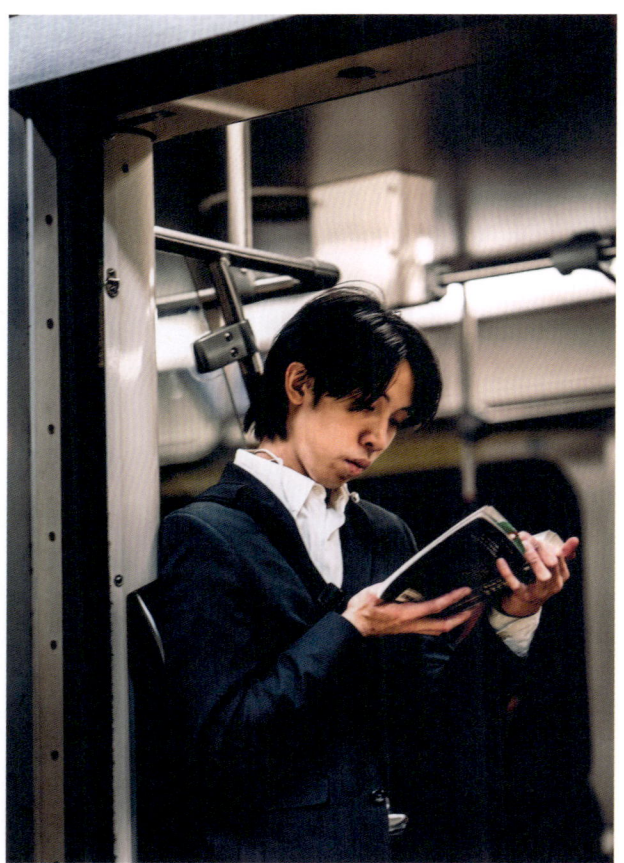

Toronto → *Canada*

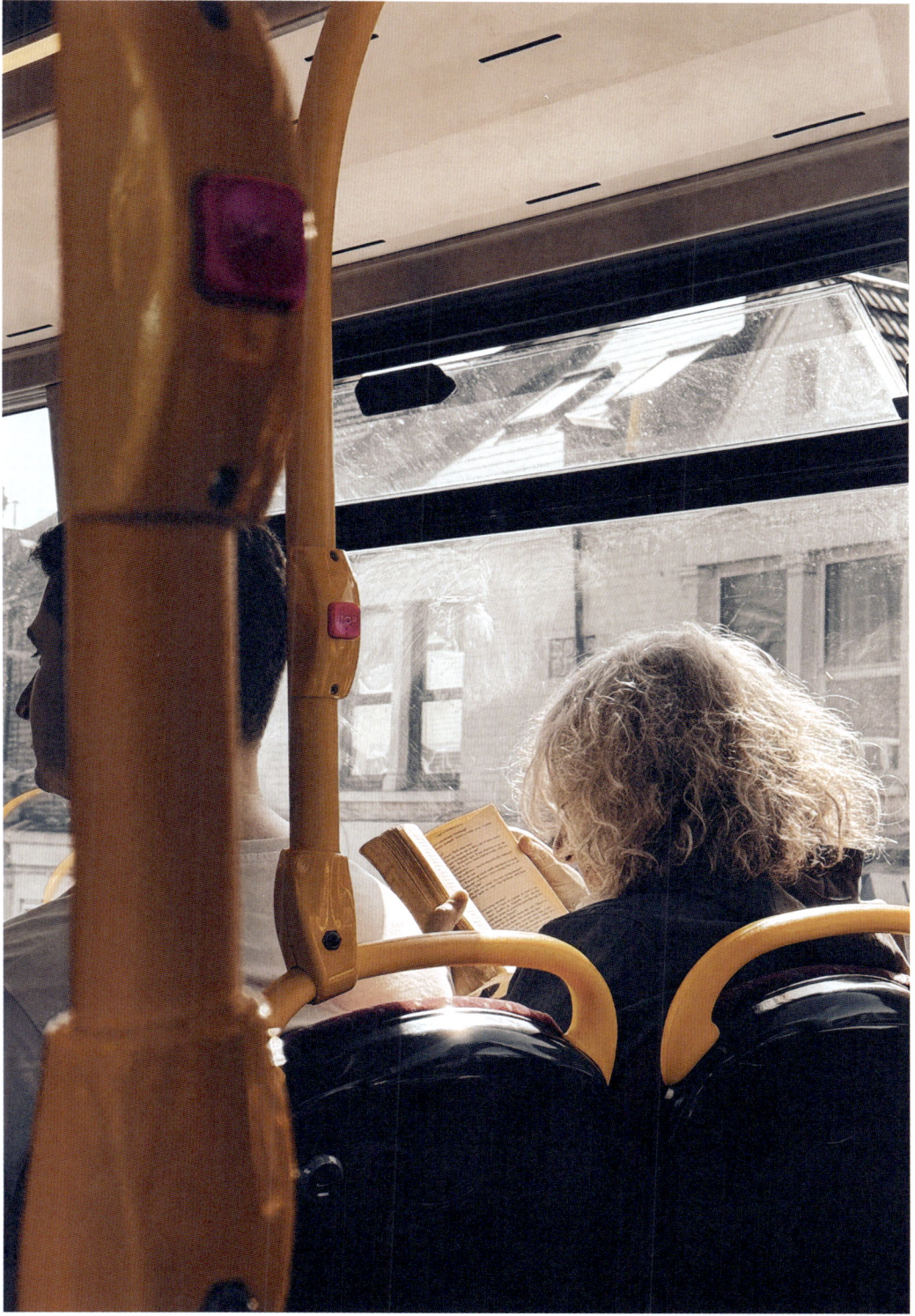

London → *England*

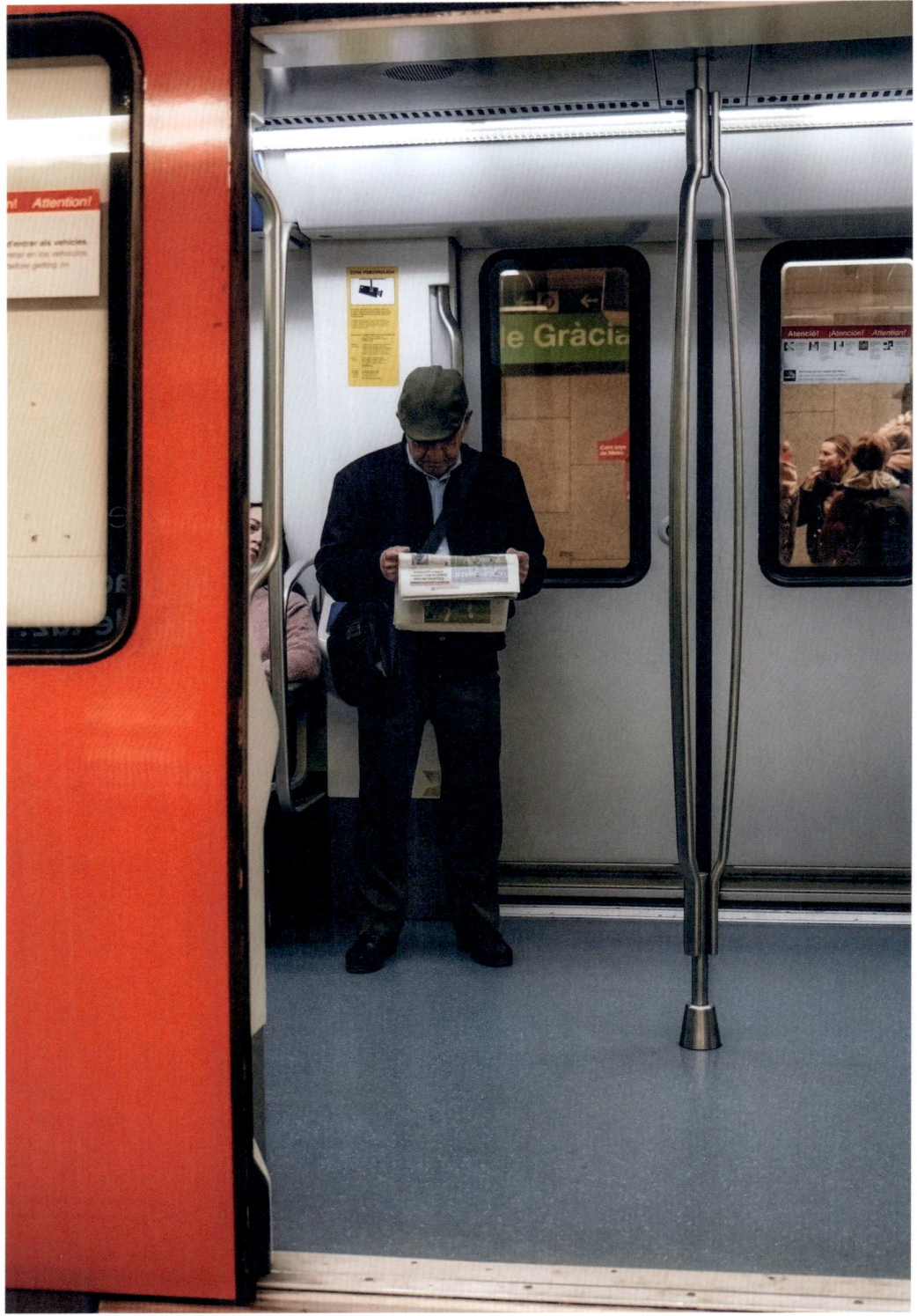

Barcelona → *Spain*

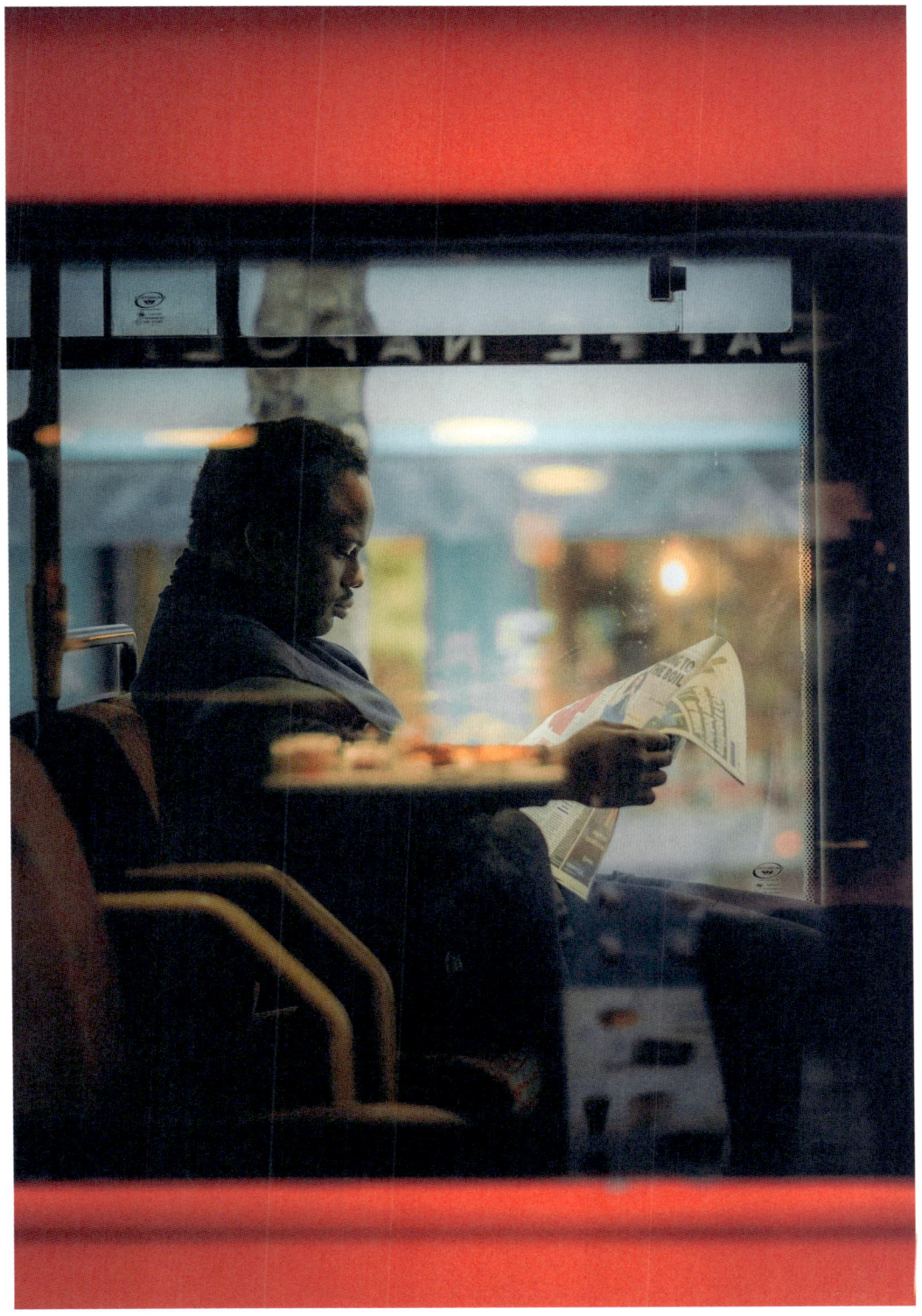

London → England

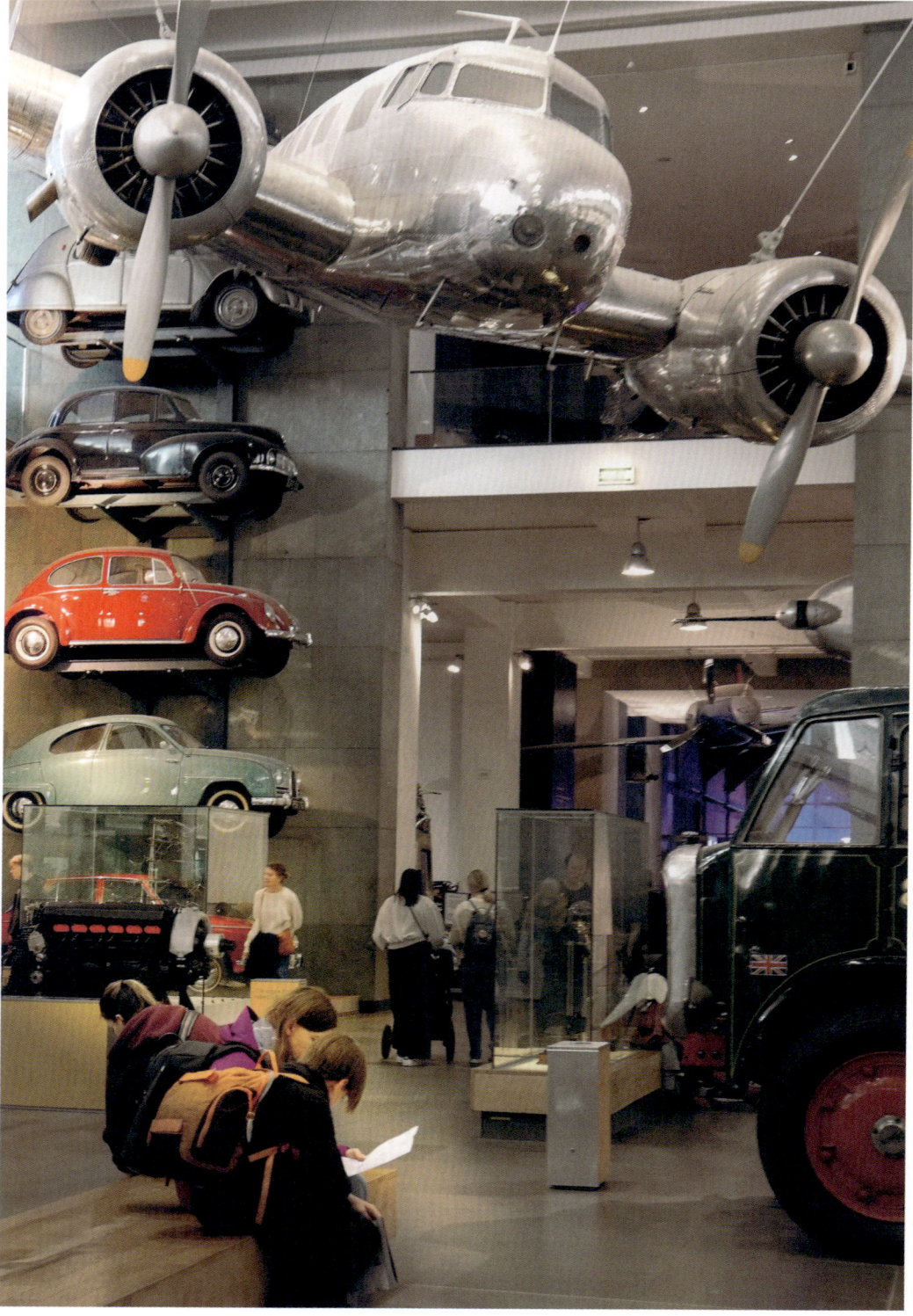

London → *England*

"When I look back, I am so impressed again with the life-giving power of literature. If I were a young person today, trying to gain a sense of myself in the world, I would do that again by reading, just as I did when I was young."

MAYA ANGELOU

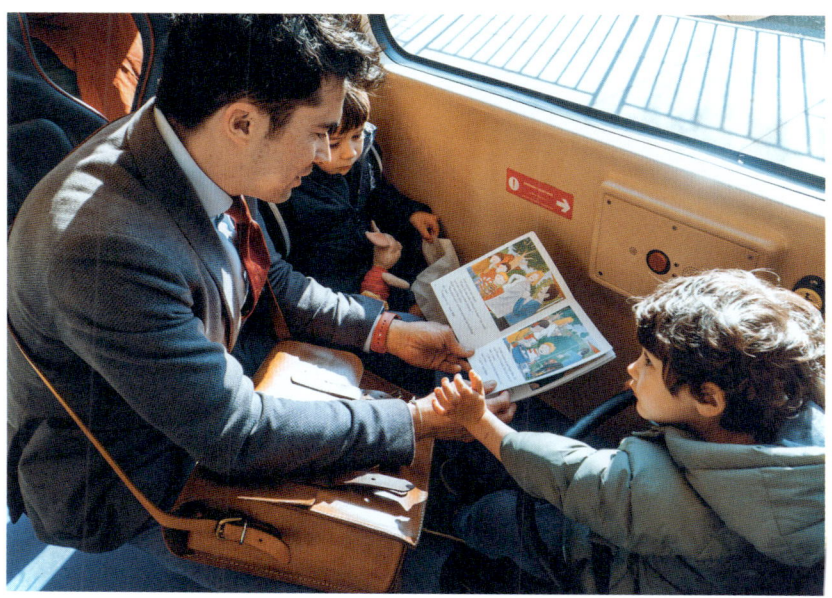

Edinburgh → *Scotland*

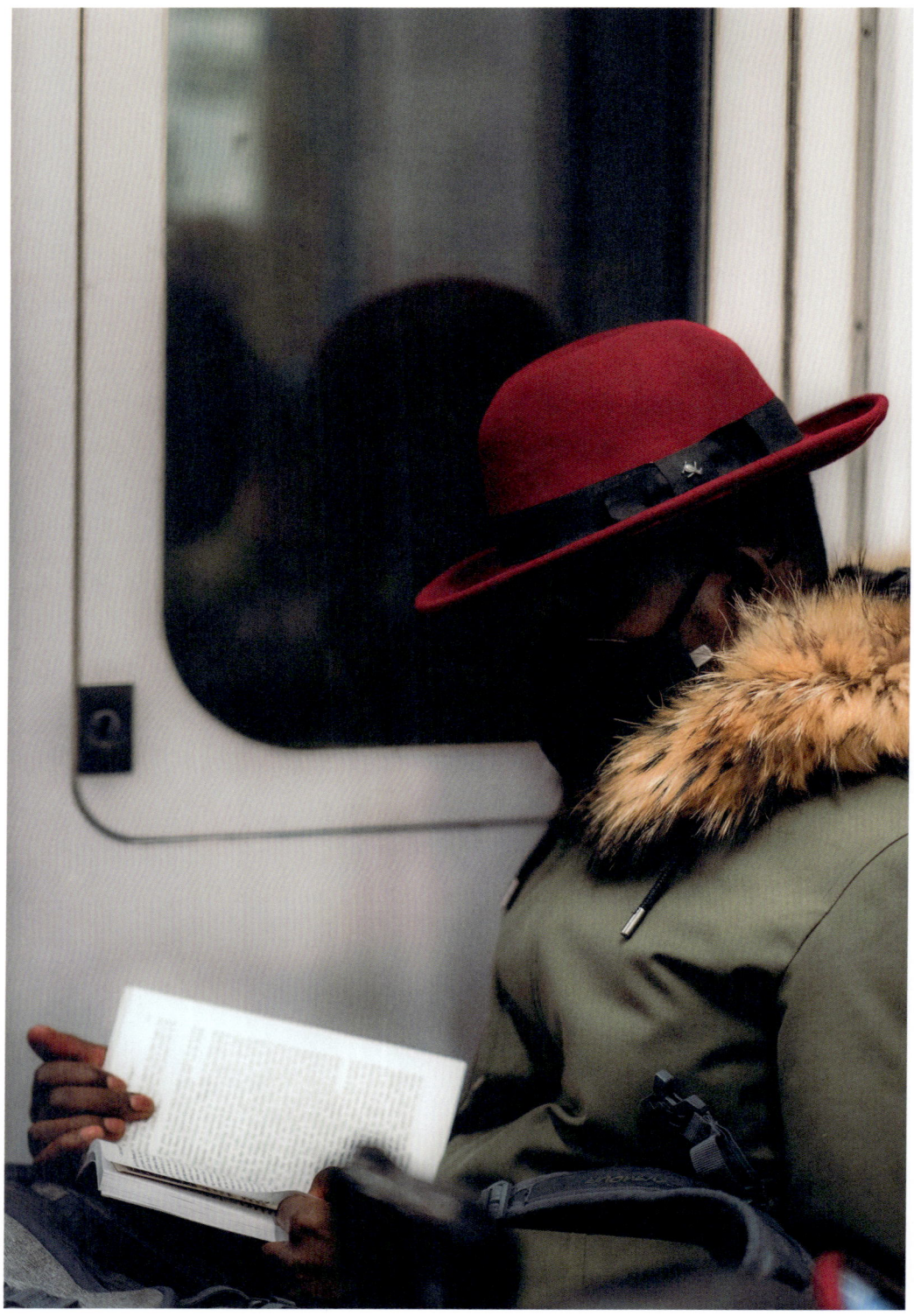

New York, New York → *United States*

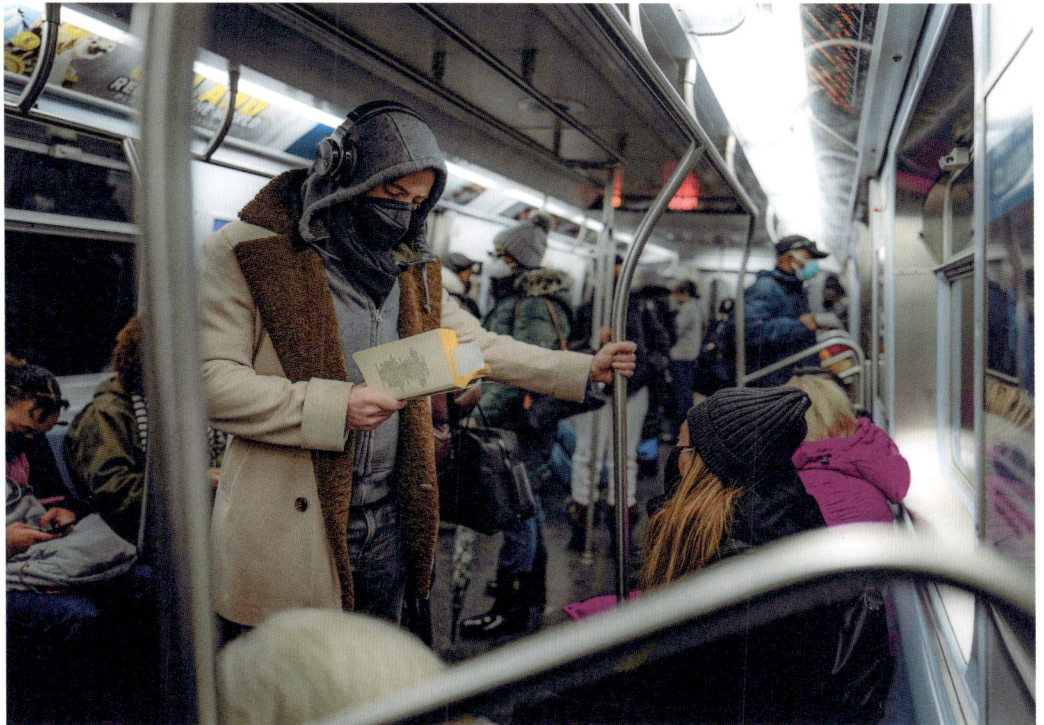

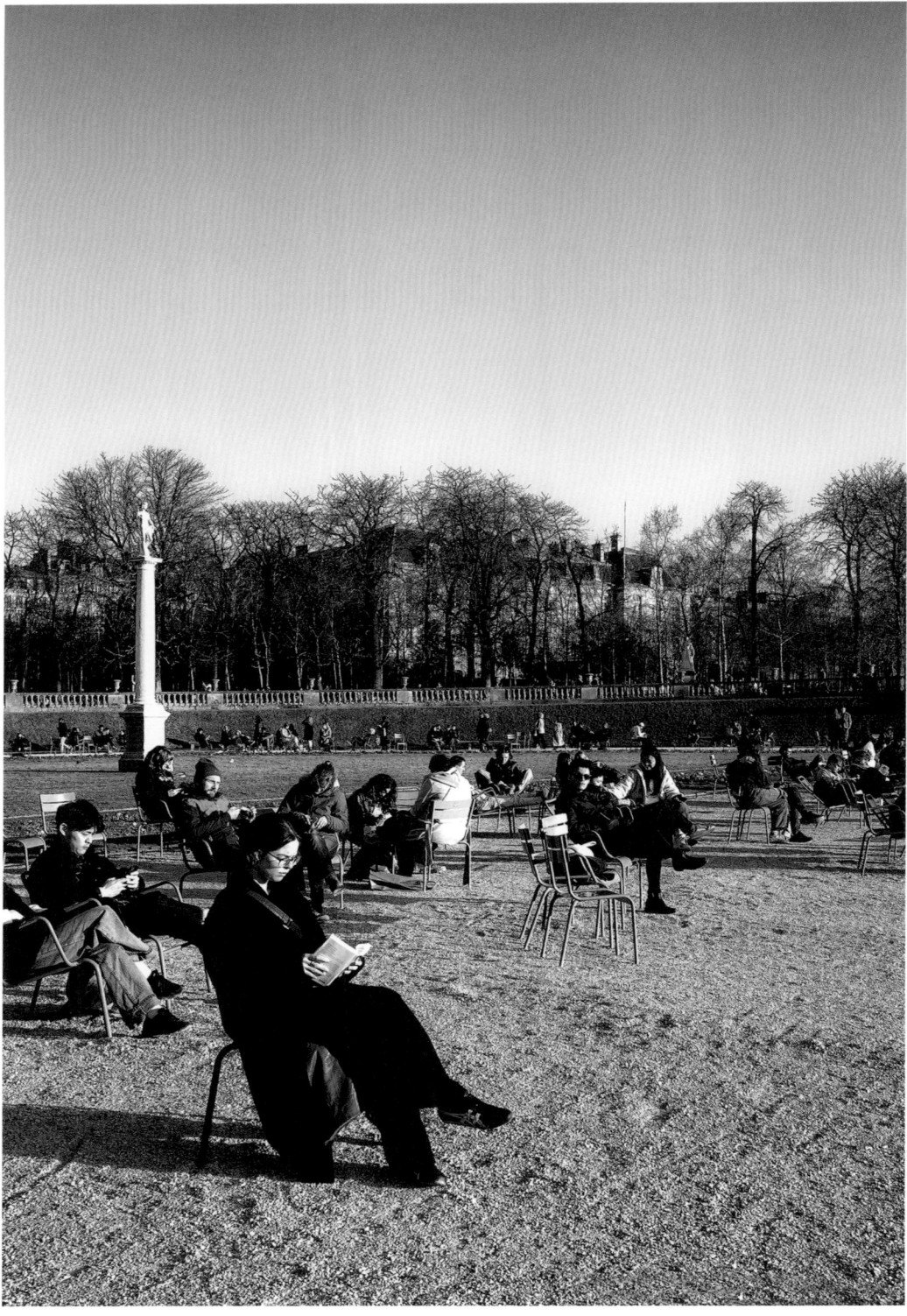

Paris → France

"Books are a uniquely portable magic."

STEPHEN KING

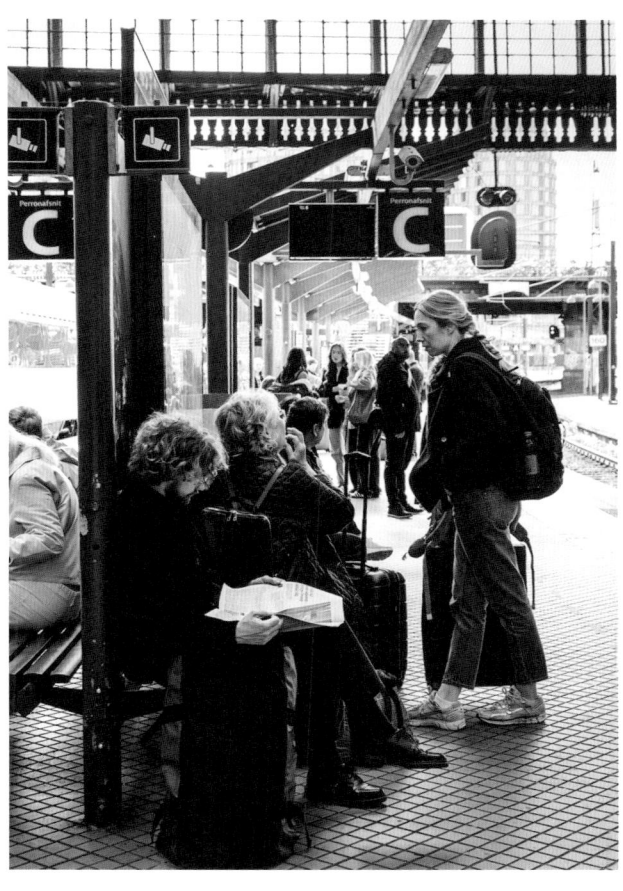

Copenhagen → *Denmark*

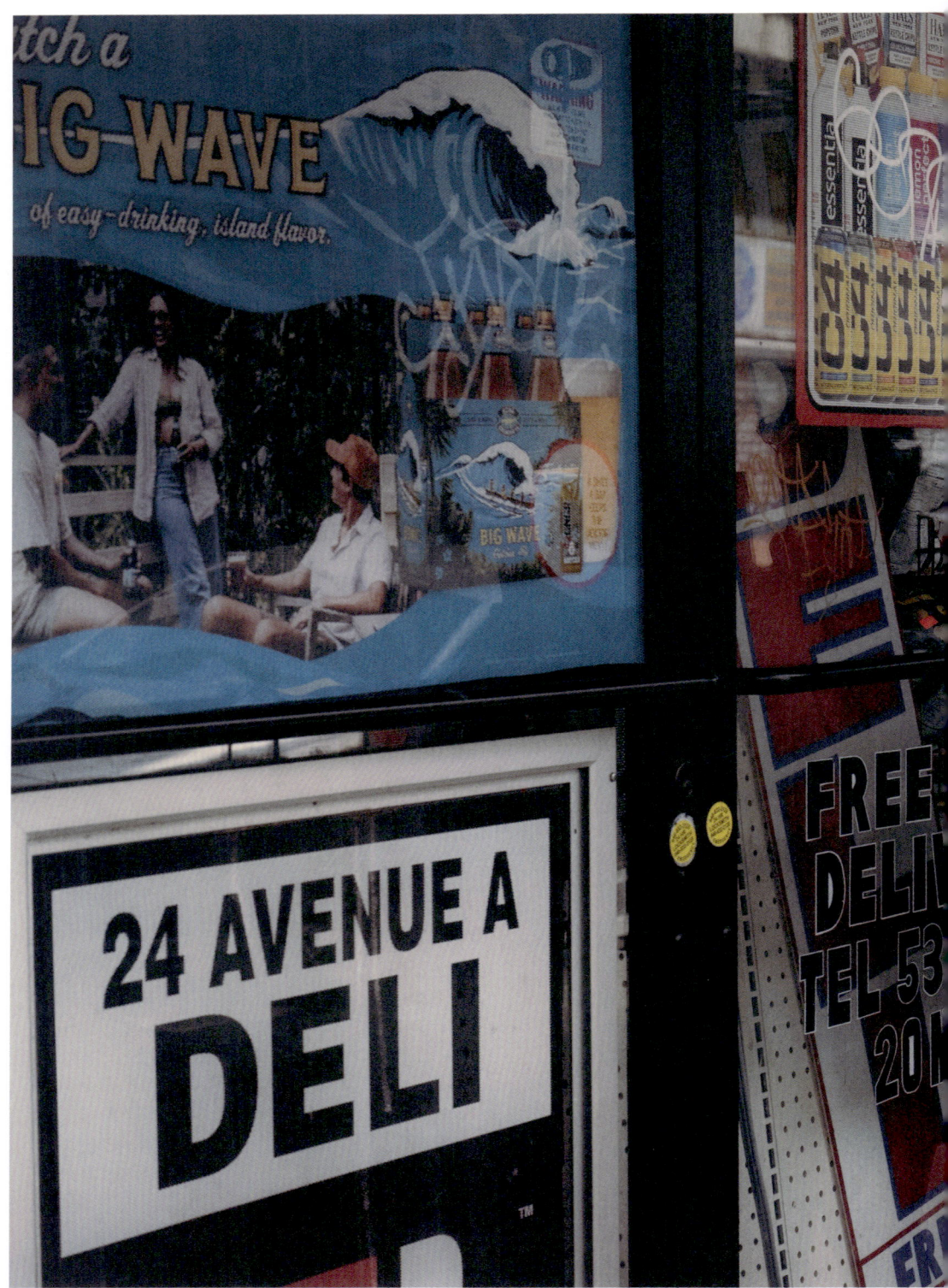

New York, New York → United States

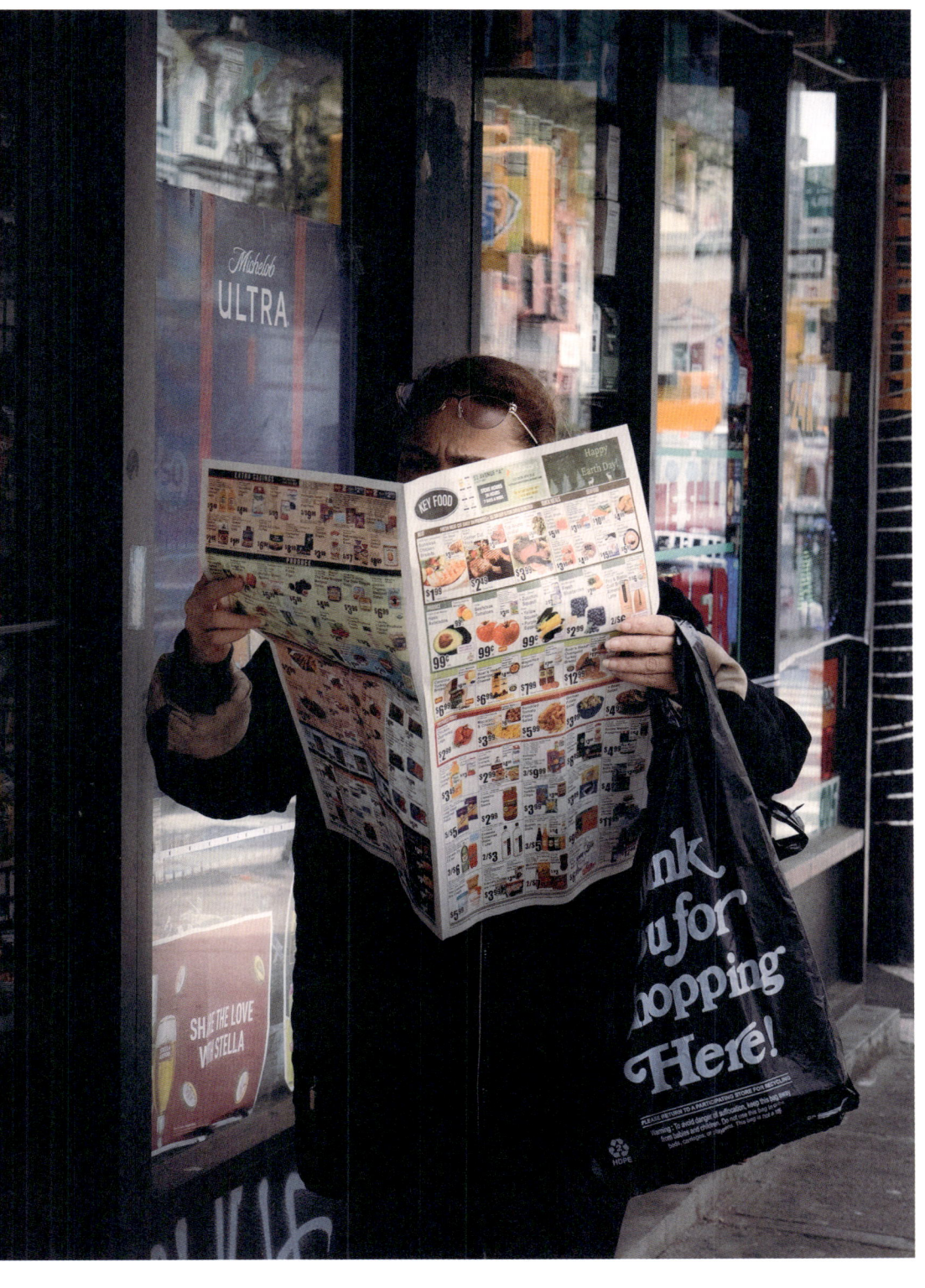

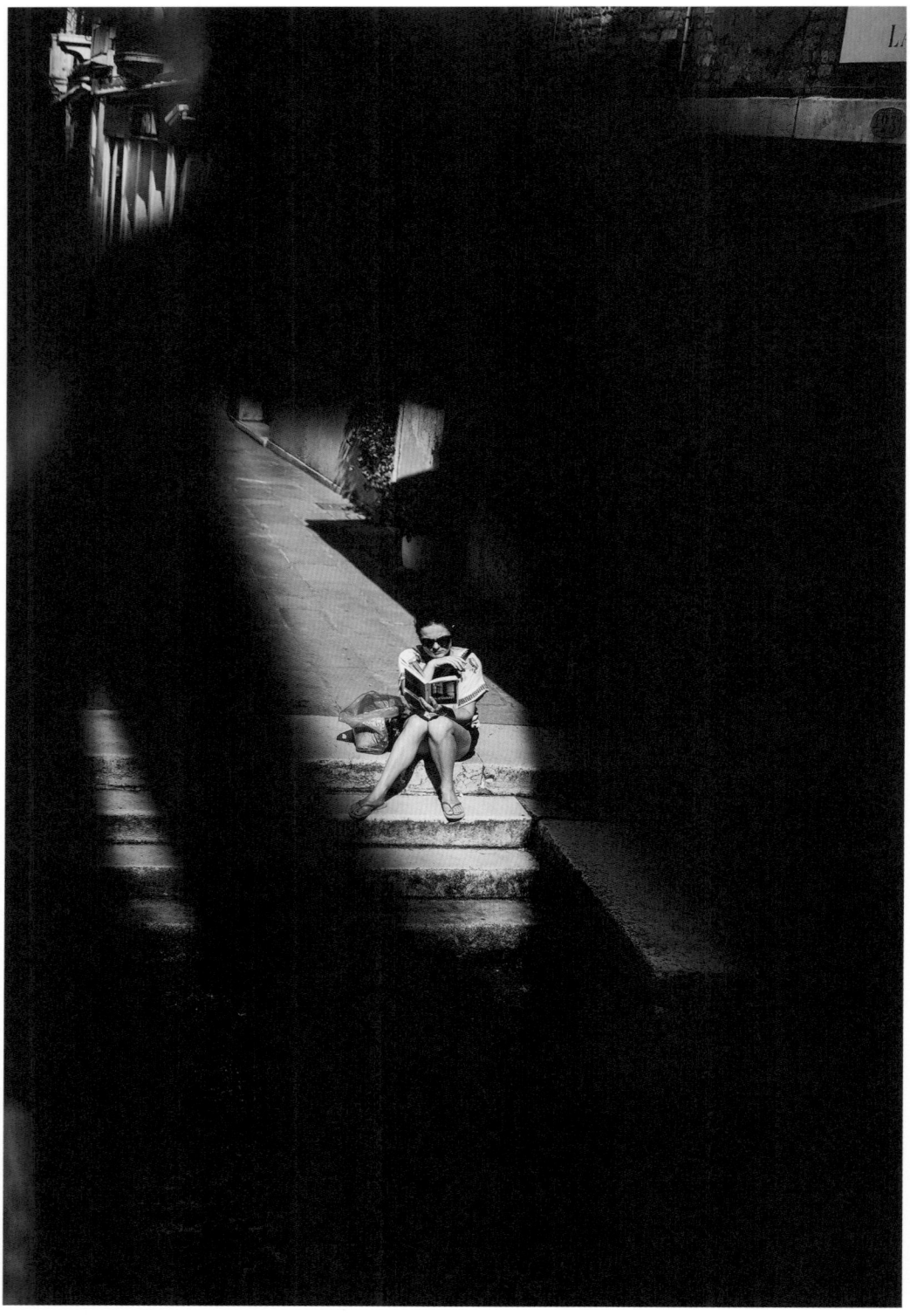

Venice → *Italy*

"Read a lot. Expect something big, something
exalting or deepening from a book. No book
is worth reading that isn't worth re-reading."

SUSAN SONTAG

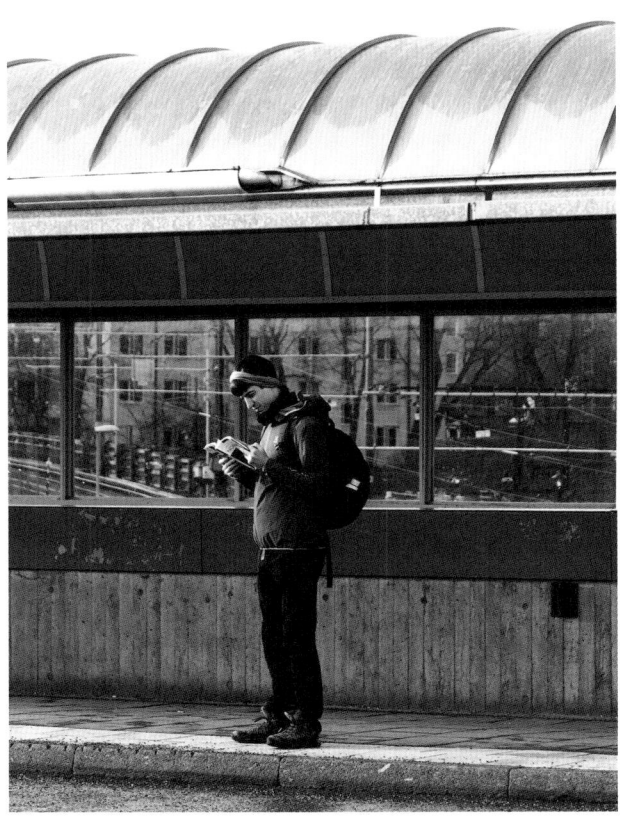

Stockholm → *Sweden*

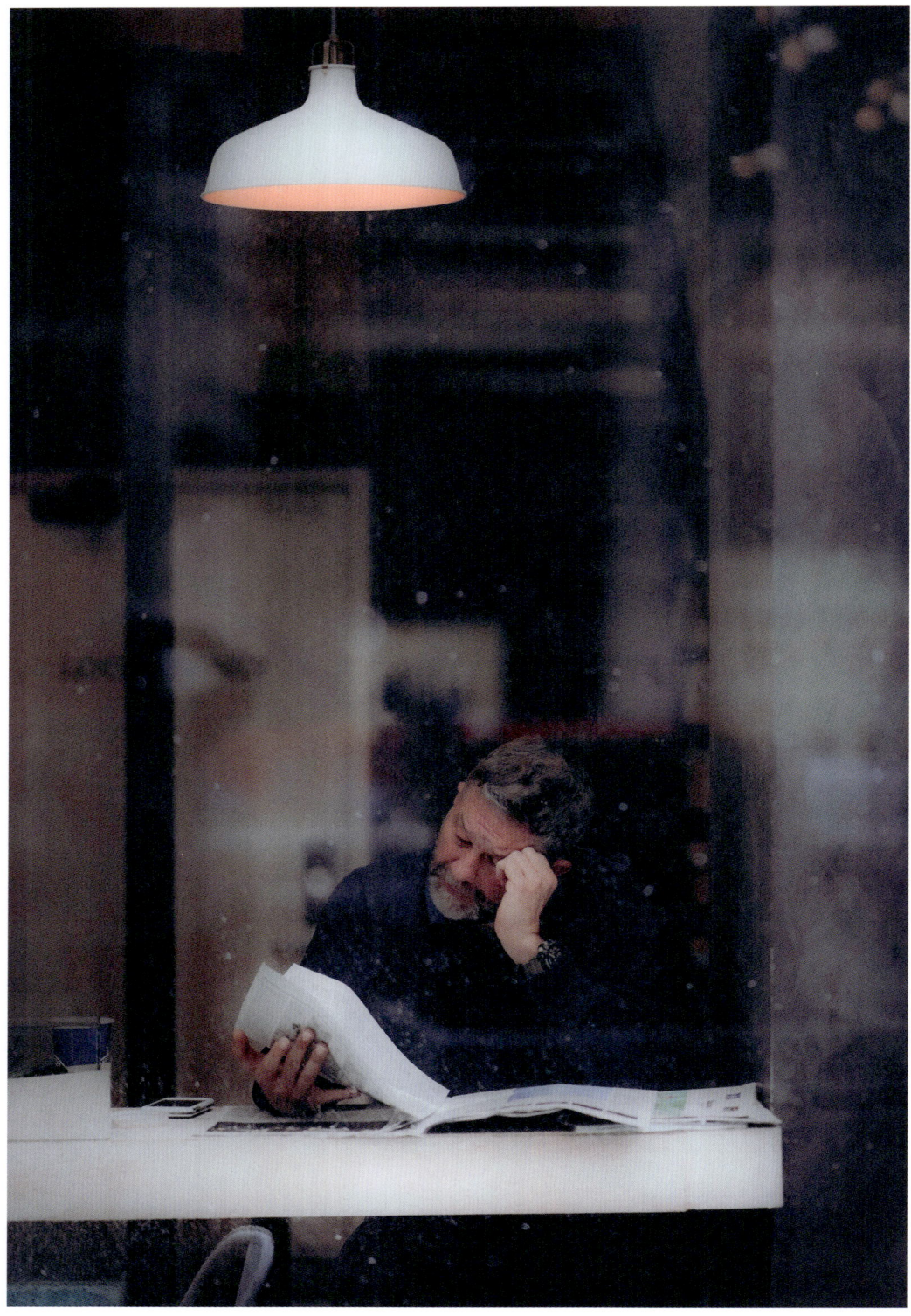

New York, New York → *United States*

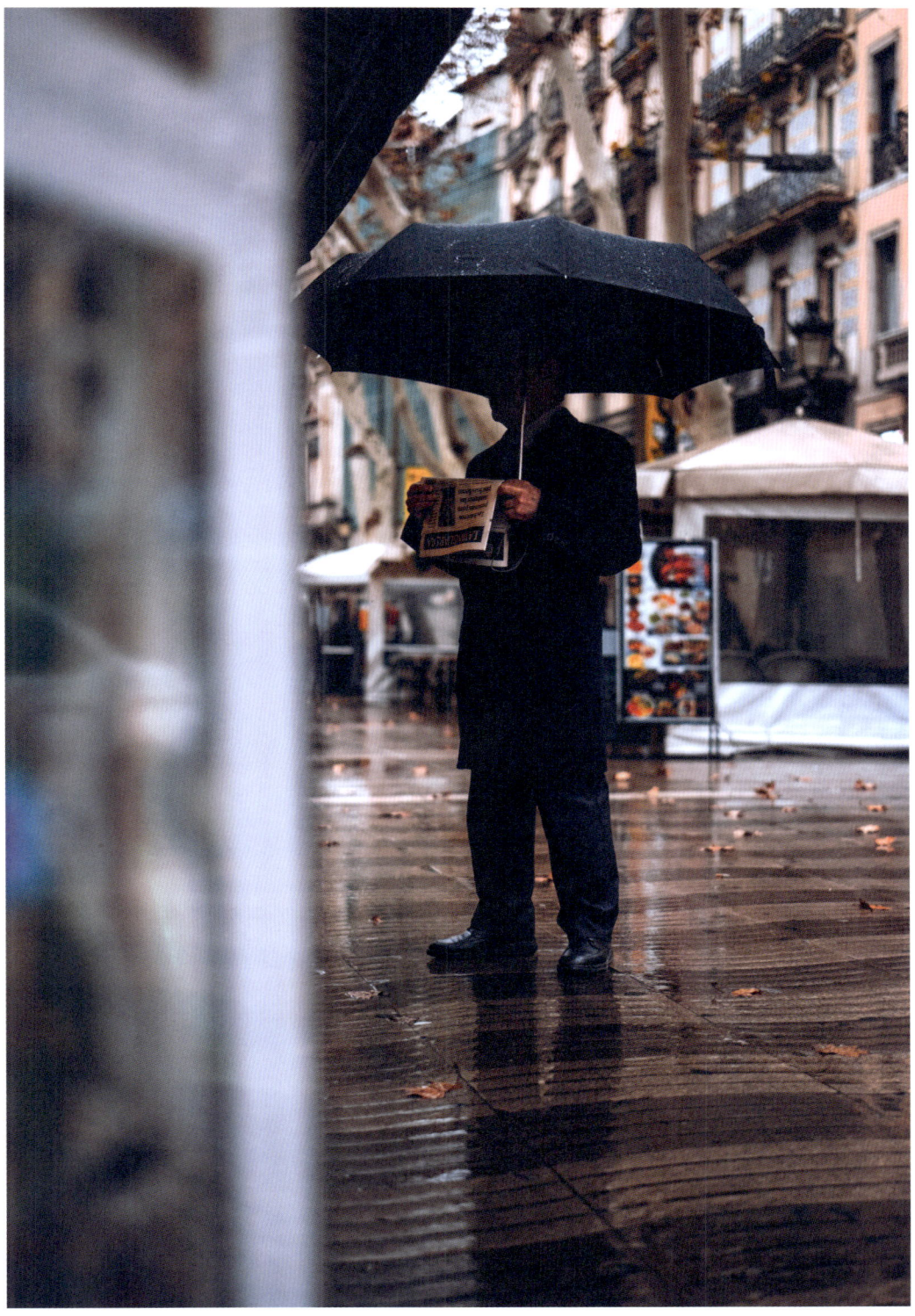

Barcelona → *Spain*

"Once you've read a book you care about,
some part of it is always with you."

LOUIS L'AMOUR

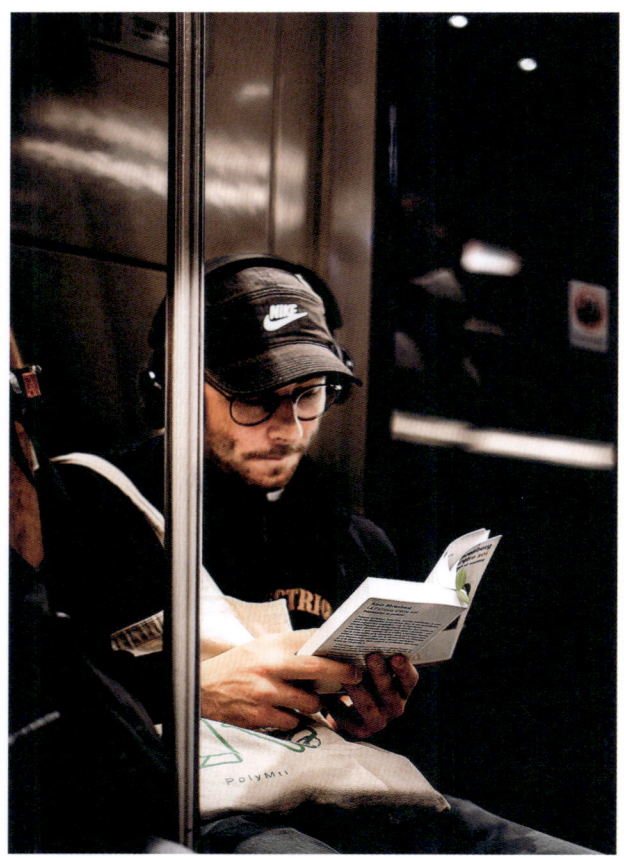

Montreal → *Canada*

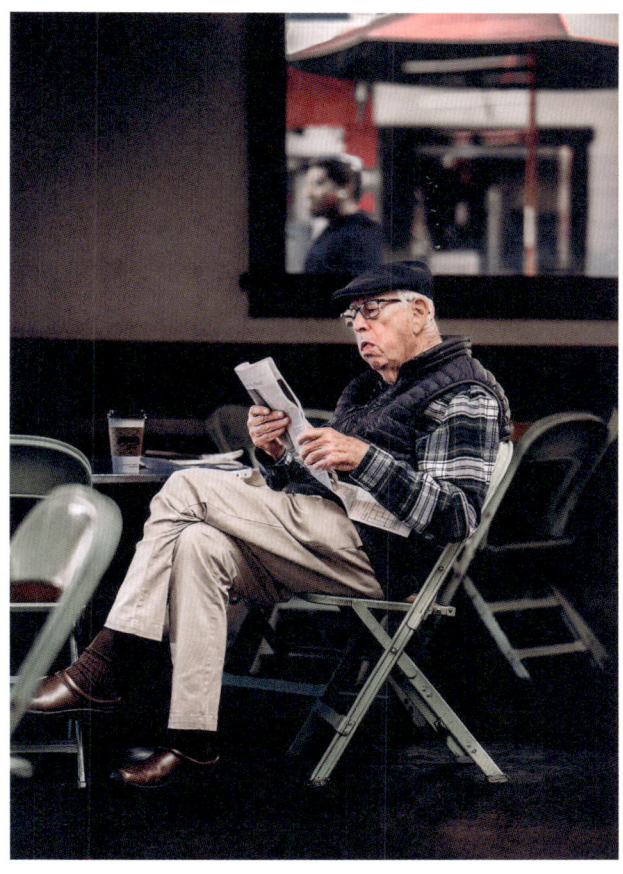

"Have books 'happened' to you? Unless your
answer to that question is 'yes,' I'm unsure
how to talk to you."

HARUKI MURAKAMI

Los Angeles, California → *United States*

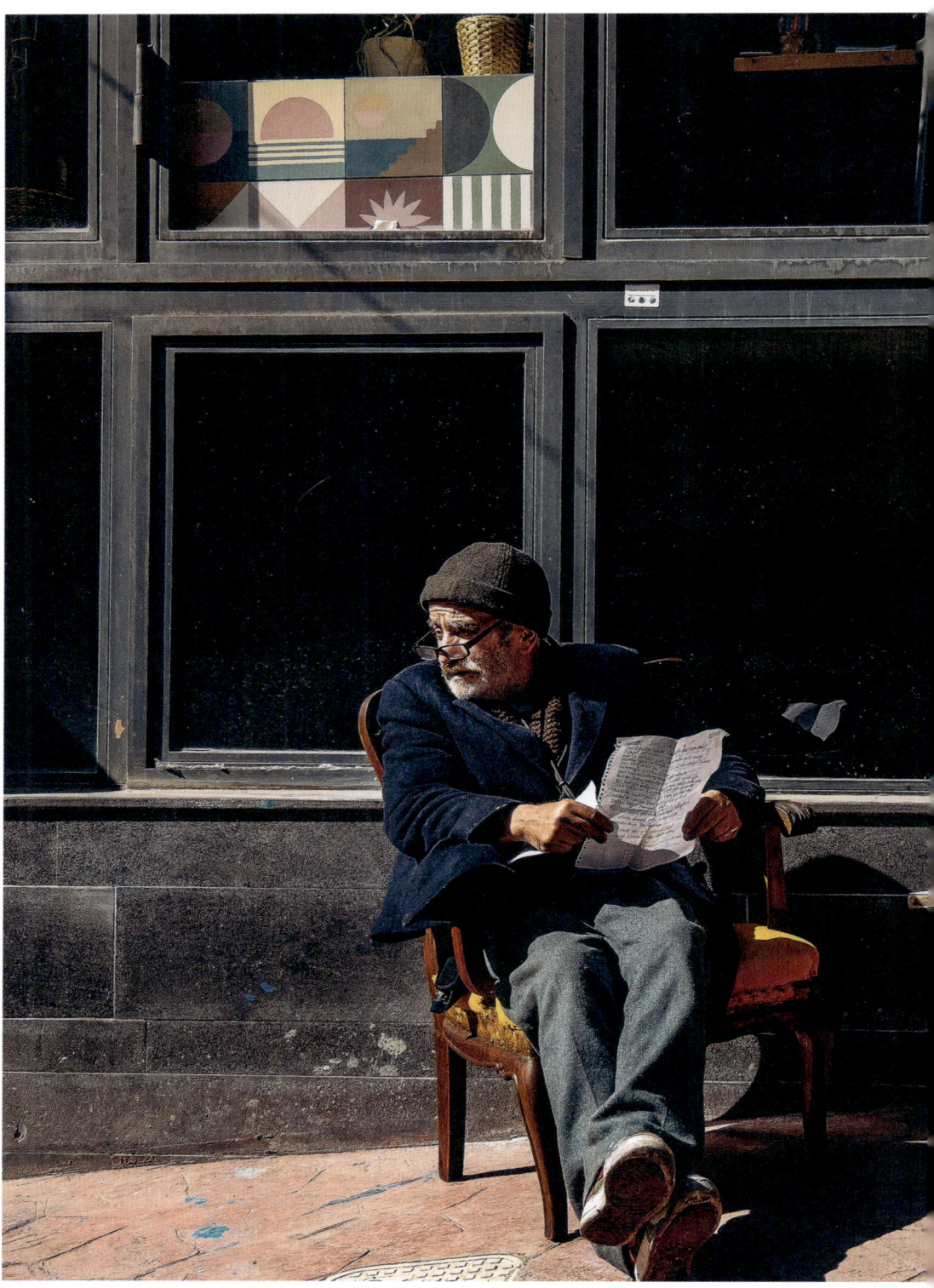

Istanbul → *Turkey*

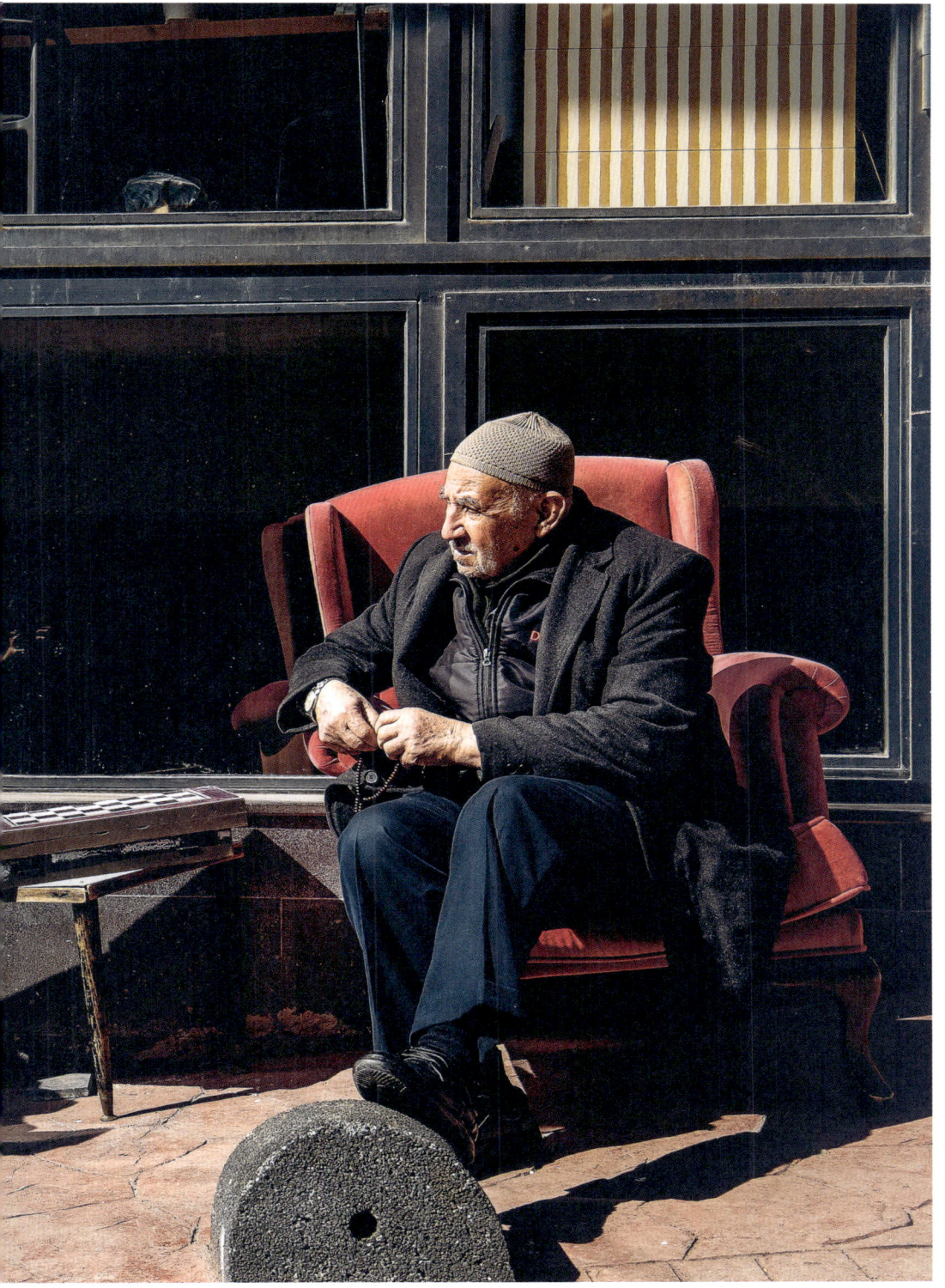

"I think books are like people, in the sense that they'll turn up in your life when you most need them."

EMMA THOMPSON

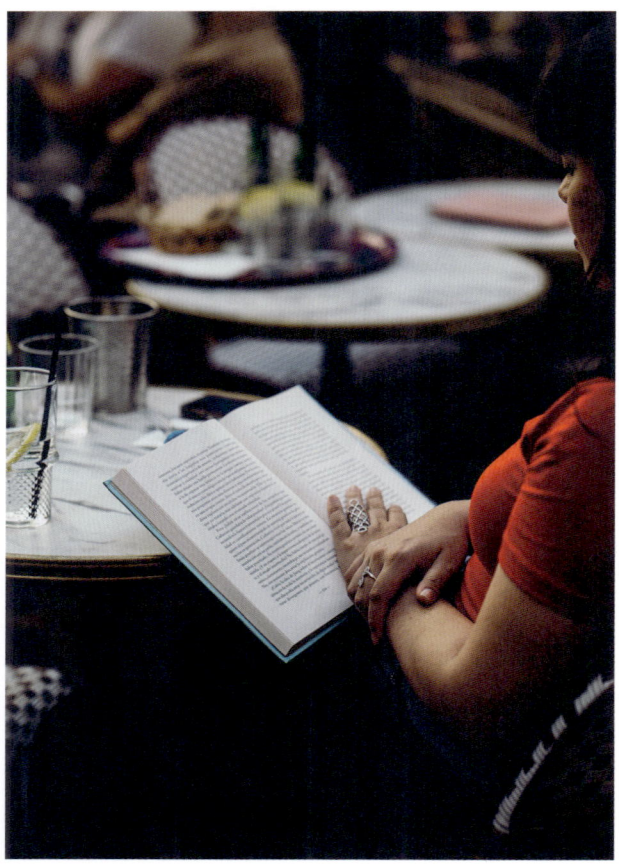

Montpellier → *France*

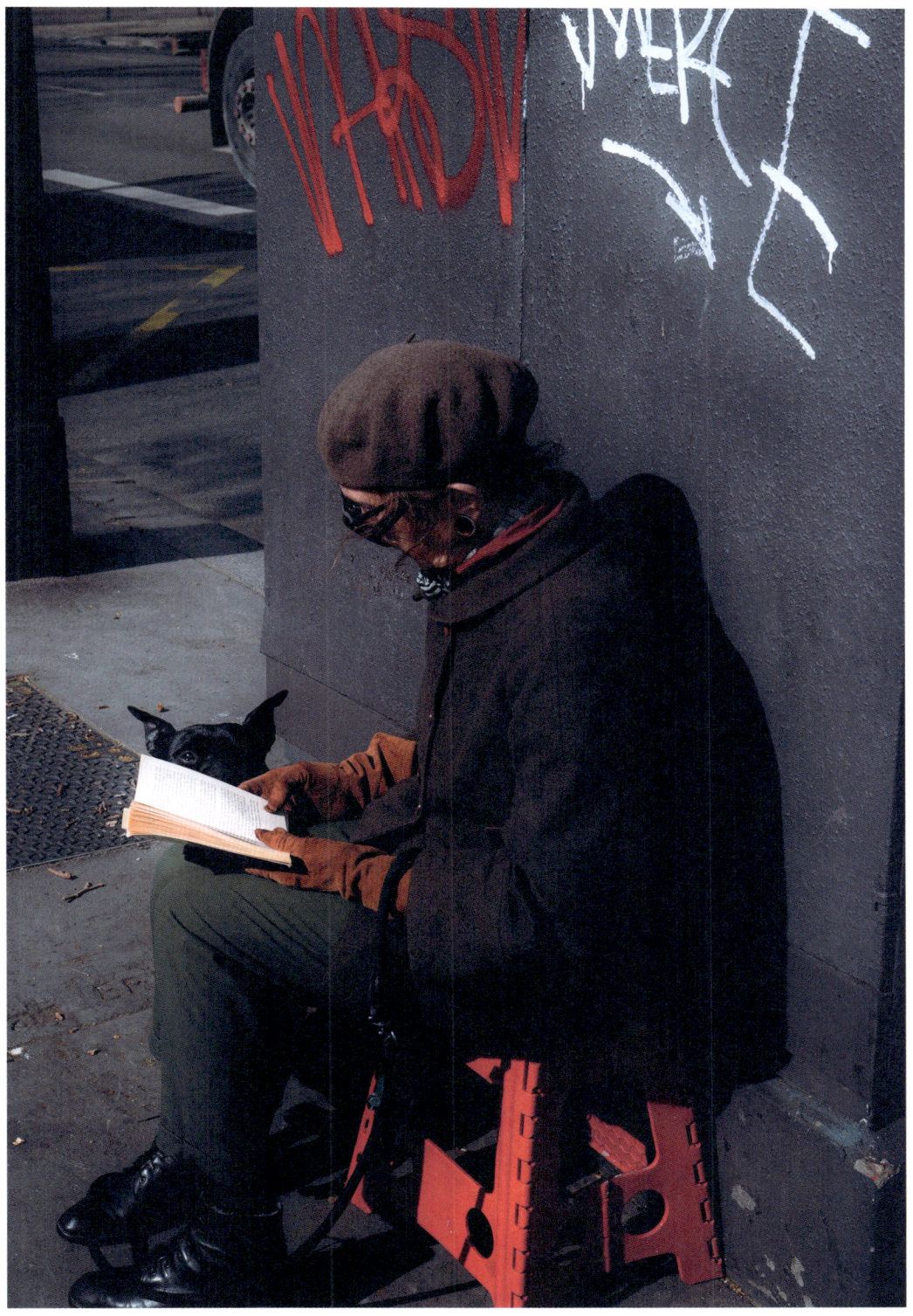

New York, New York → *United States*

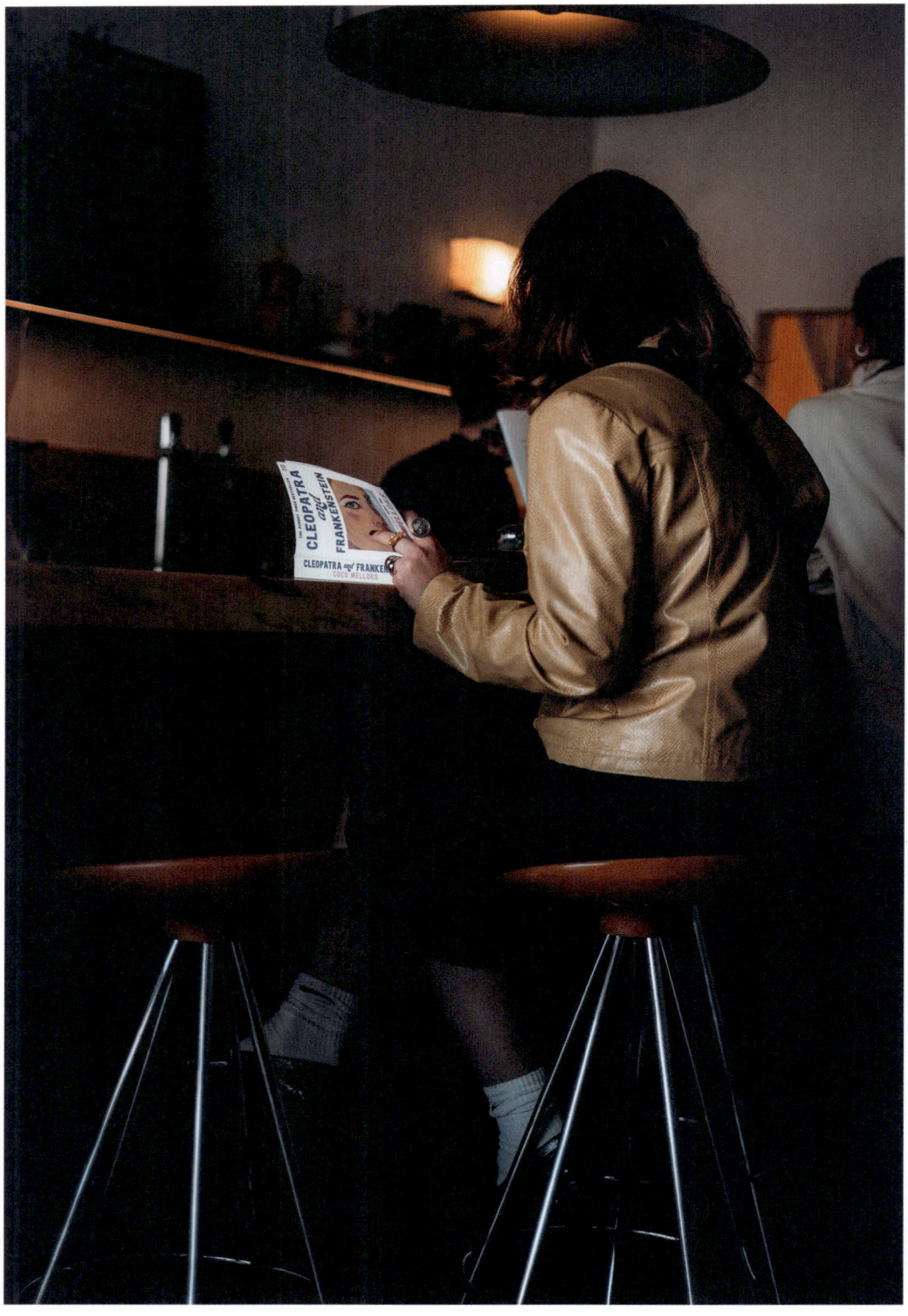

Barcelona → *Spain*

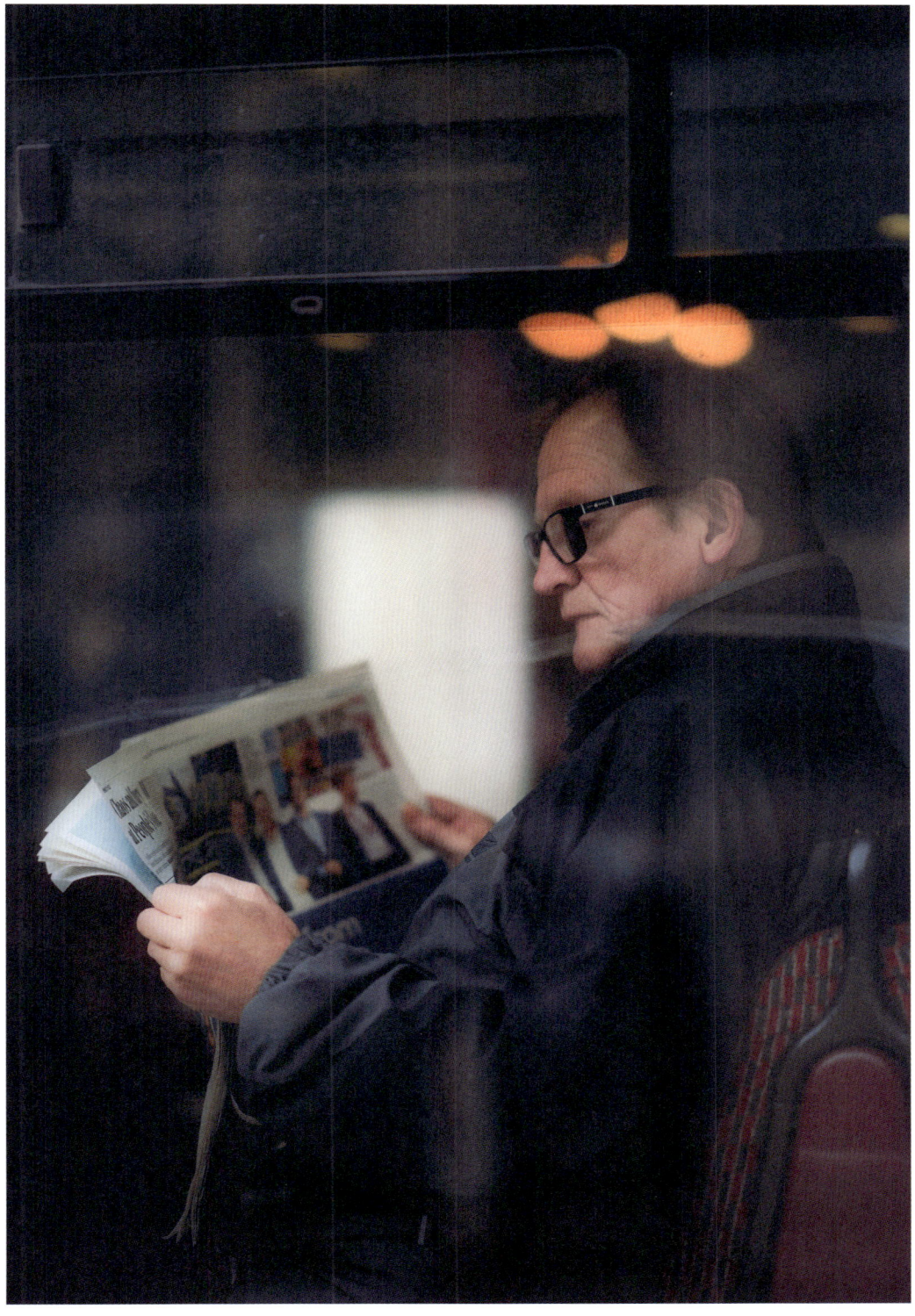

London → England

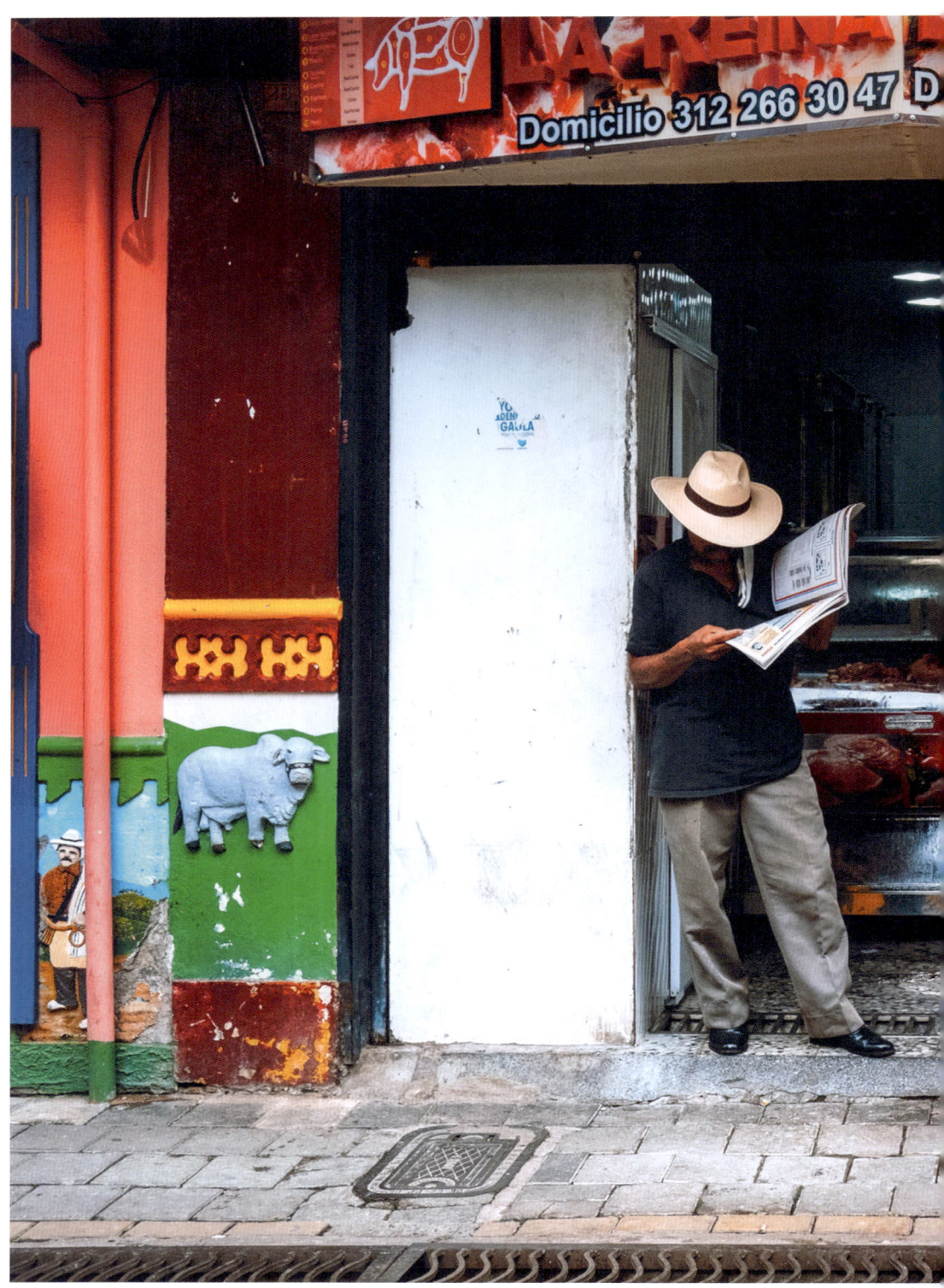

Guatapé → *Colombia*

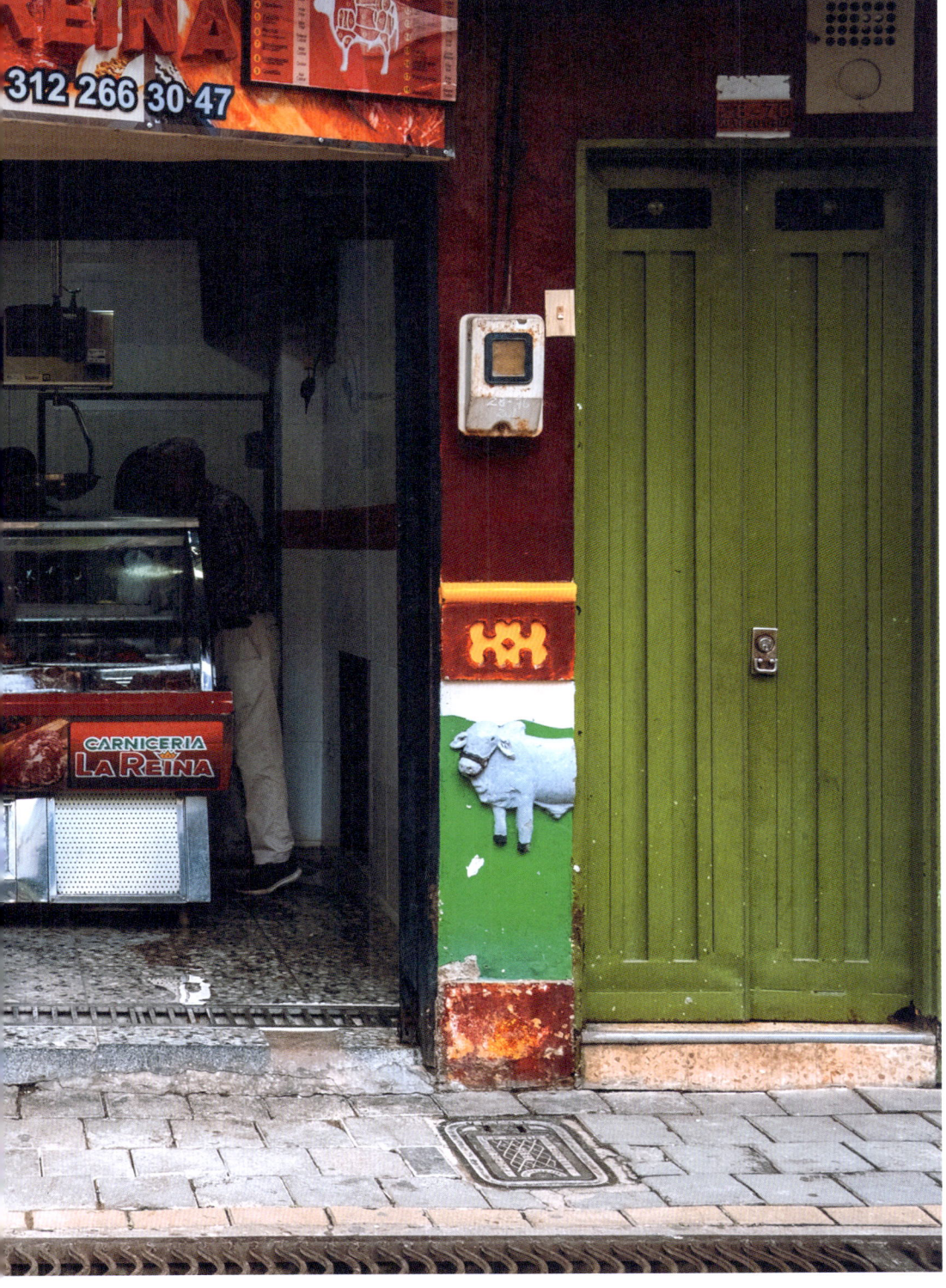

"You can never get a cup of tea large enough
or a book long enough to suit me."

C.S. LEWIS

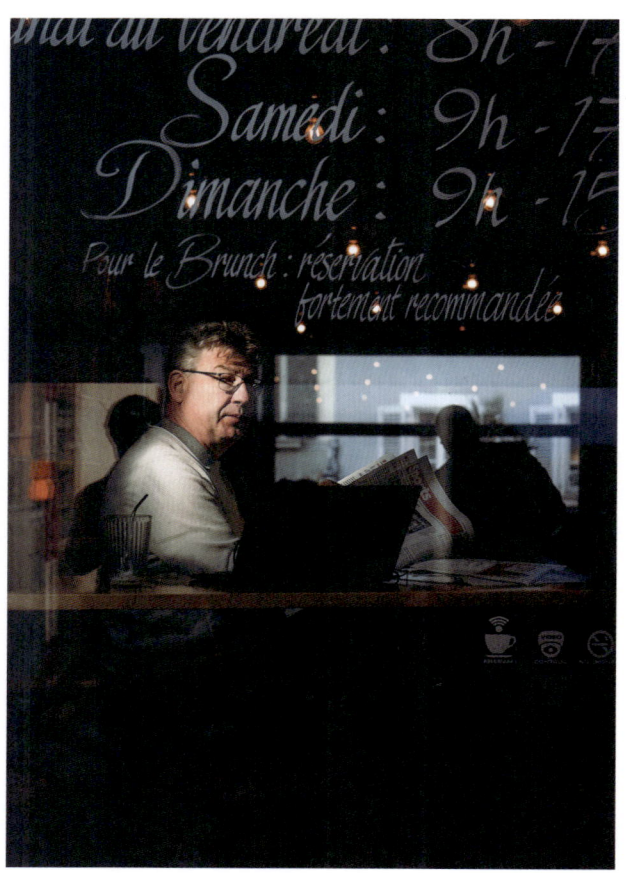

Paris → *France*

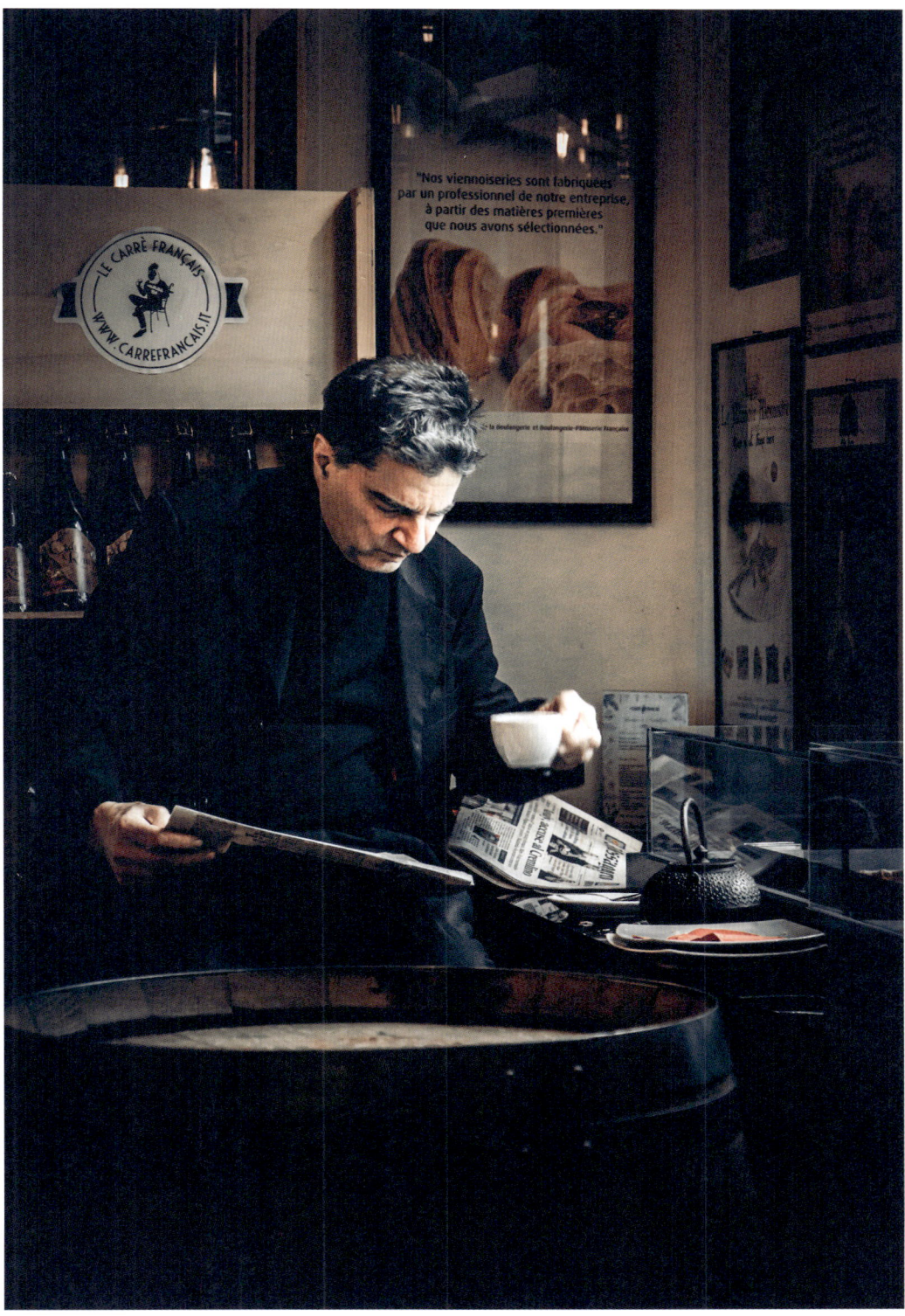

Rome → *Italy*

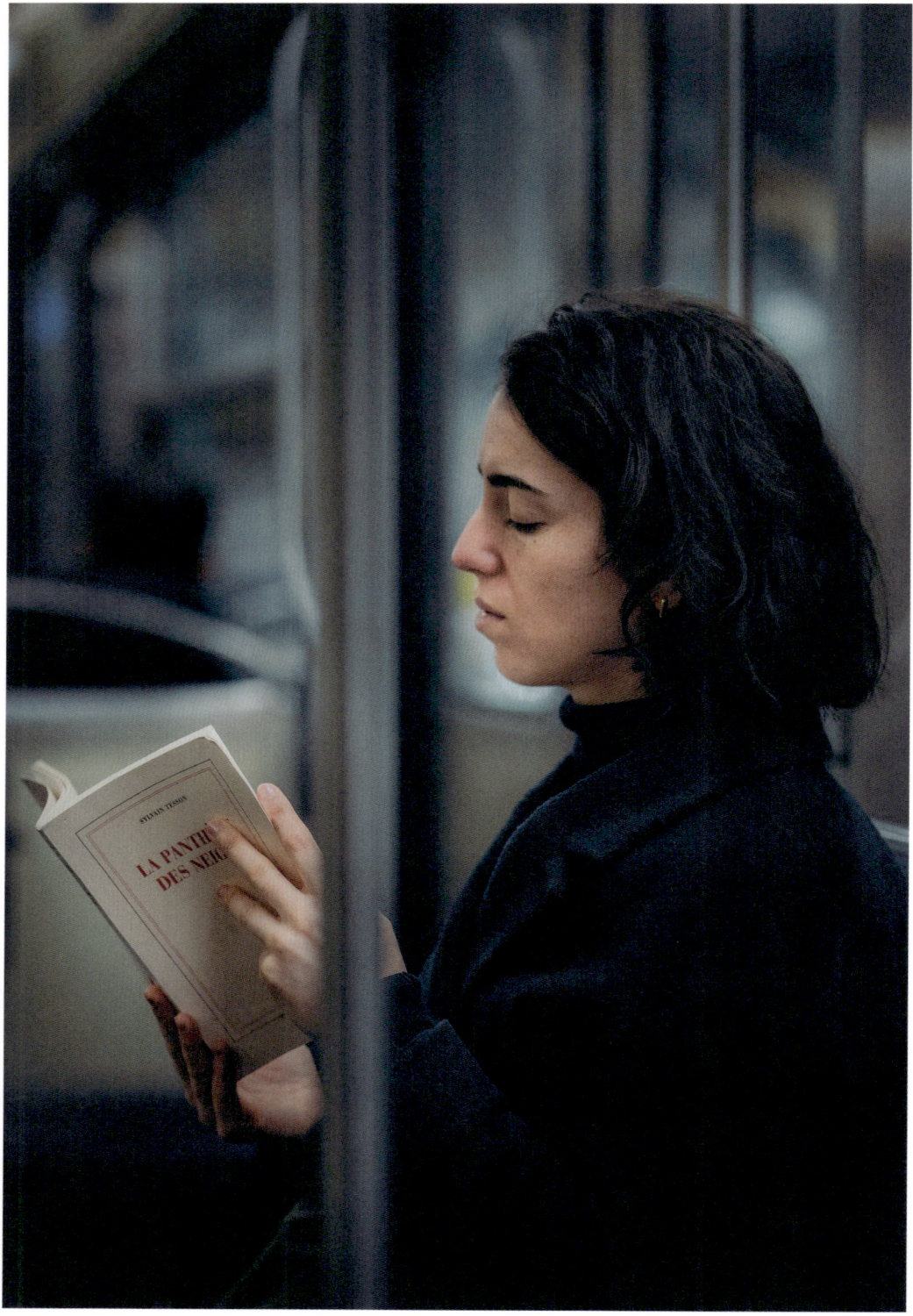

Paris → France

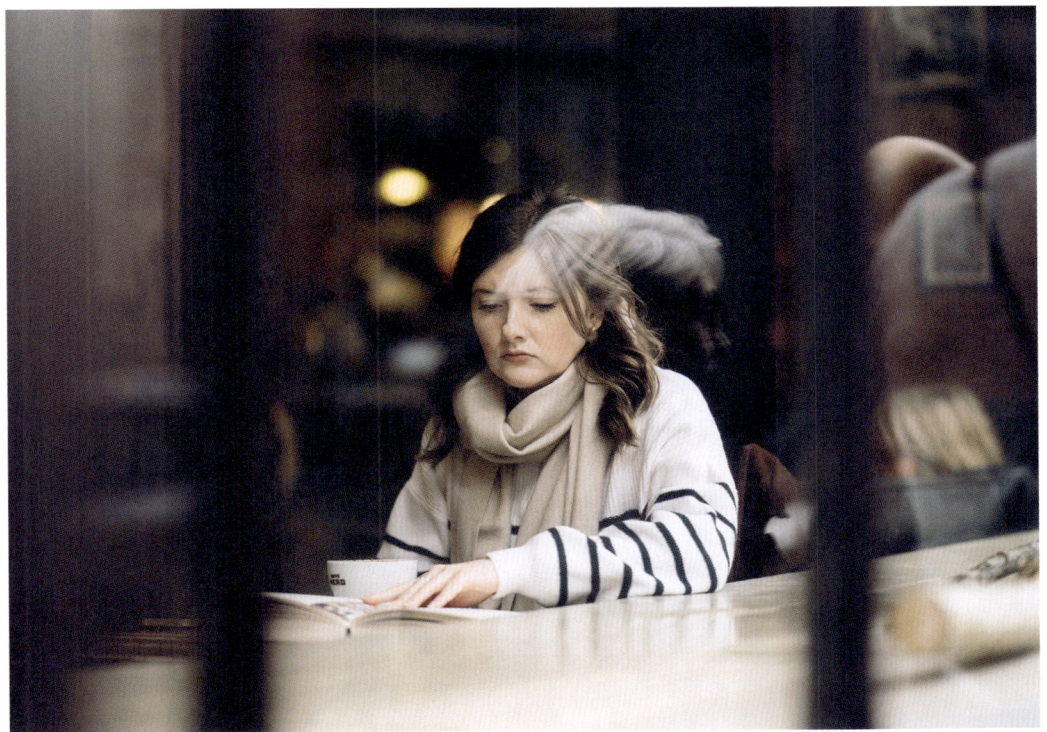

London → *England*

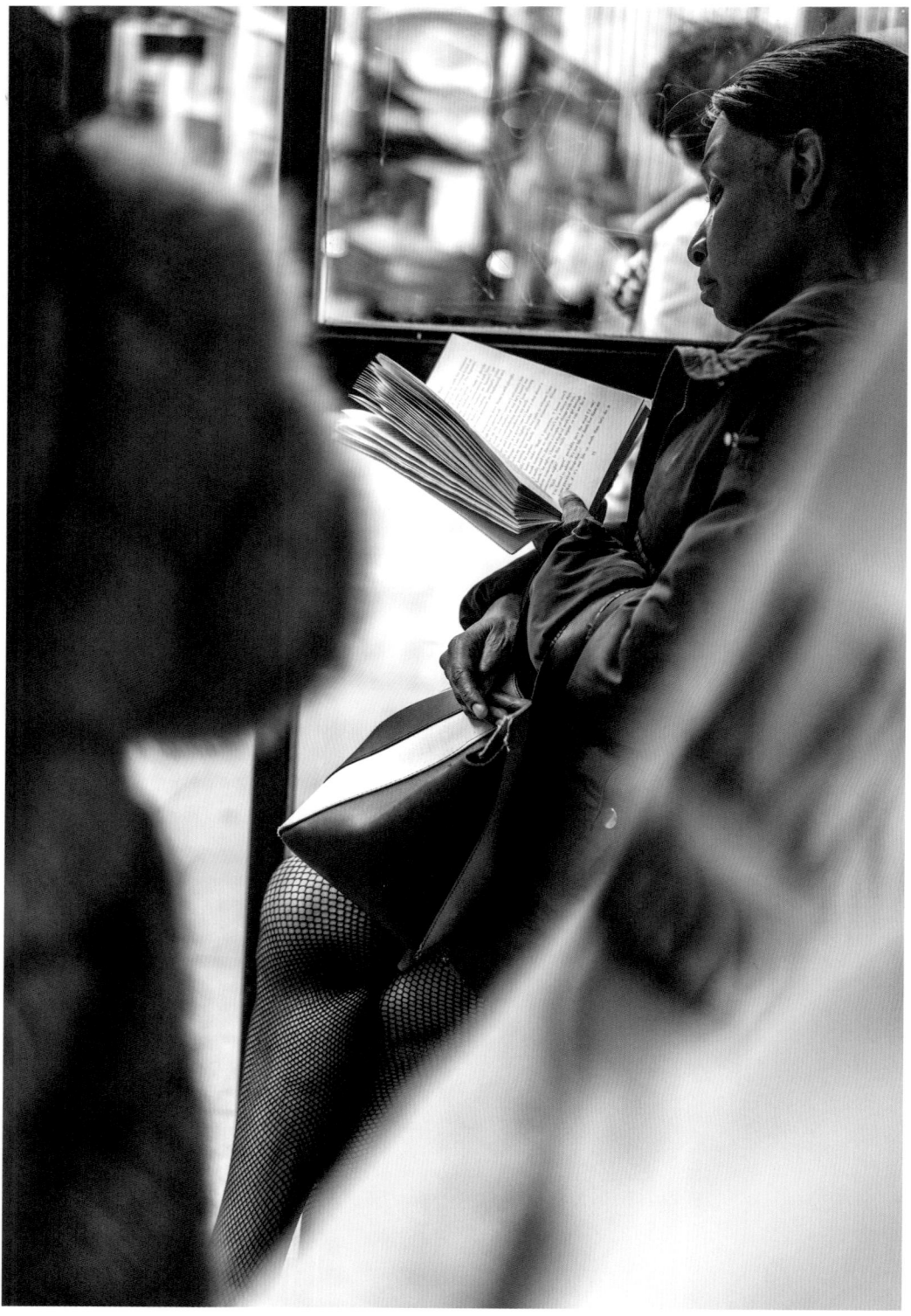

London → England

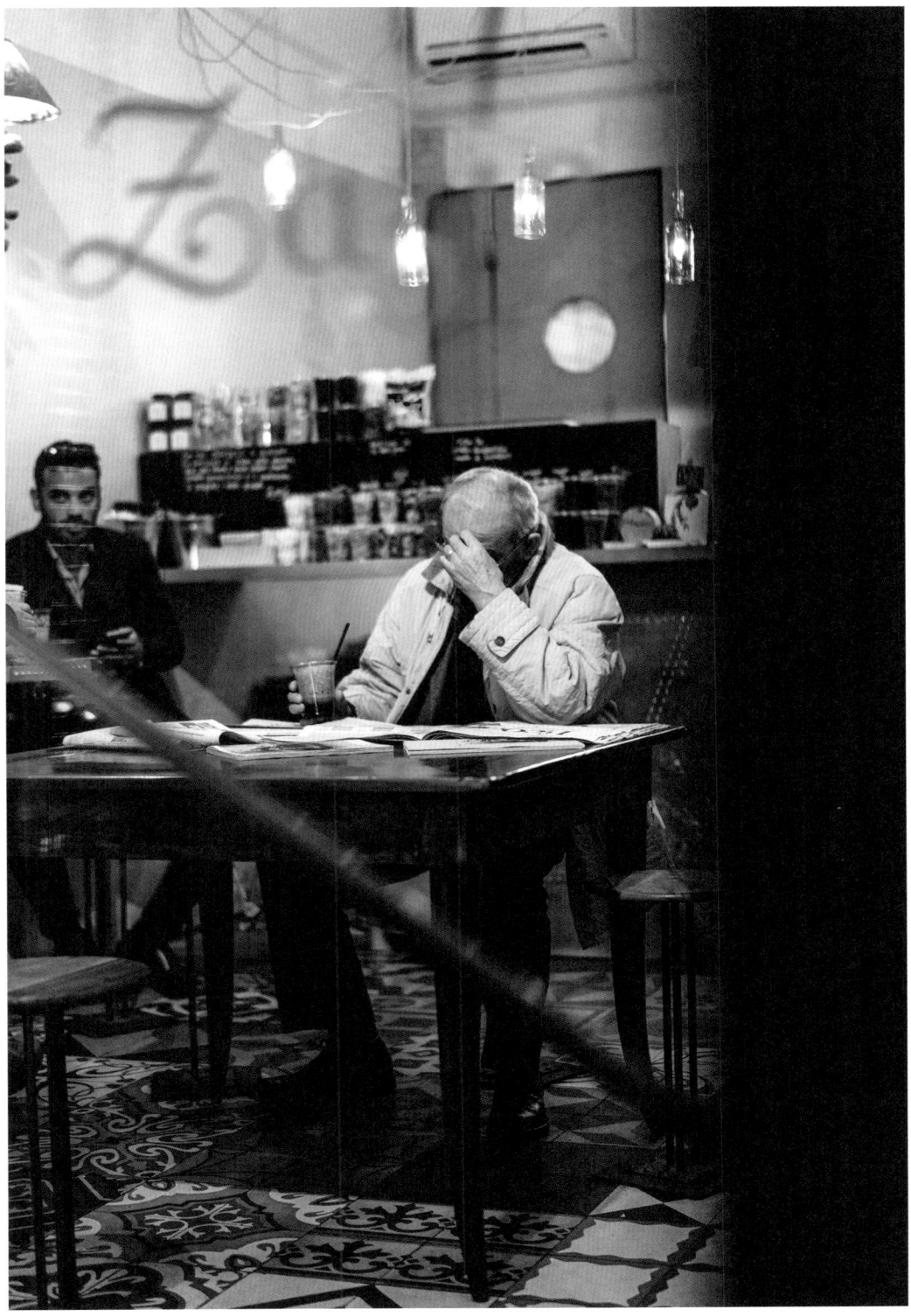

Bologna → *Italy*

Milan → *Italy*

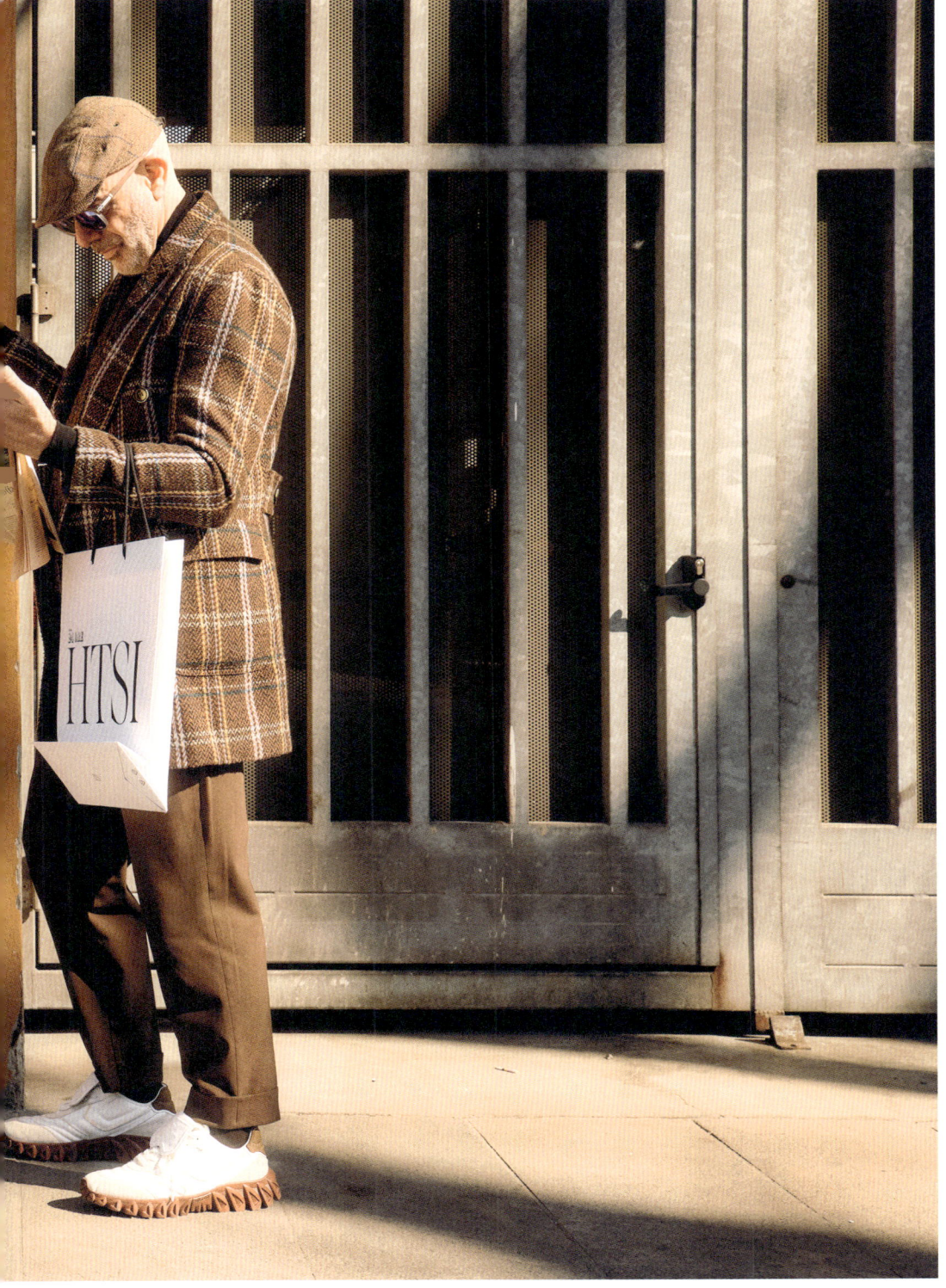

"Reading is an active, imaginative act;
it takes work."

KHALED HOSSEINI

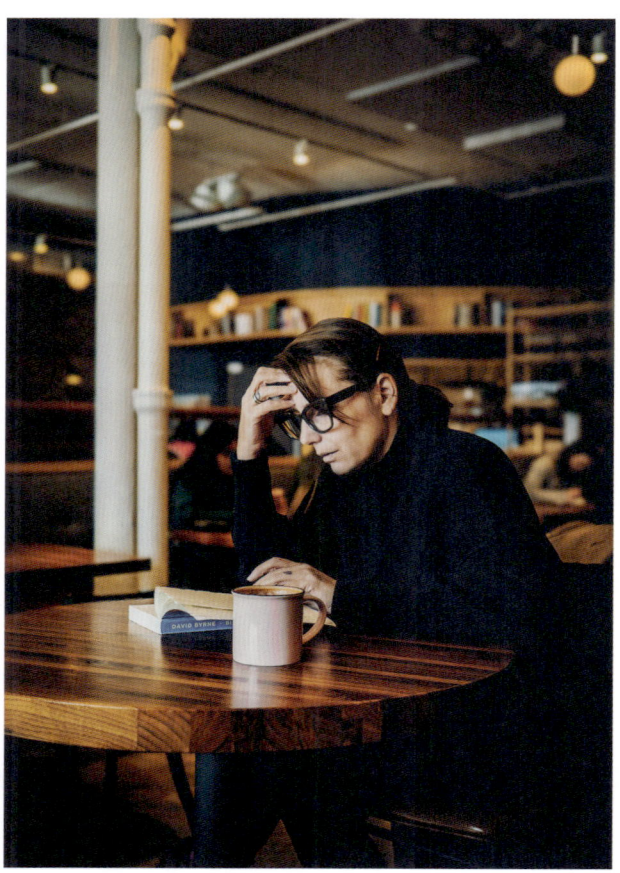

Chicago, Illinois → *United States*

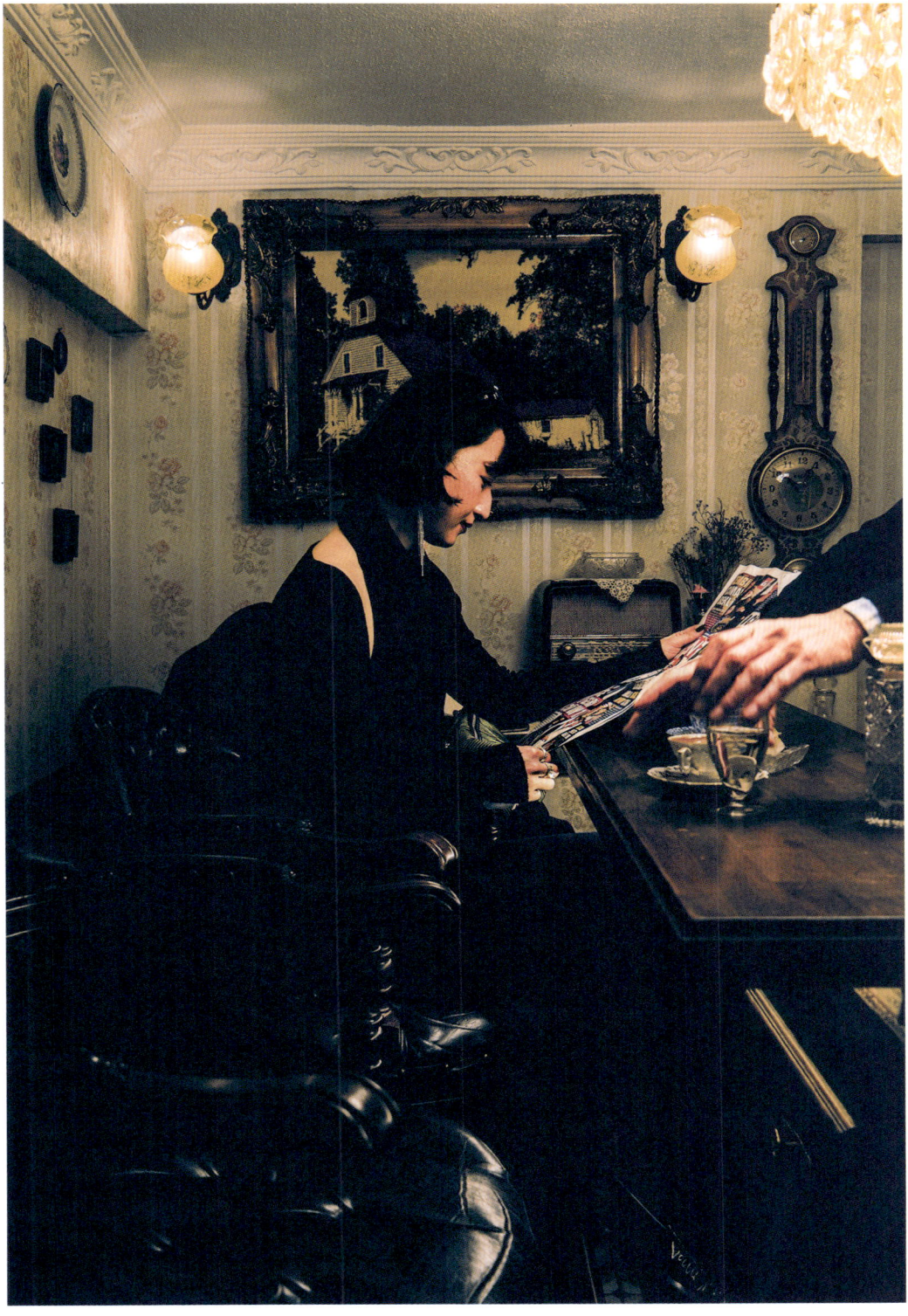

Istanbul → *Turkey*

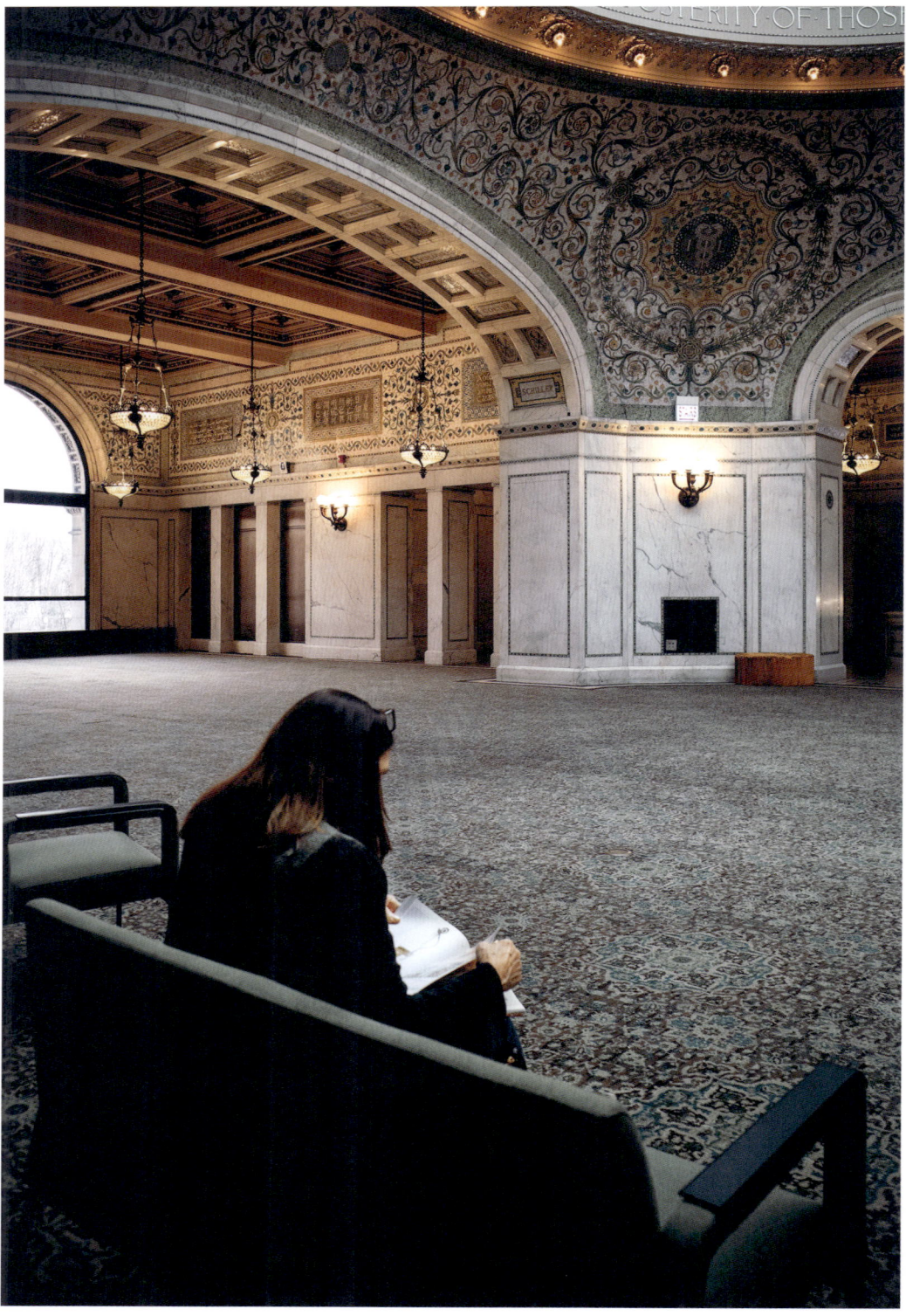

Chicago, Illinois → *United States*

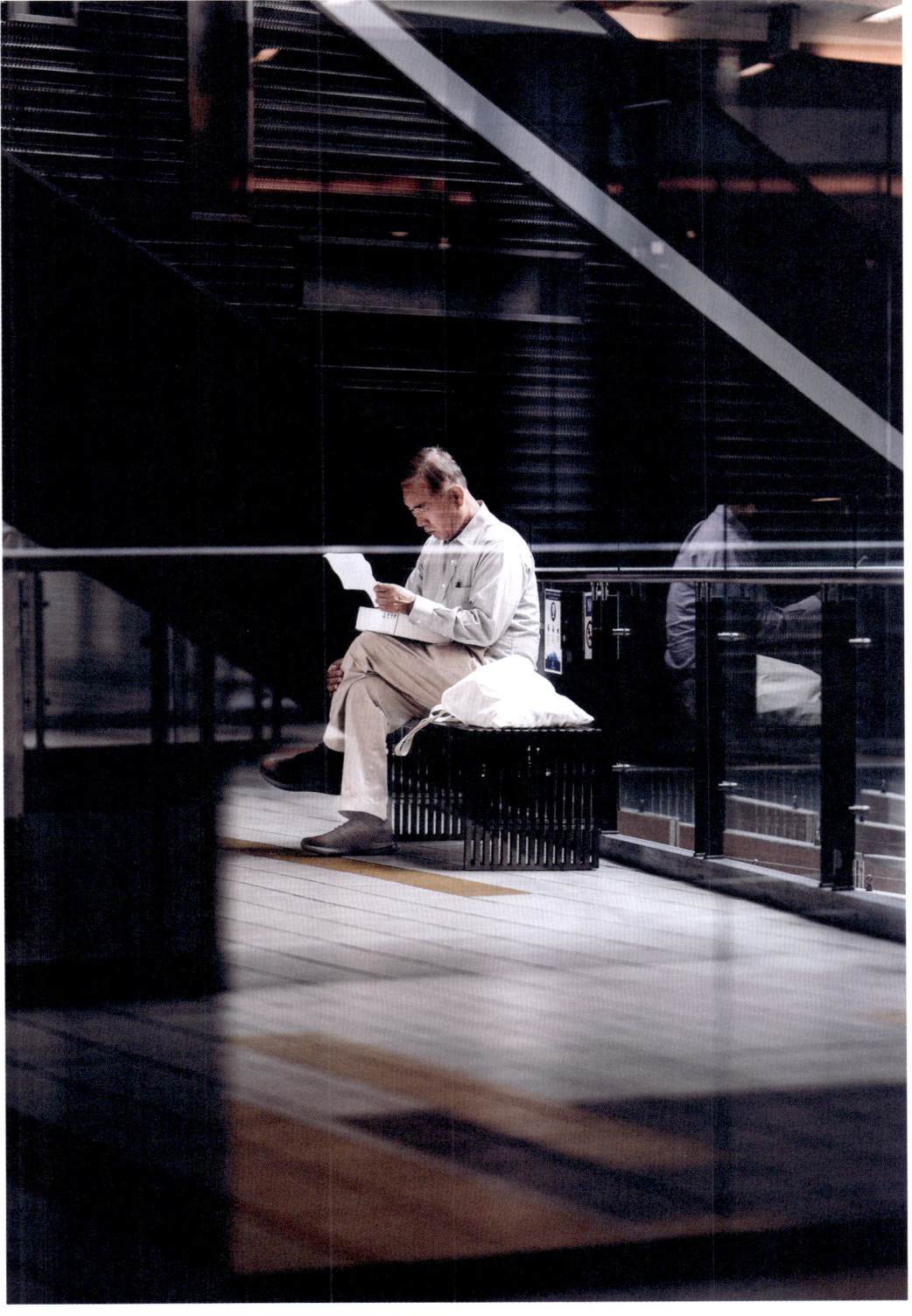

Los Angeles, California → *United States*

"I believe that within every great reader
there are multitudes of people."

SARAH MCNALLY

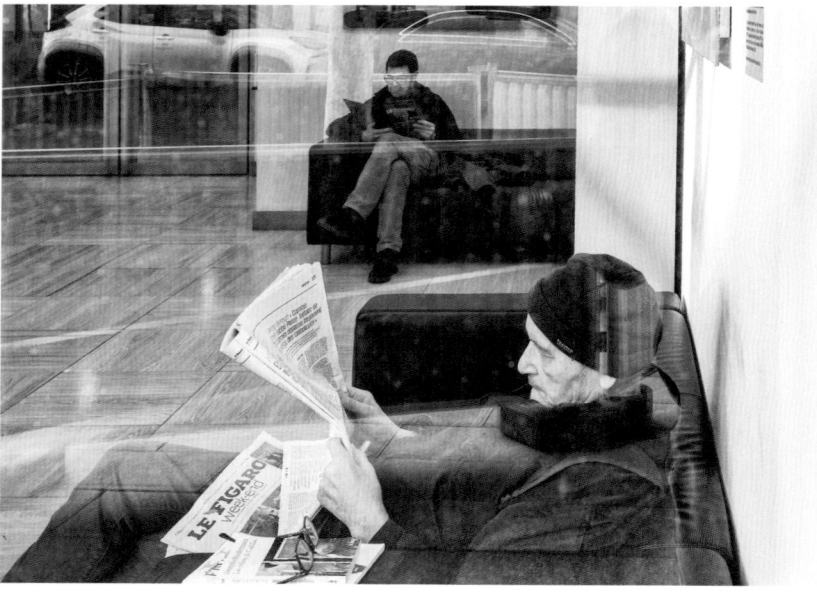

Paris → France

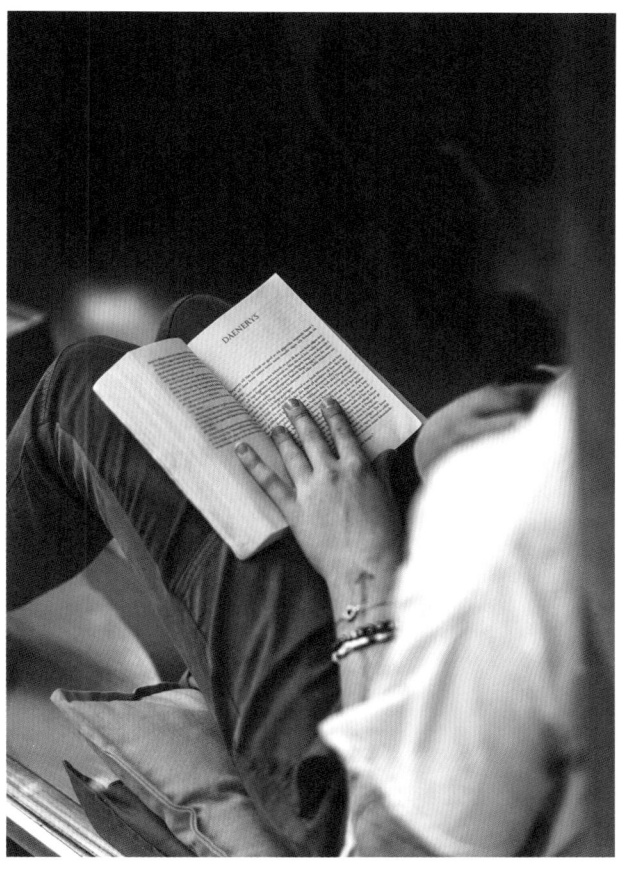

"A reader lives a thousand lives before he dies...
The man who never reads lives only one."

GEORGE R. R. MARTIN

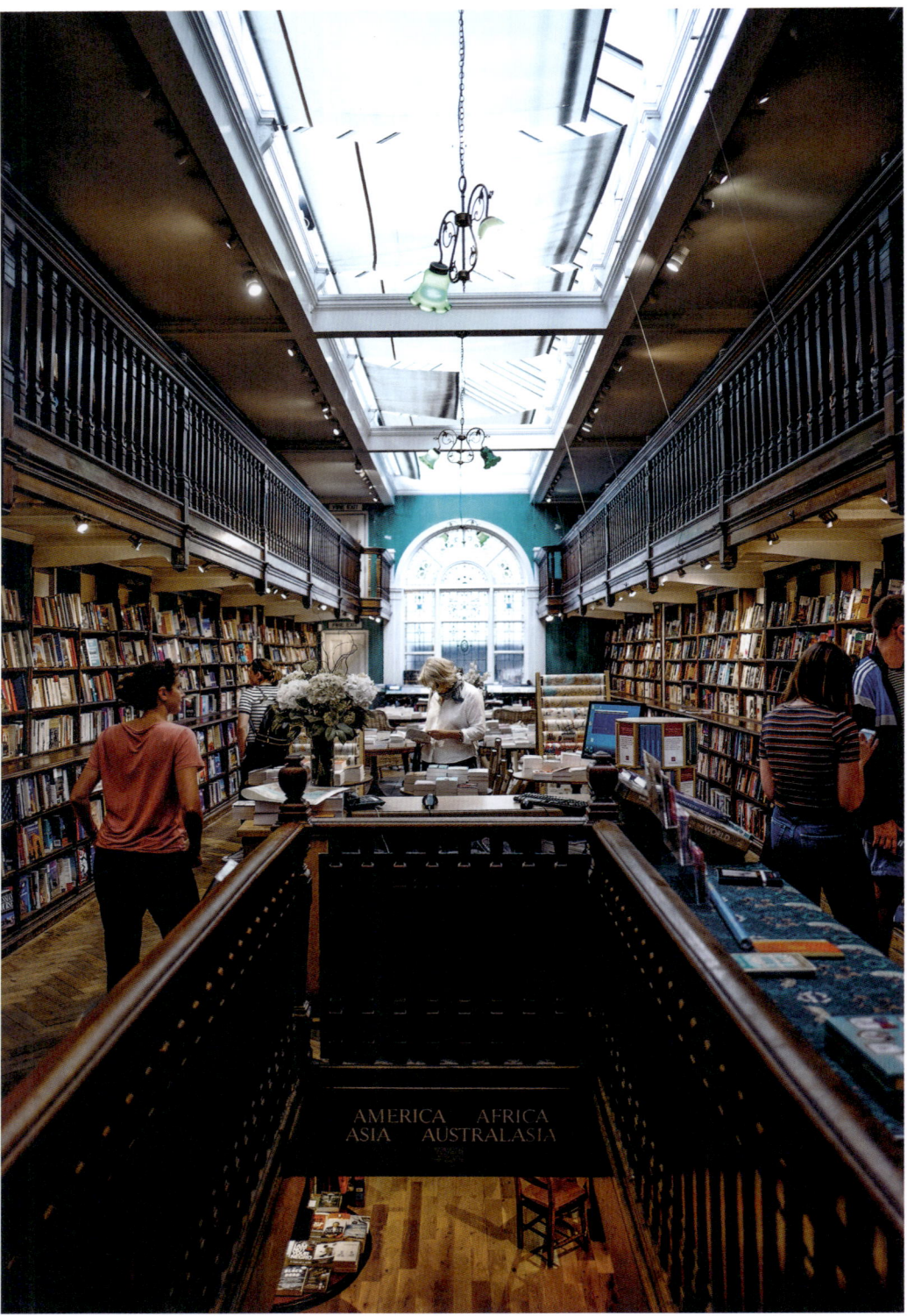

London → England

"A room without books is like
  a body without a soul."

CICERO

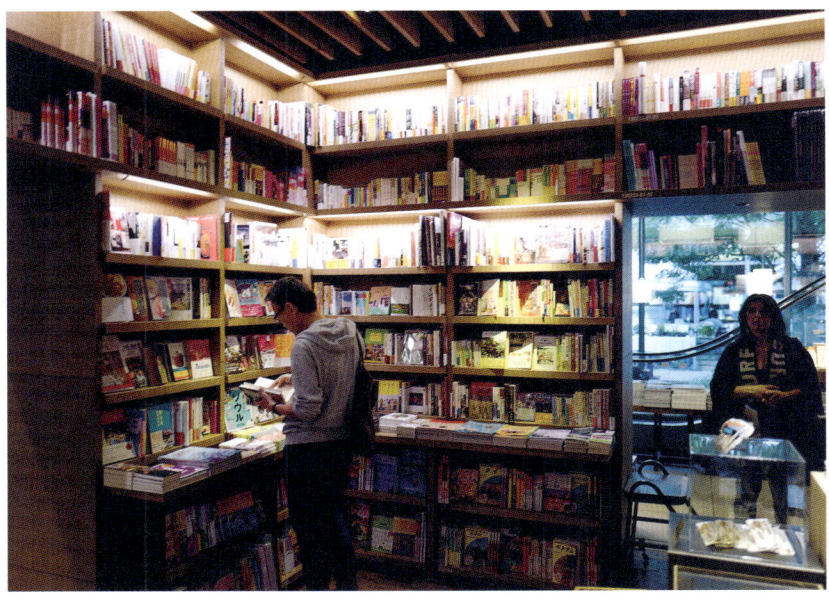

Tokyo → *Japan*

JONATHON SANCHEZ, *Owner*
Blue Bicycle Books → Charleston, South Carolina

We need books in order to live.

There are books we read for school, or to help us fall asleep at night, or to feel less lonely while eating a burrito.

There are books we read for pleasure, in our favorite reading spots.

And then there are those books that become major life moments. A specific copy, the cover, the paper, the typeface, where you read it, when you read it — everything adds up to something completely transcendent.

I've been lucky enough to have a few. One was a $3.95 pocket paperback of *The Great Gatsby*. The original eyes-of Dr.-T.J.-Eckleburg cover, in that *Gatsby* blue — not royal, not navy — a twilight of the infinite promise of a summer night.

I was on a two-week backpacking trip in the North Carolina mountains. I was 15 years old. I couldn't have packed a more perfect book. The lavish parties, waiters carrying in crates of oranges, Daisy swimming in Jay's closet of beautiful shirts, a perfect foil to the freeze-dried meals and crusty socks of the trek.

Then again, it was also the other way around. Those two weeks of beef jerky lunches, campfires, blisters and hacky-sack sessions were my own West Egg. I was having the time of my life. Gatsby and Daisy and Myrtle were caught in the trappings of civilization, flitting back and forth between Manhattan and the lawns of Long Island, never really escaping the valley of ashes in between. I was walking through rhododendron tunnels in the Shining Rock Wilderness. The mountains, when you're young, can burrow in your heart and become a longtime source of solace and joy.

The thing about these magical reading moments is they're like grace, you can't force them, they just happen.

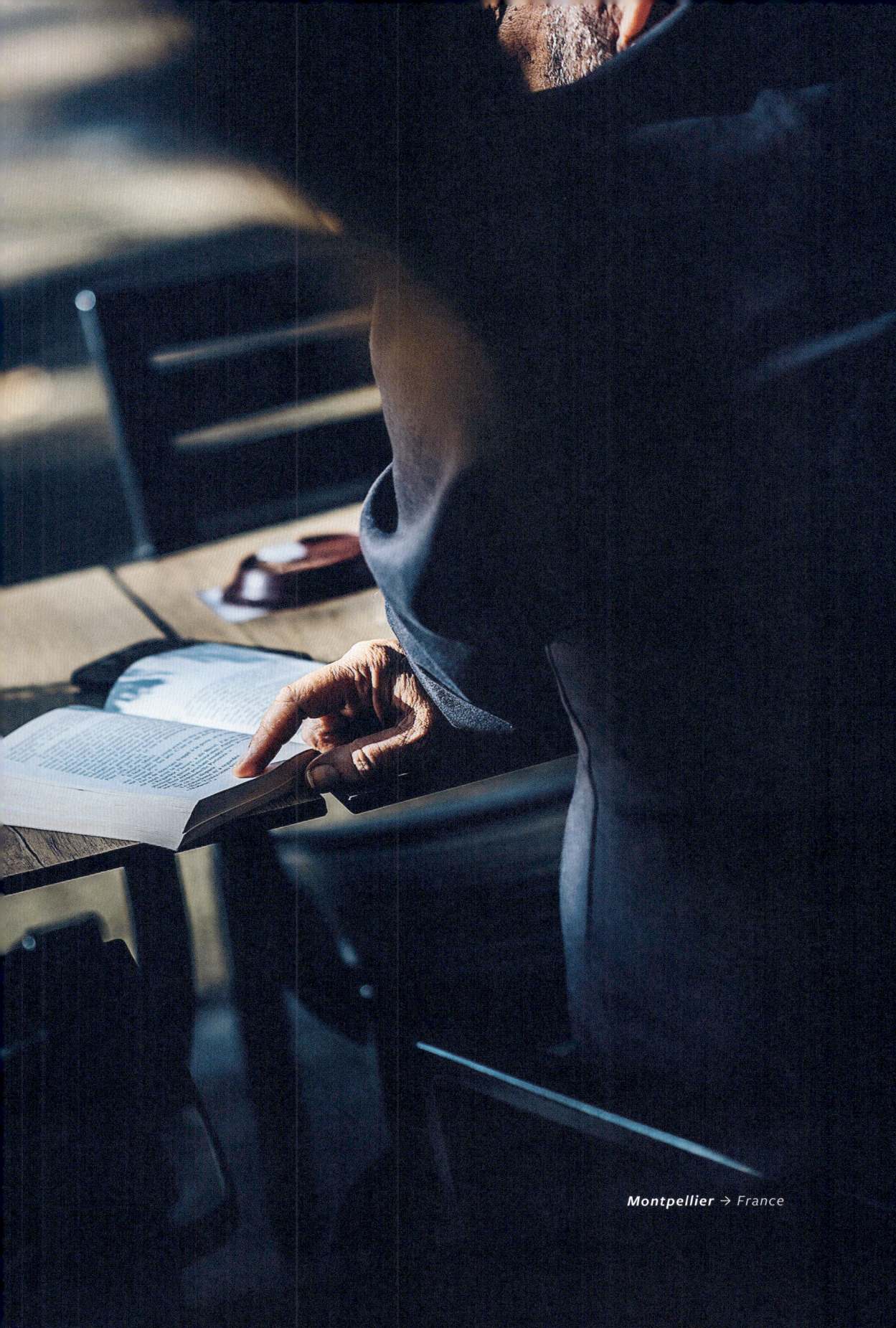

Montpellier → France

The copy of *Don Quixote* I carried around college till the cover felt worn in my hand like Rocinantes' saddle.

The Big Sleep by Raymond Chandler, L.A. noir on a bright hot beach, like ice cream on fruit cobbler.

One Hundred Years of Solitude—I still remember the wooden shelf I found it on, at a secondhand shop in Massachusetts. The sexy, rich cover had a reviewer's quote that became like a mantra: "...forces upon us at every page the wonder and extravagance of life."

I started reading *Anna Karenina* while we were living in a small rented house. Our young children shared a bedroom, there was a den with a plush Ikea chair. A cup of black tea, two toddlers playing at my feet, Levin and Oblonsky snipe hunting in the Russian woods. I wished it could last forever. (In a way it did, it took me eight years to finish it.)

There's a whole industry now, selling the complete reading experience. You can get a box with a book, thoughtfully paired with a scented candle, snacks, beverages, other appropriate accoutrements. As a retailer and a believer in the total book experience, I admire the hustle, even if I have to admit the whole thing feels store-bought and inorganic.

Yet how tragically and perfectly American, this urge to artificially recreate a moment.

Had we the means, I think we all, in some way or another, would build a big house across the water from our long-lost love, throw huge jazzy parties, invite everyone we knew—all in the hopes that Daisy Buchanan will one day show up.

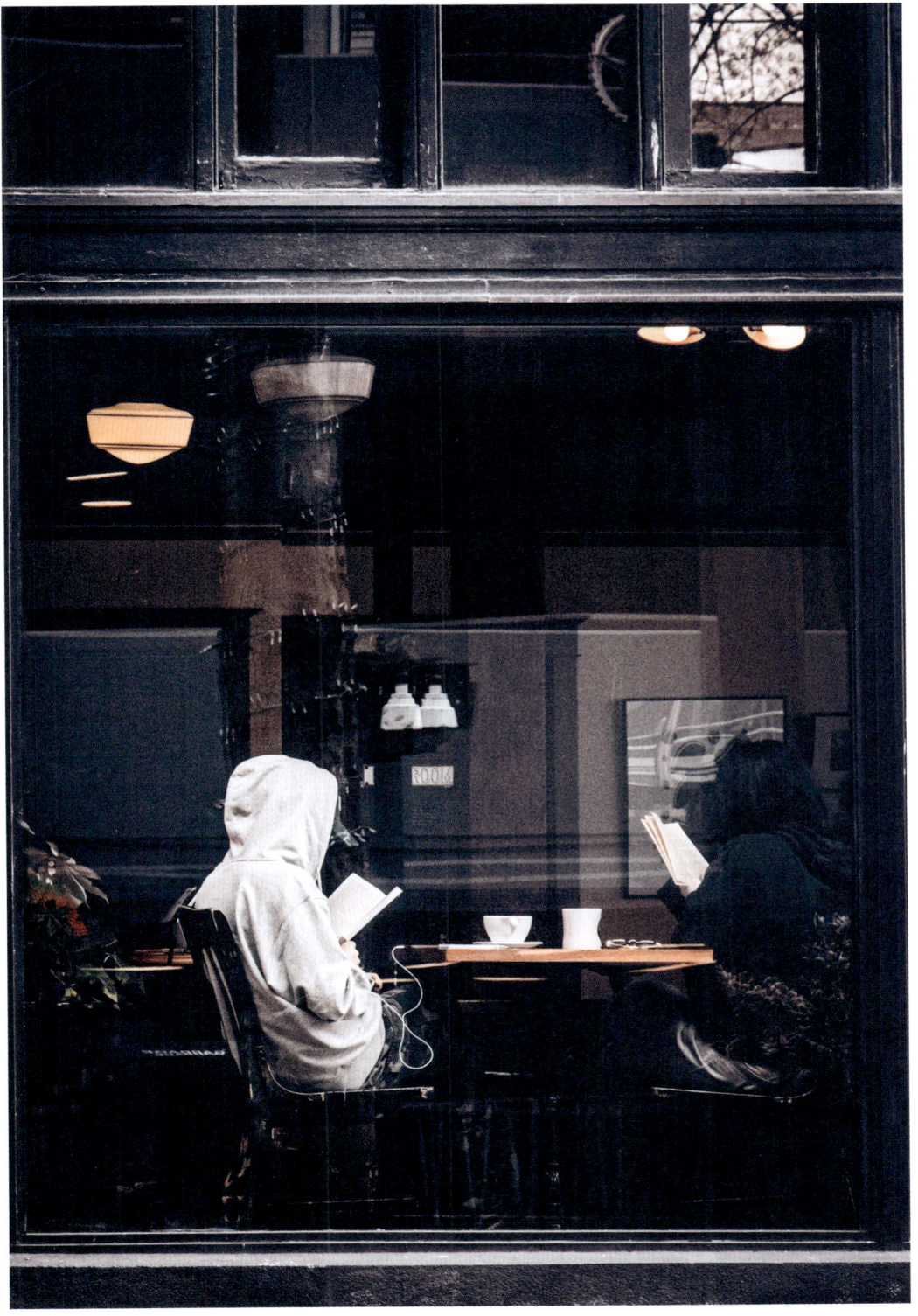

Portland, Oregon → *United States*

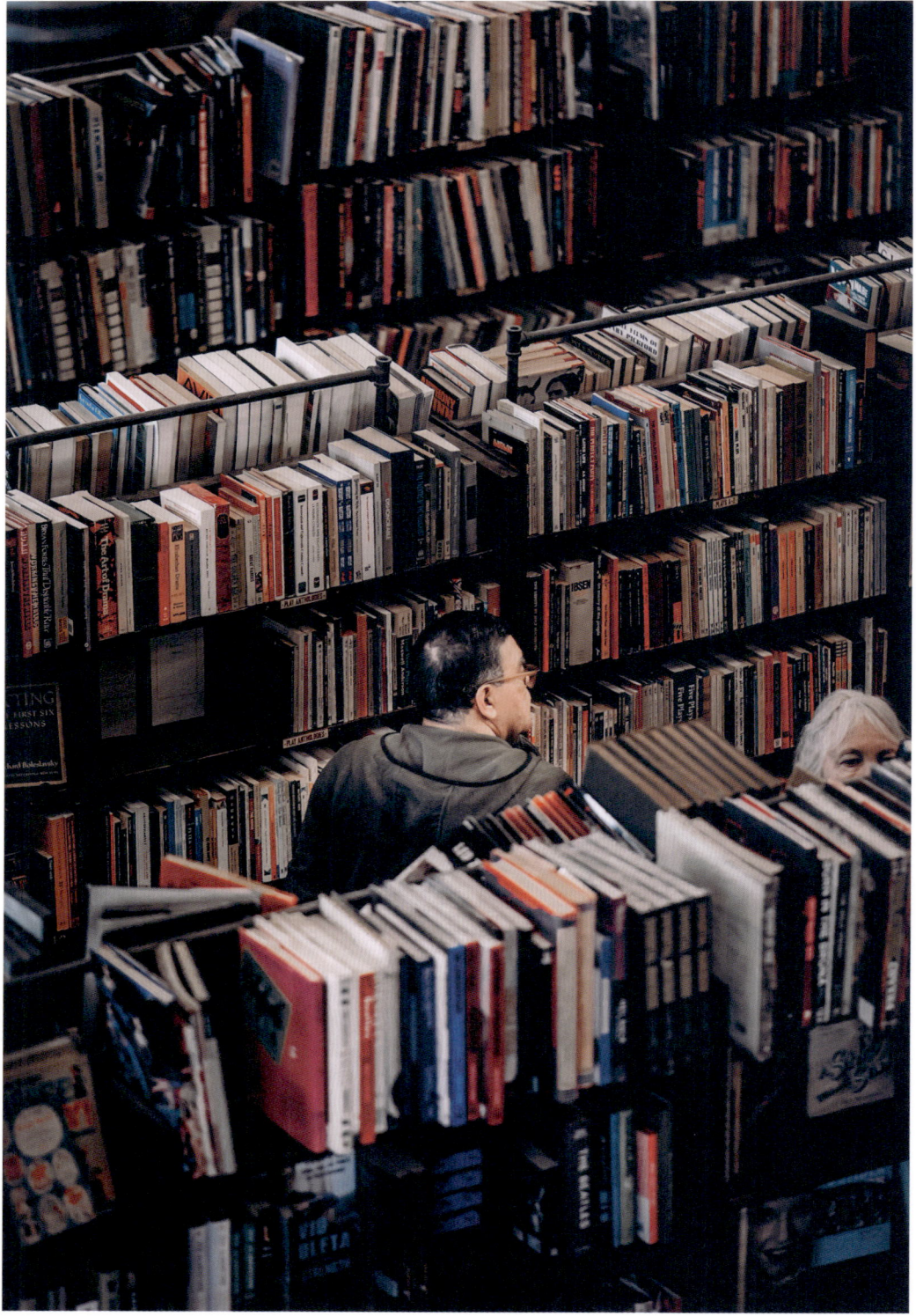

Los Angeles, California → *United States*

"Books are good company, in sad times and happy times, for books are people—people who have managed to stay alive by hiding between the covers of a book."

E.B. WHITE

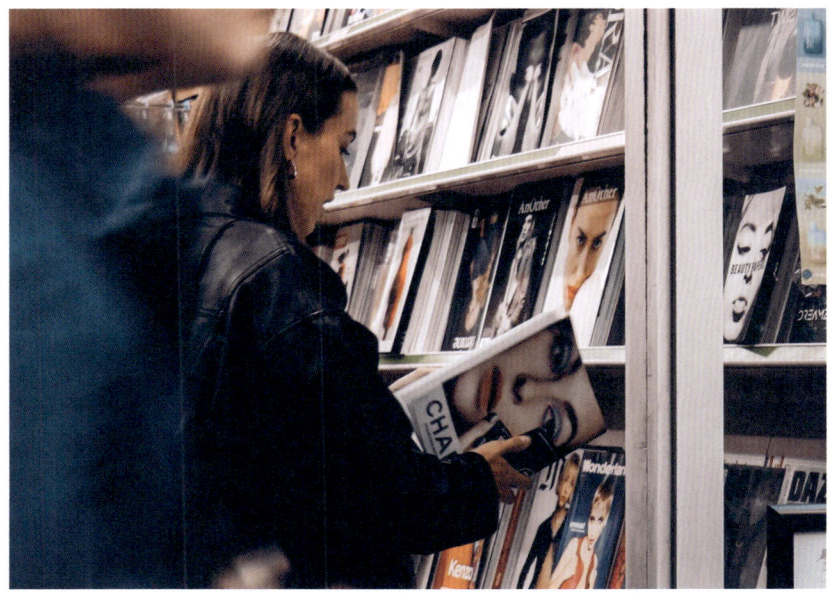

London → *England*

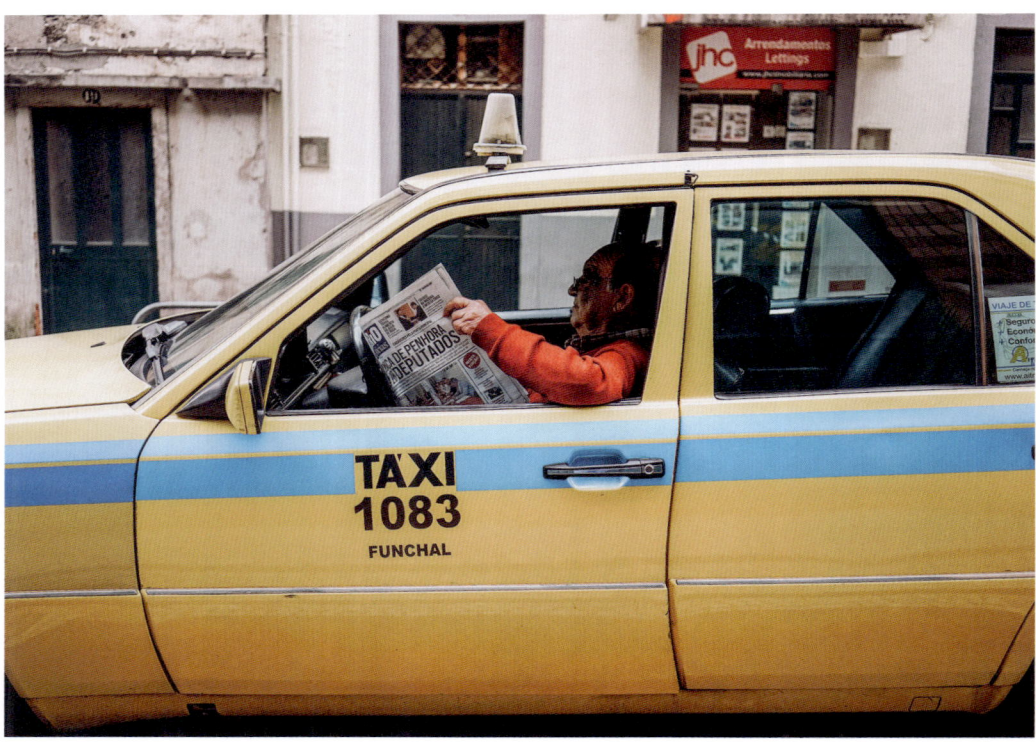

Madeira → *Portugal*

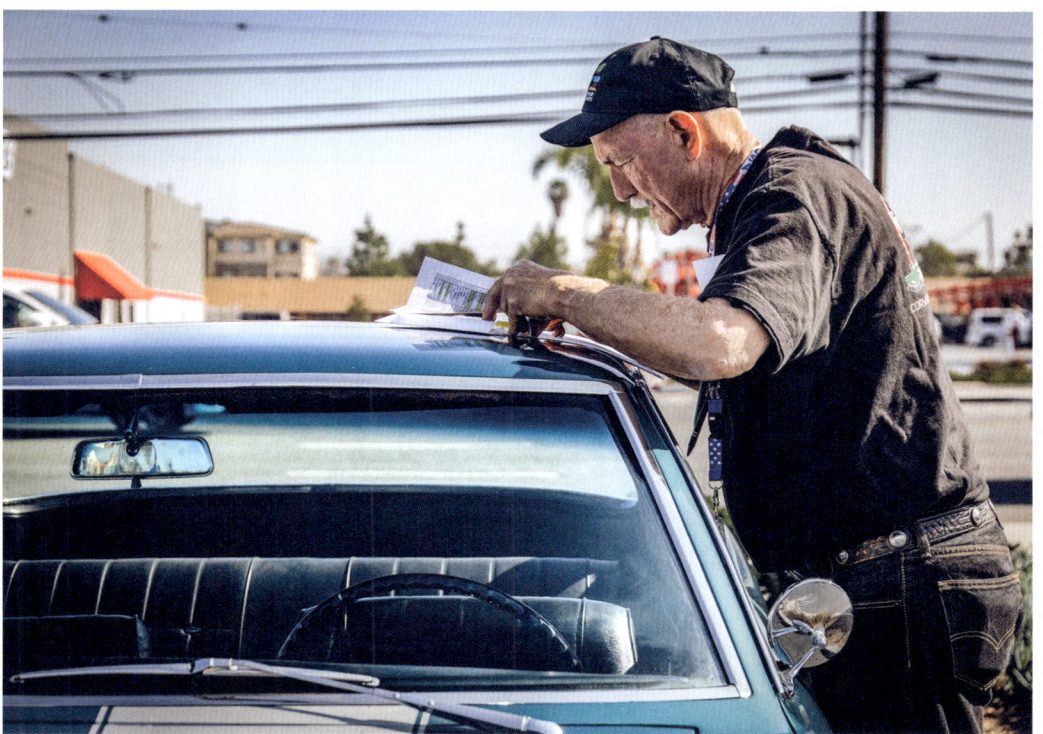

Los Angeles, California → *United States*

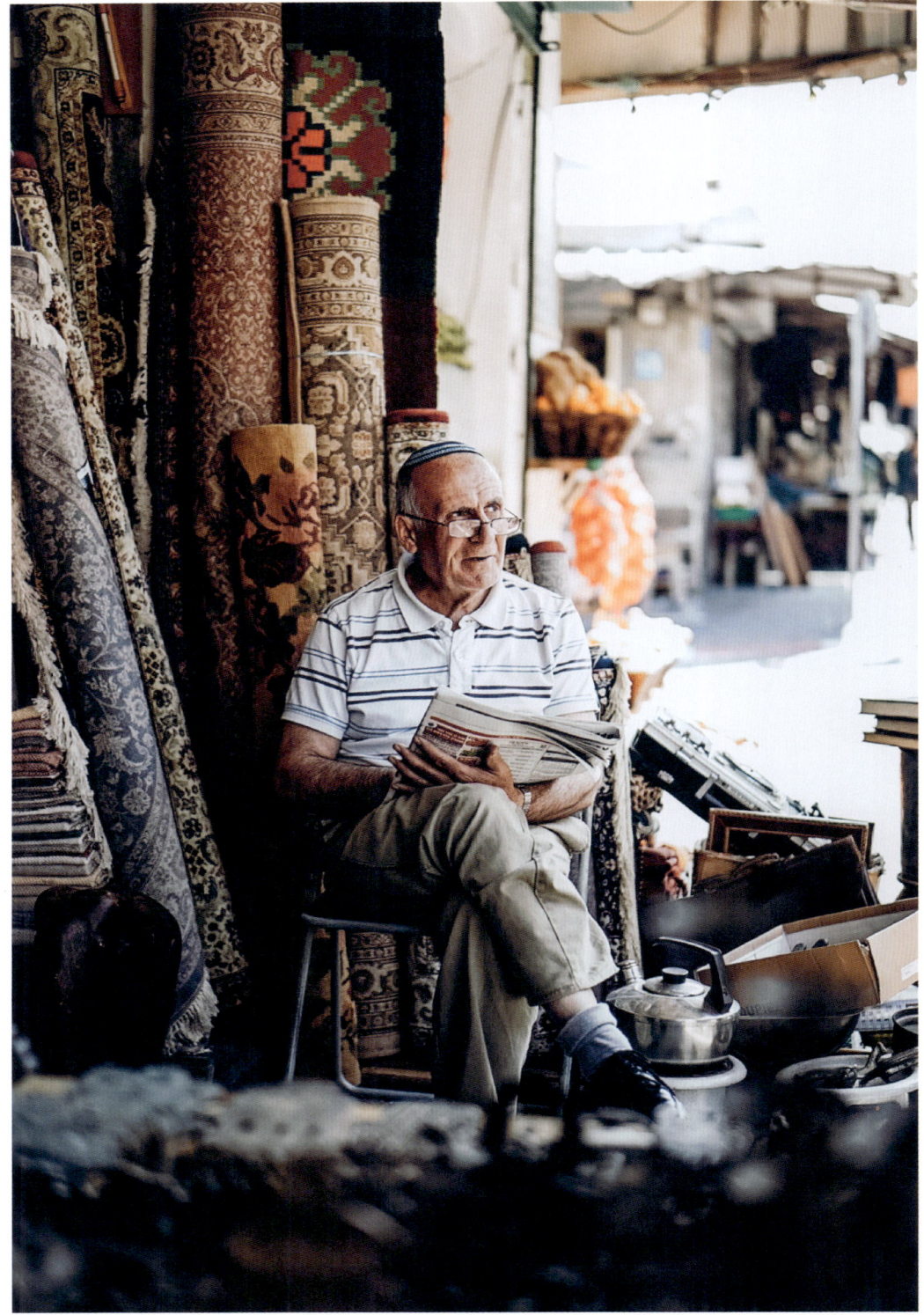

Jaffa → *Israel*

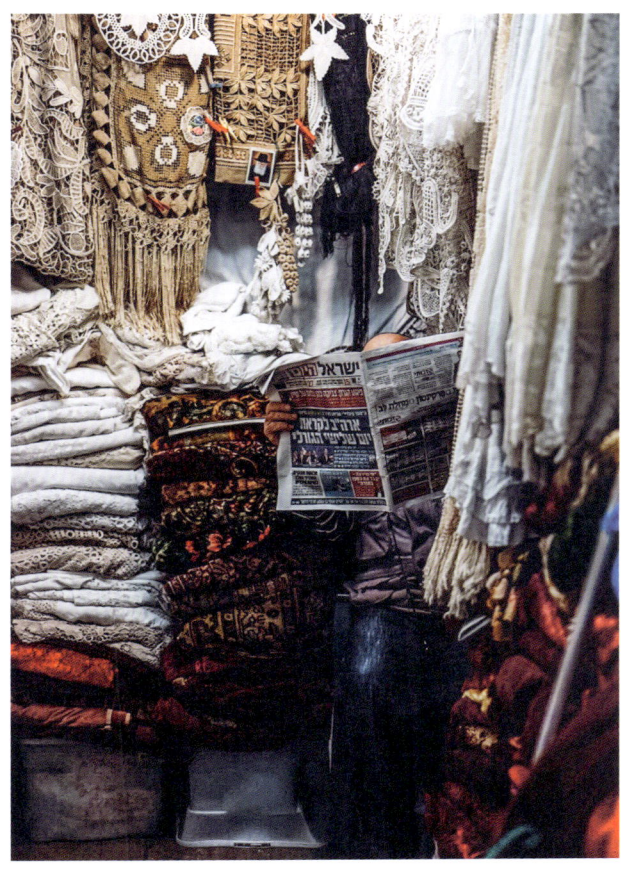

"Reading is the sole means by which we slip, involuntarily, often helplessly, into another's skin, another's voice, another's soul."

JOYCE CAROL OATES

Tel Aviv → Israel

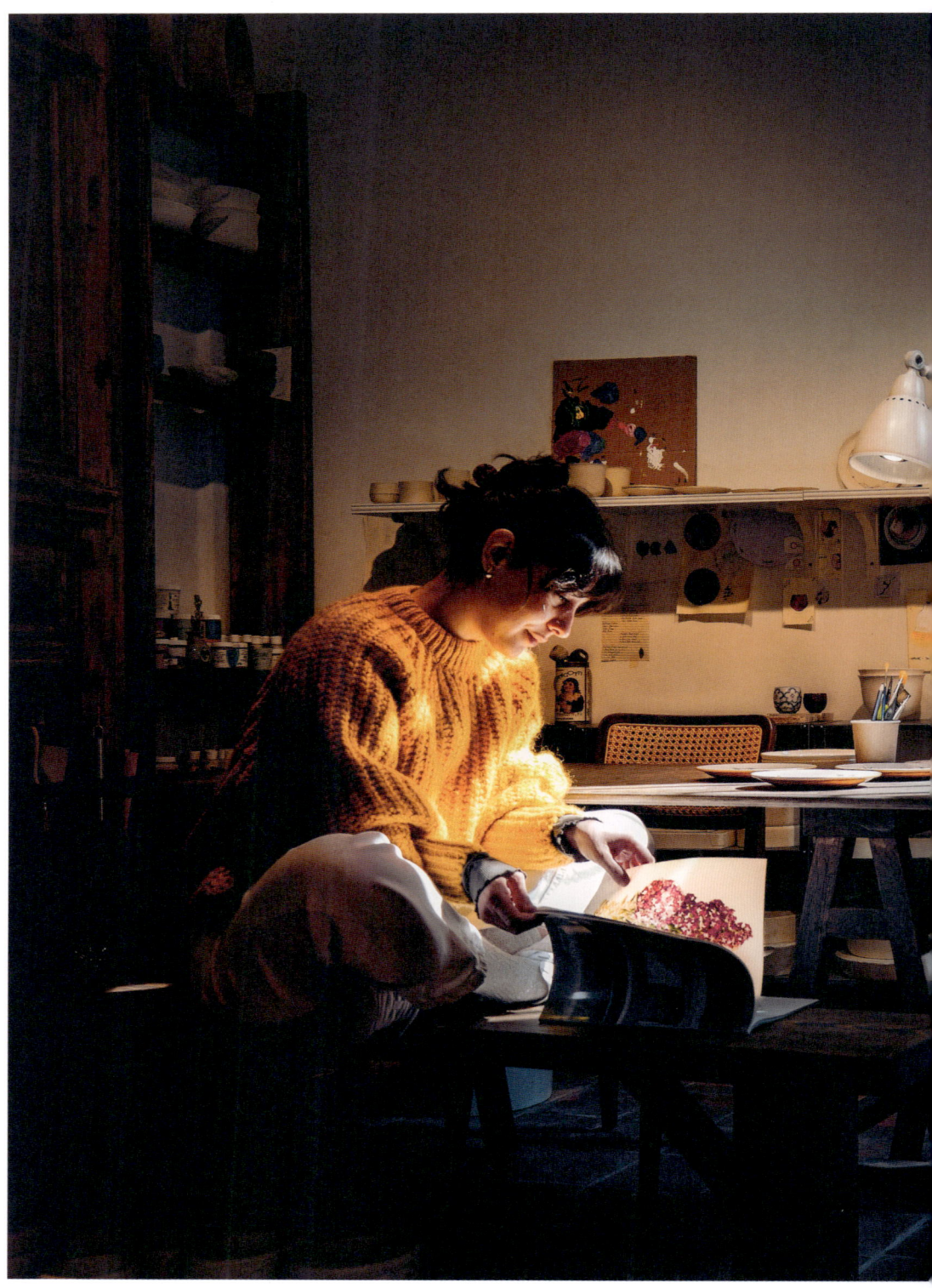

Istanbul → *Turkey*

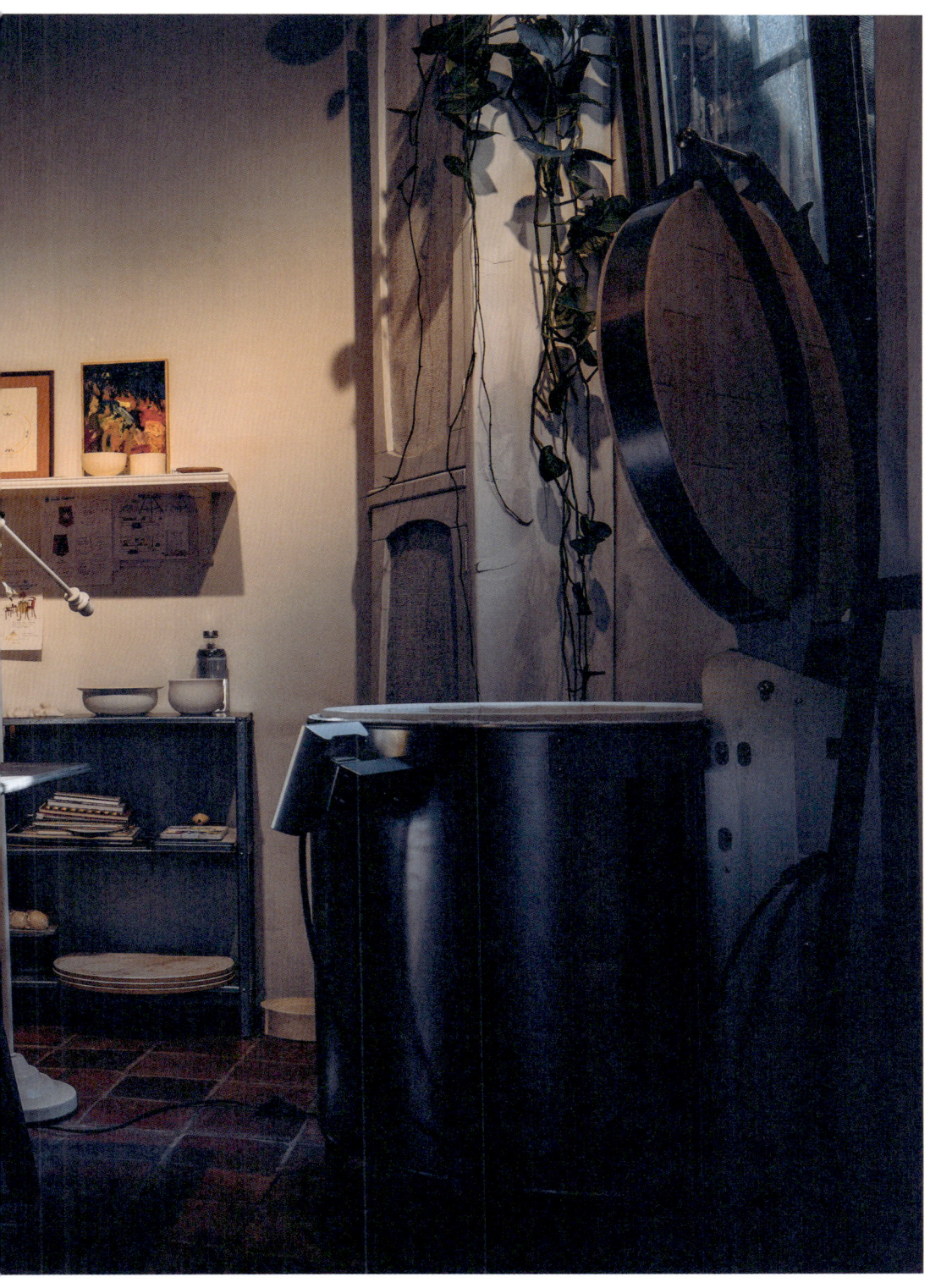

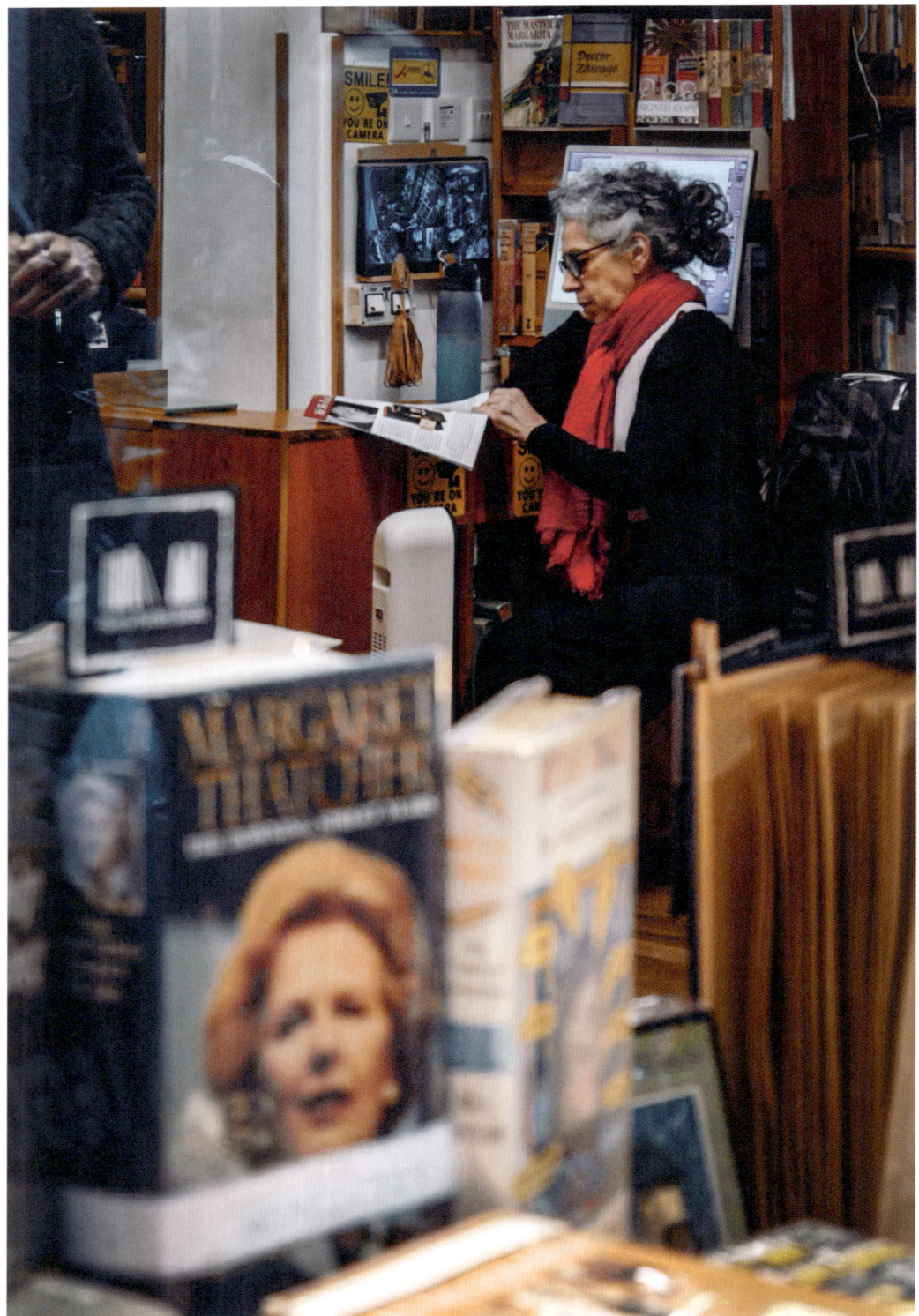

London → England

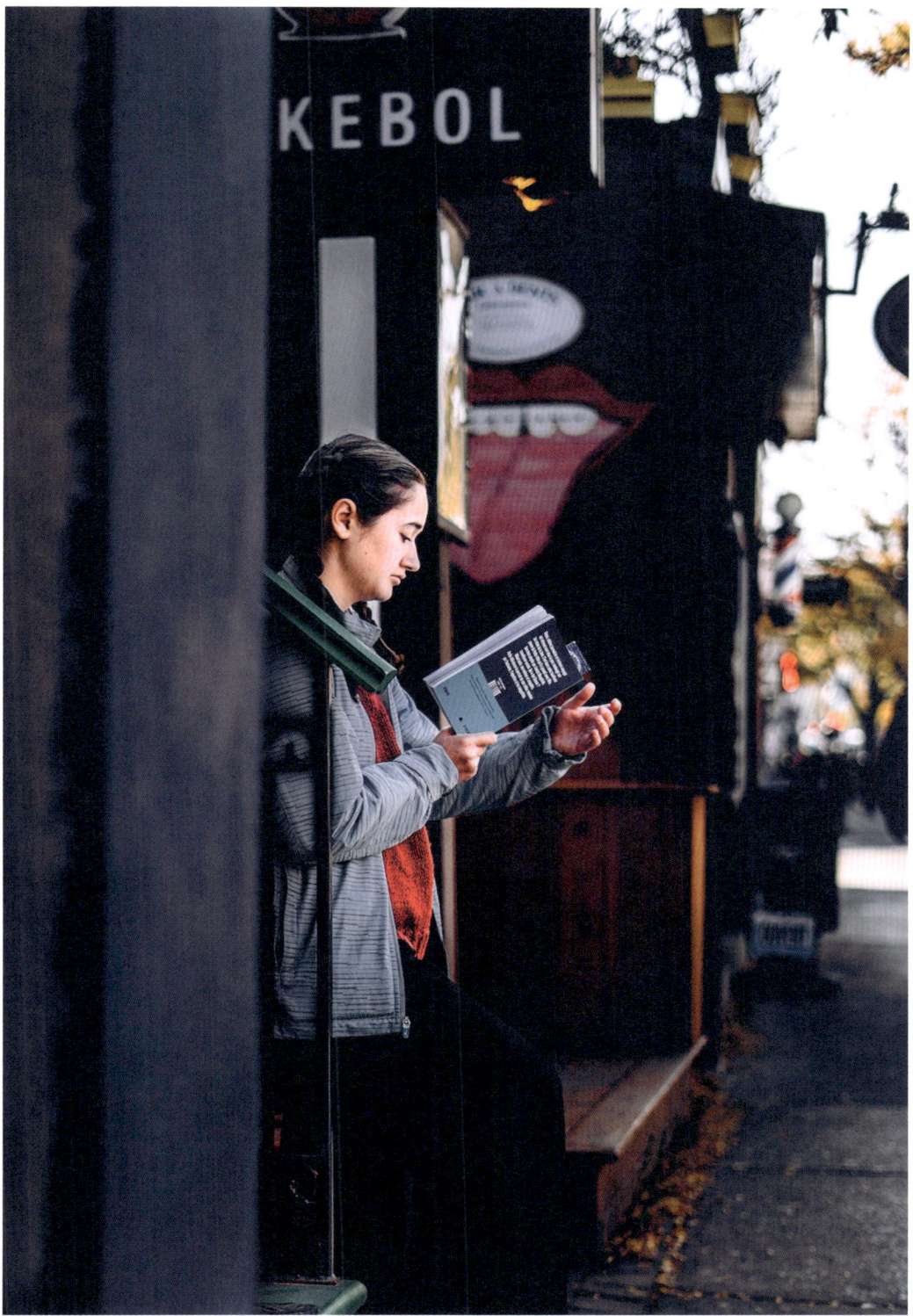

Montreal → *Canada*

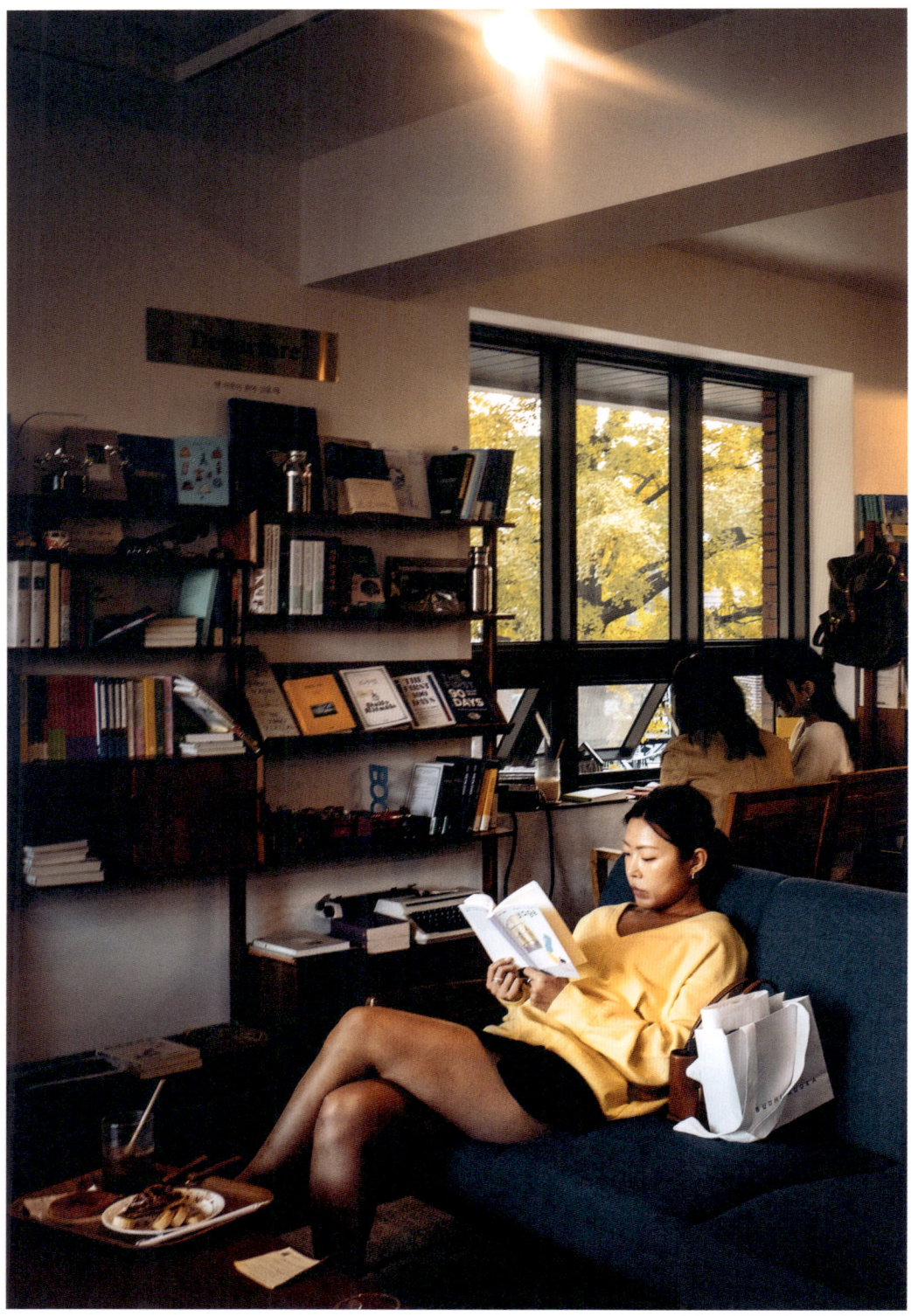

Seoul → *South Korea*

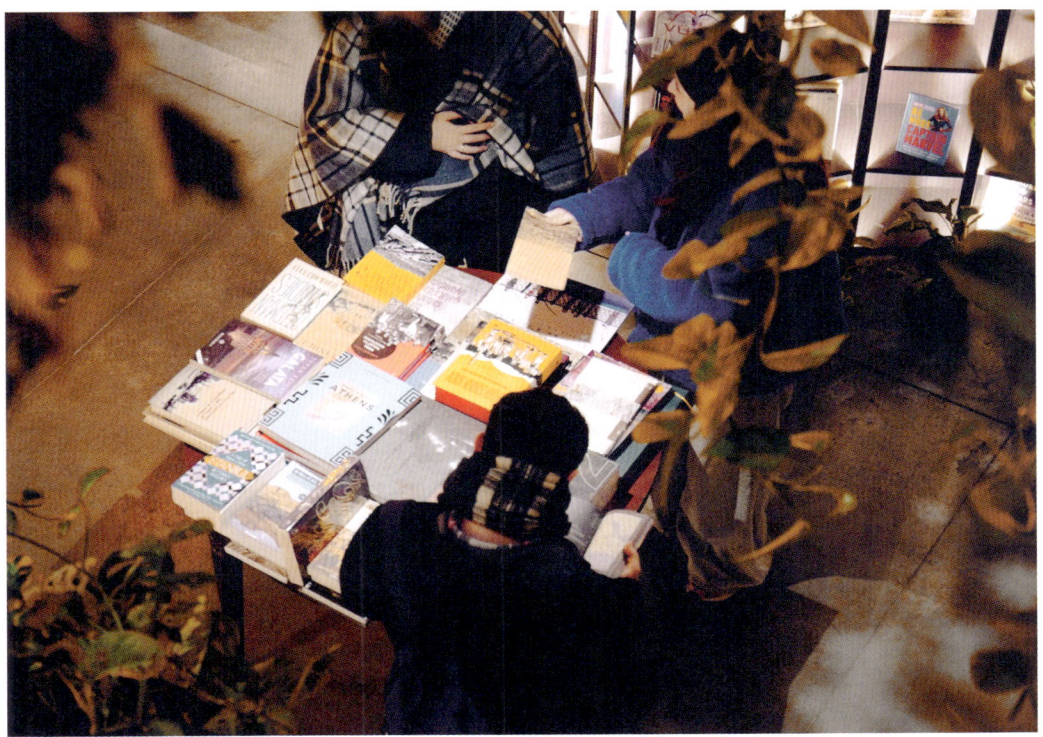

Istanbul → *Turkey*

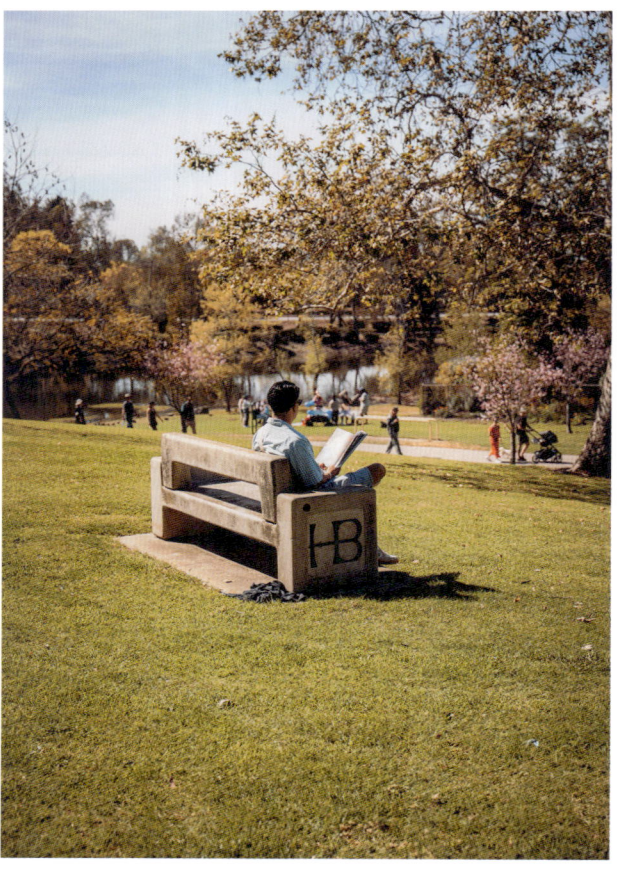

"I kept always two books in my pocket,
one to read, one to write in."

ROBERT LOUIS STEVENSON

Huntington Beach, California → *United States*

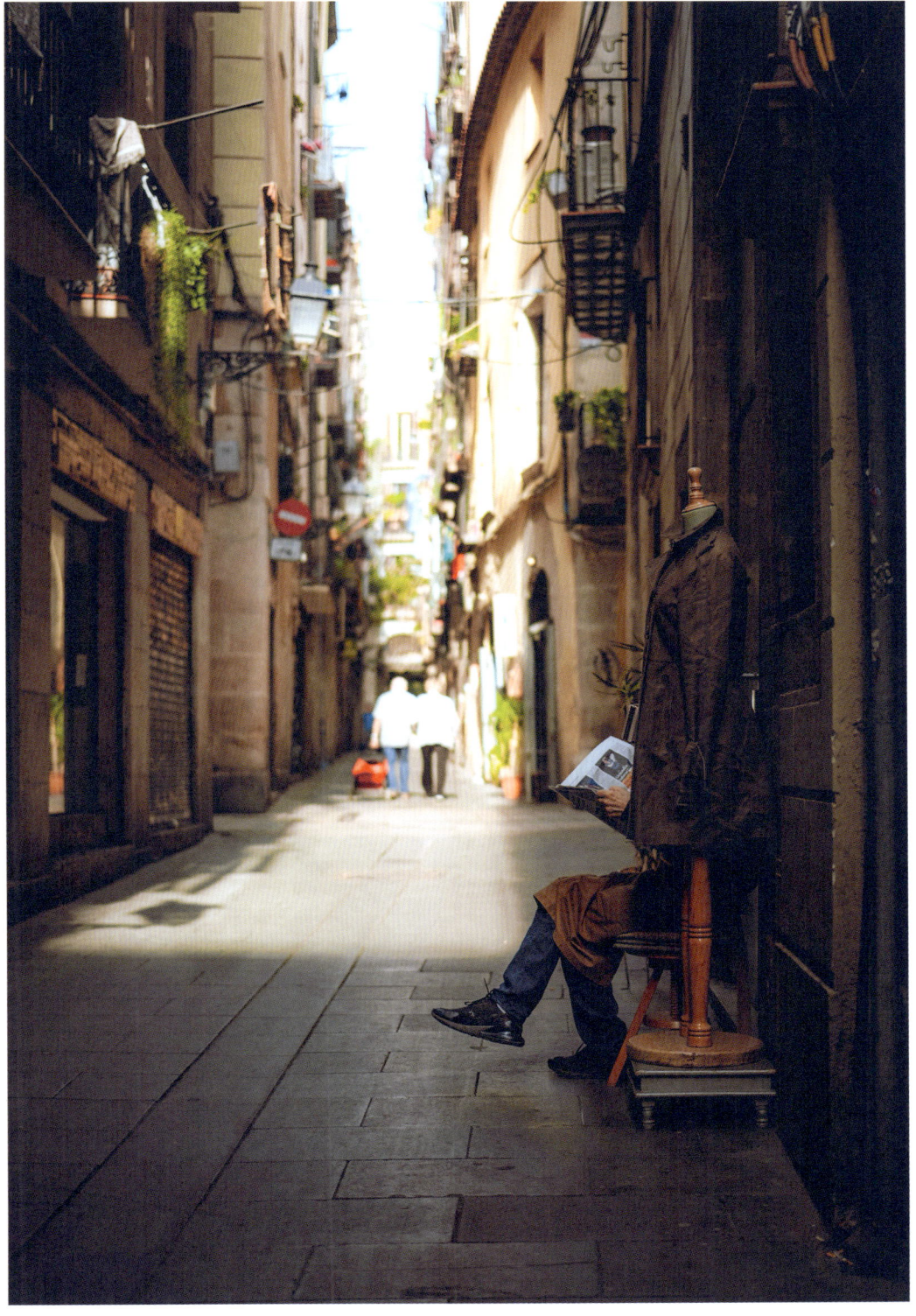

Barcelona → *Spain*

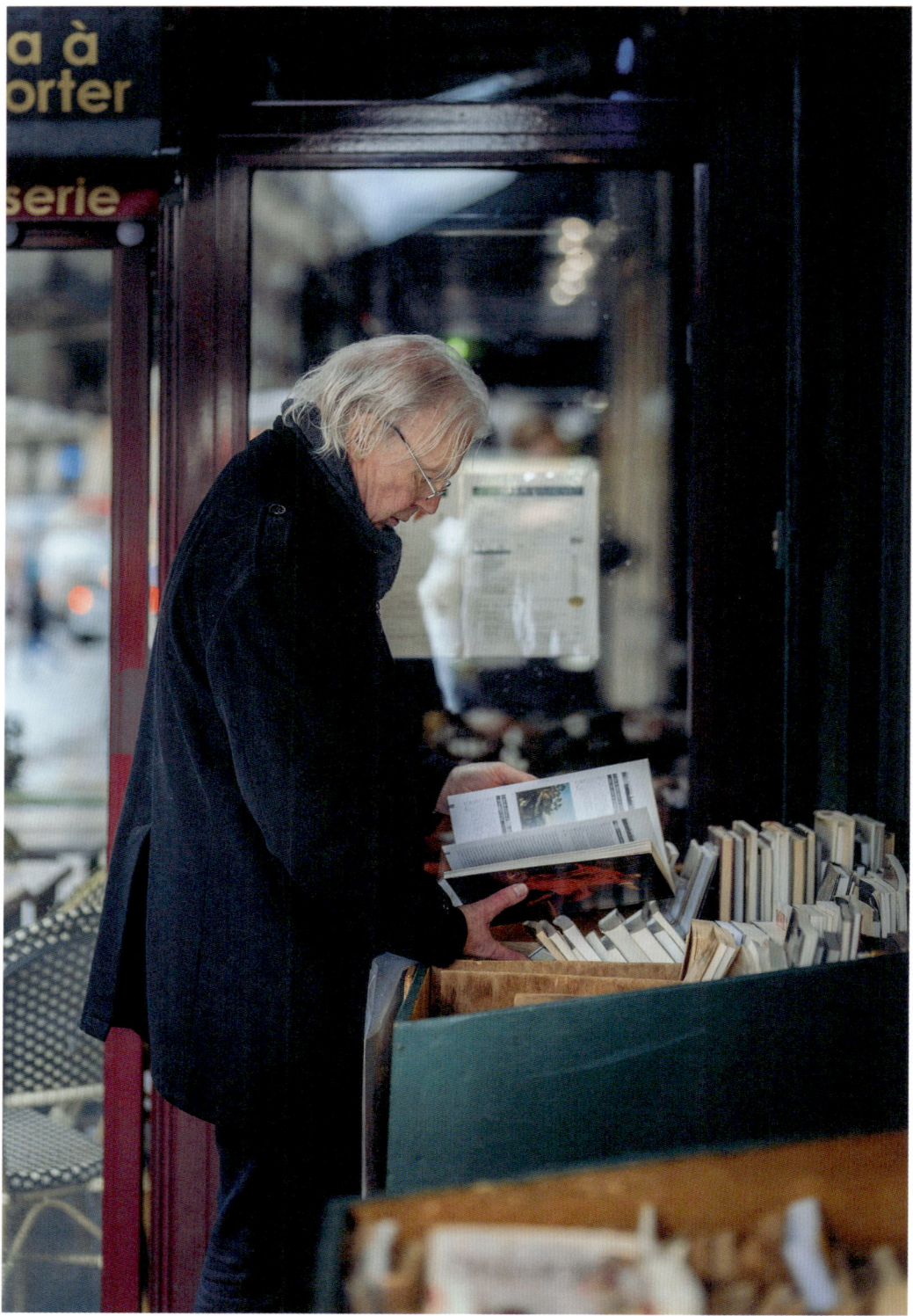

Paris → France

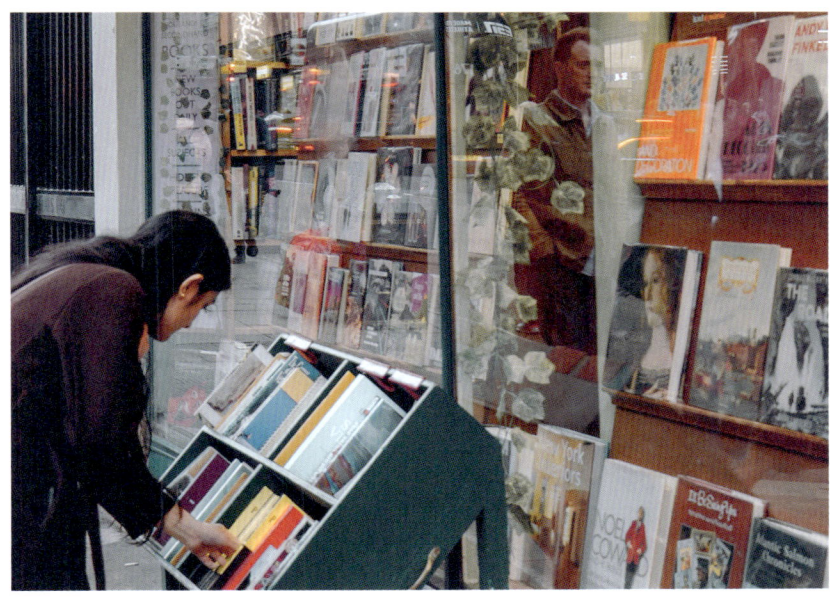

"The more that you read, the more things
you will know. The more that you learn,
the more places you'll go."

DR. SEUSS

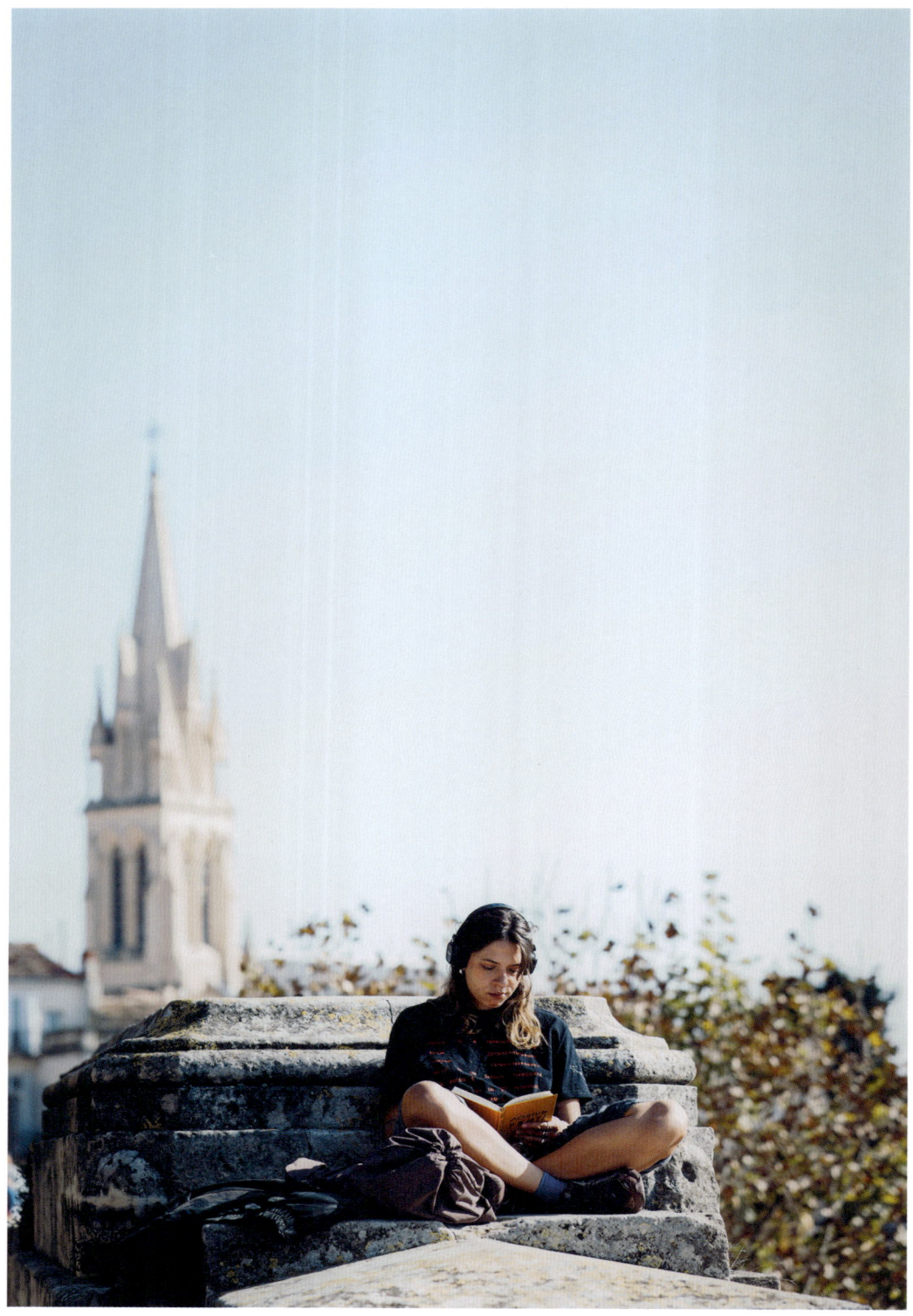

Montpellier → *France*

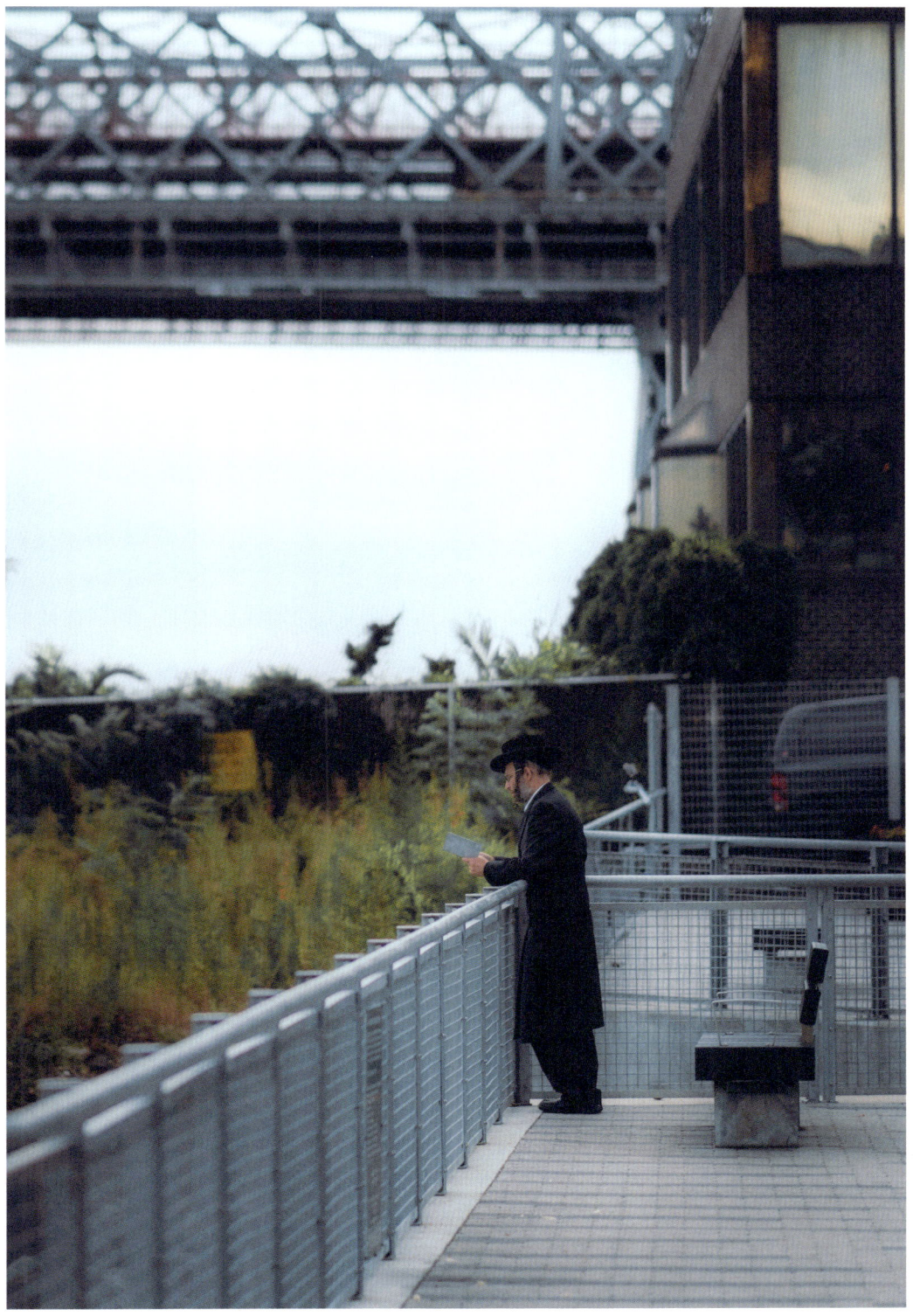

New York, New York → *United States*

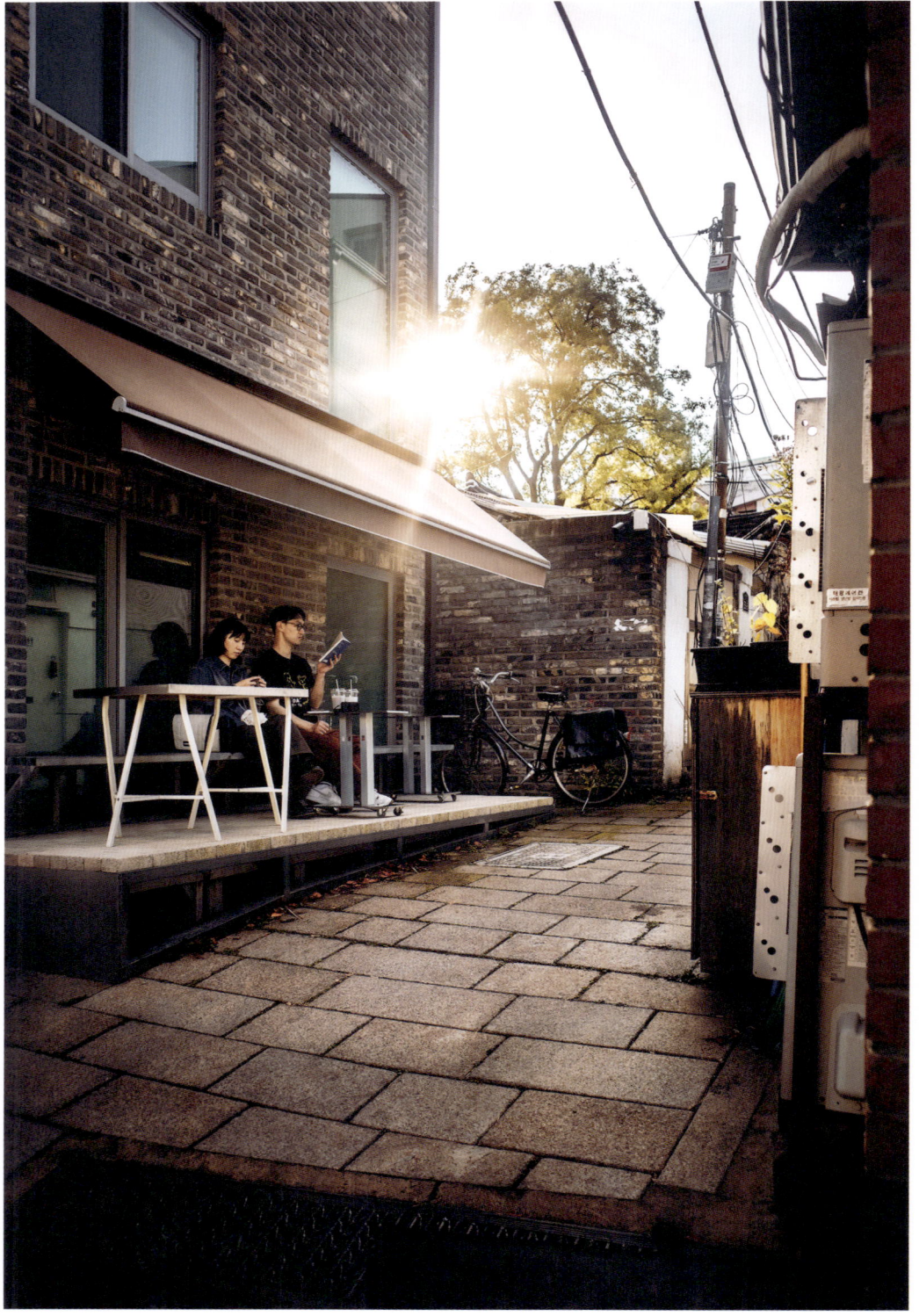

Seoul → *South Korea*

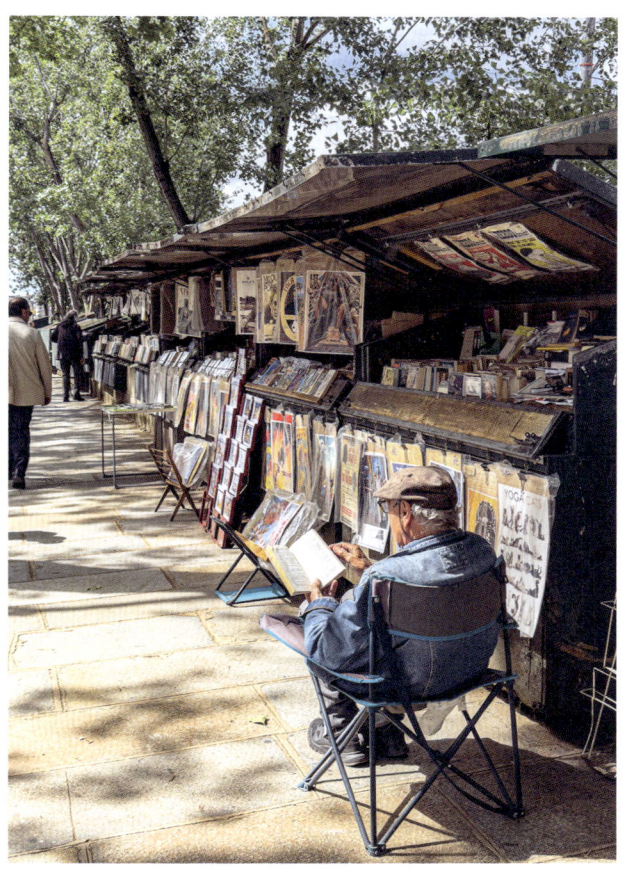

"We read books to find out who we are. What other people, real or imaginary, do and think and feel... is an essential guide to our understanding of what we ourselves are and may become."

URSULA K. LE GUIN

Paris → *France*

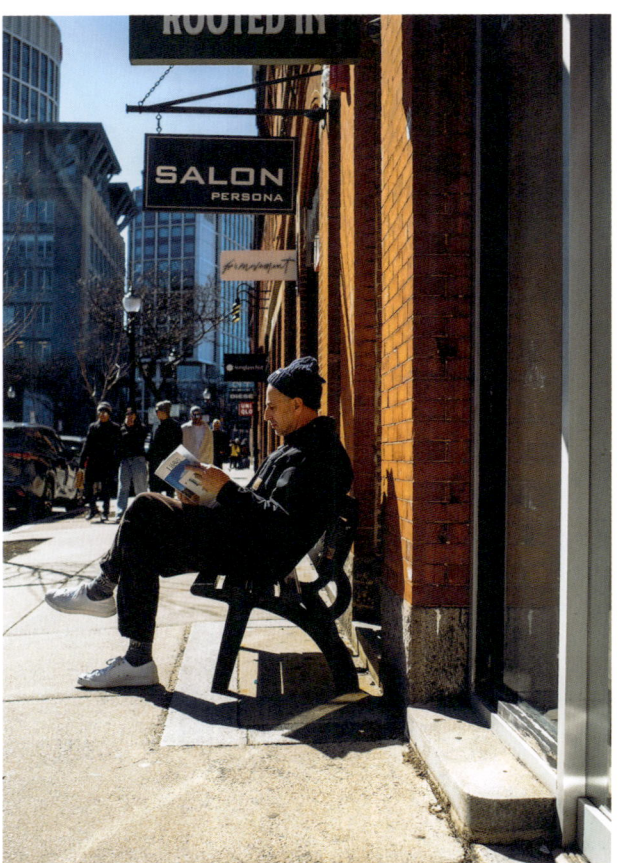

"A word after a word after a word is power."

MARGARET ATWOOD

Boston, Massachusetts → *United States*

"The reading of all good books is like
a conversation with the finest minds
of past centuries."

RENÉ DESCARTES

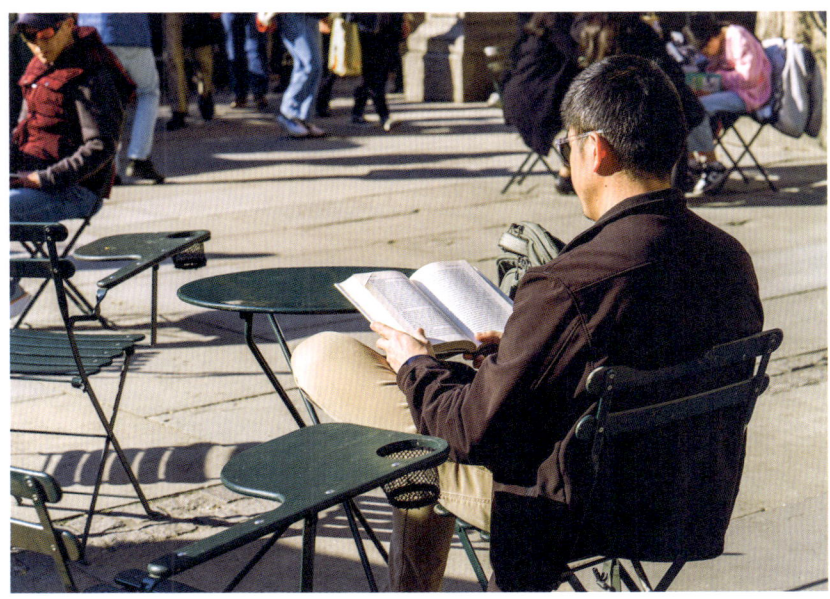

New York, New York → *United States*

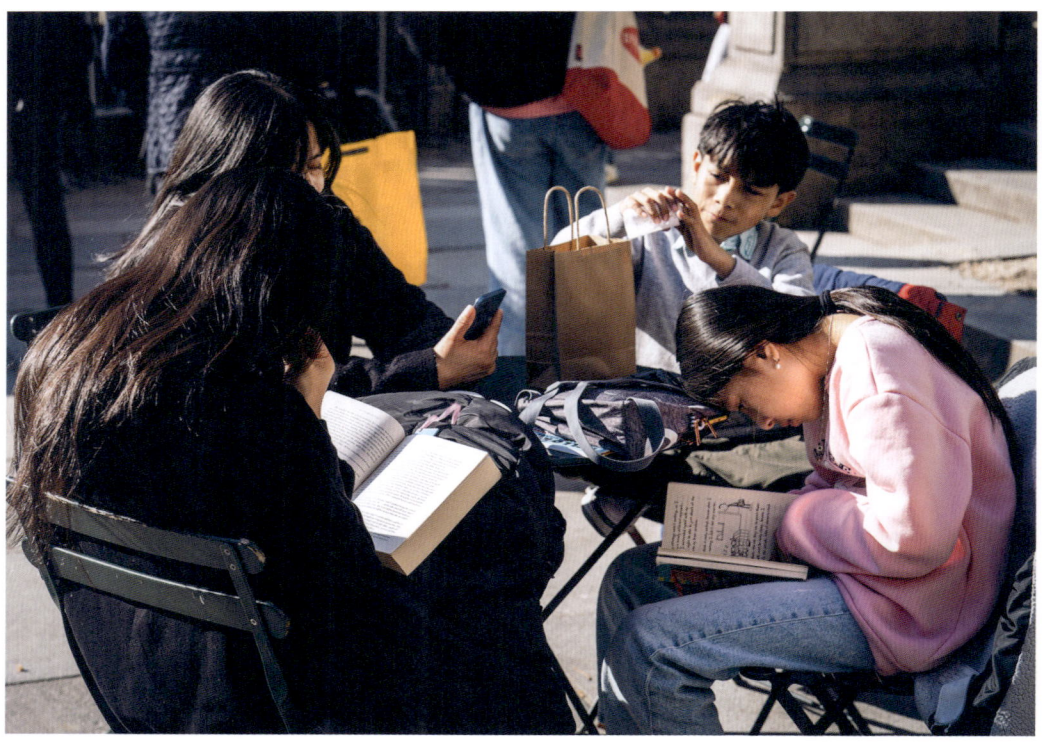

New York, New York → *United States*

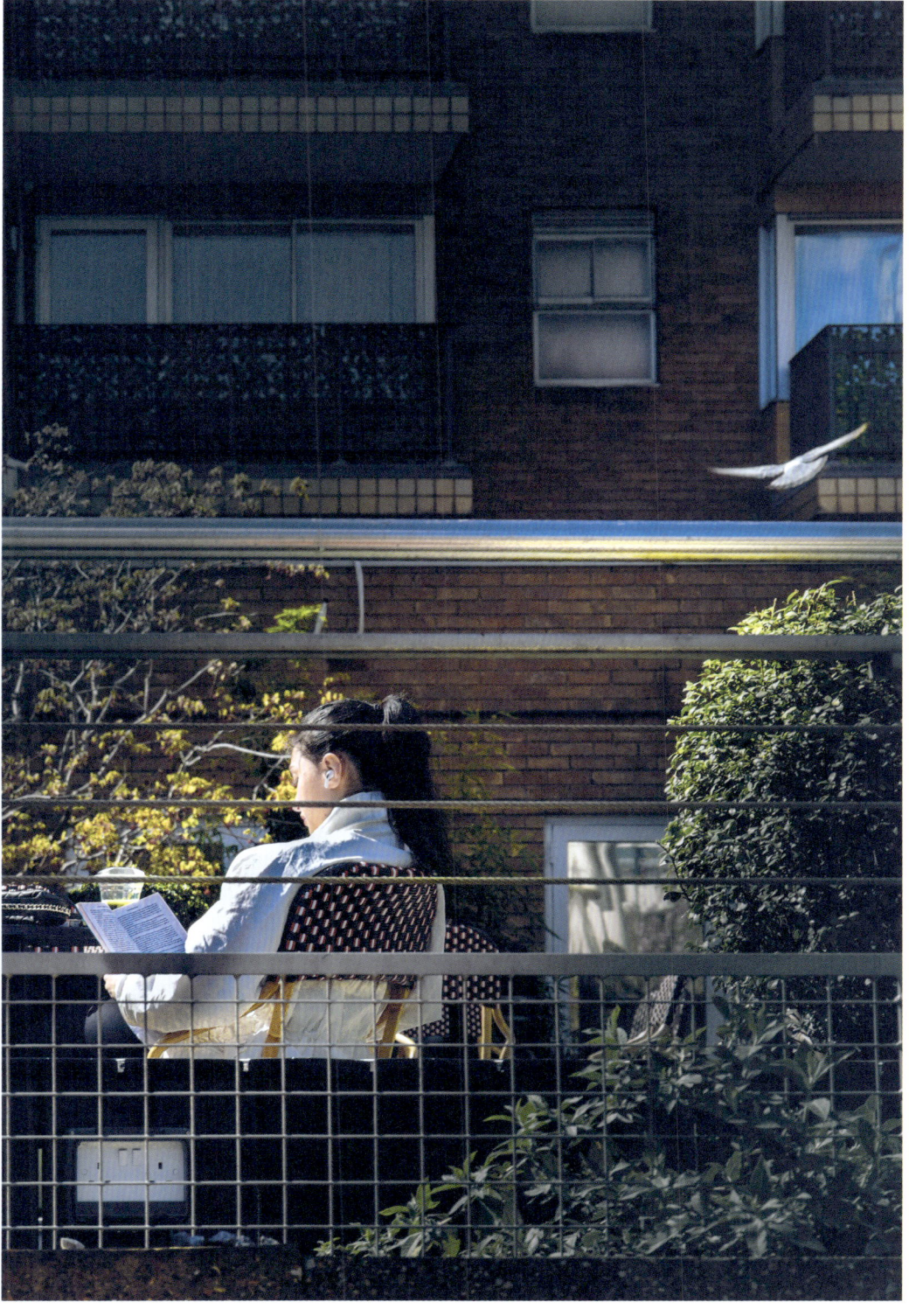

London → England

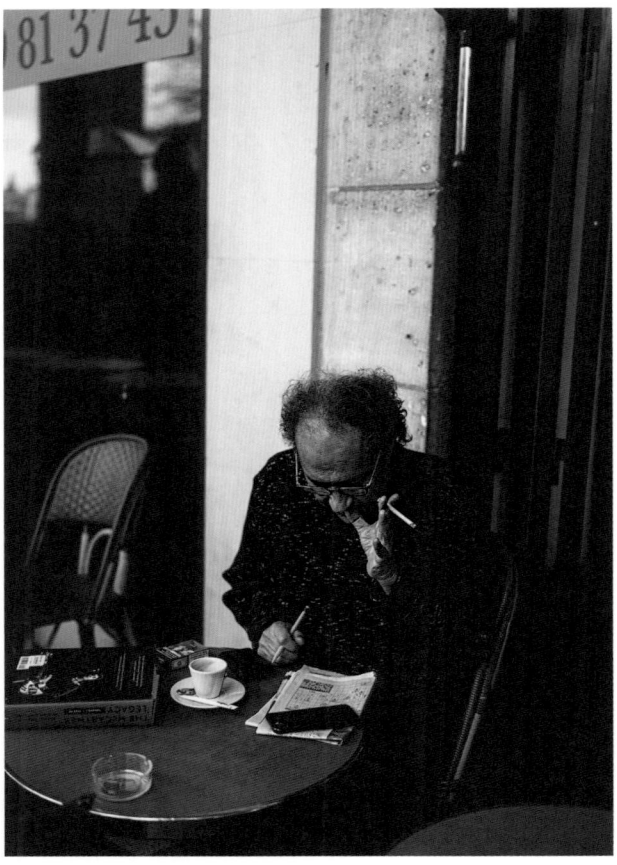

"I find television very educating. Every time
somebody turns on the set, I go into the other
room and read a book."

GROUCHO MARX

"I guess there are never enough books."

JOHN STEINBECK

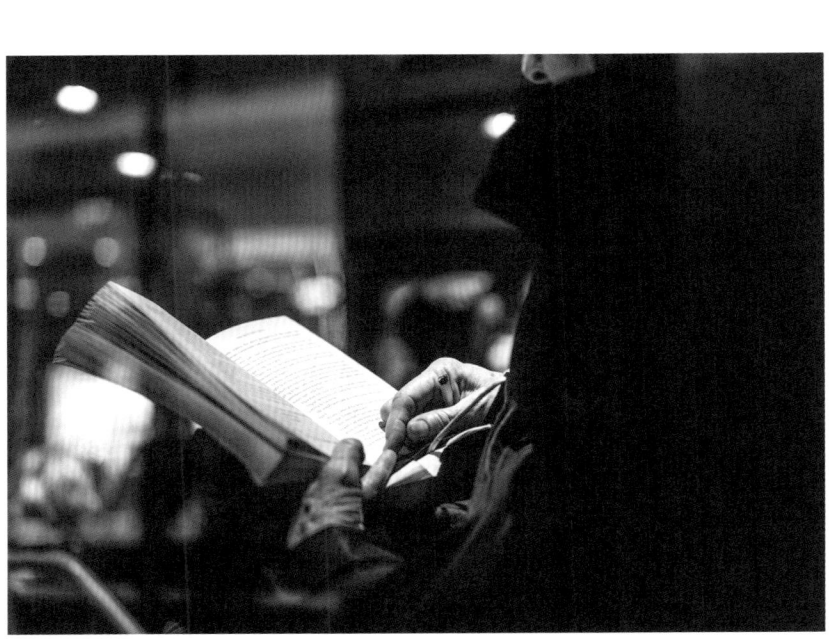

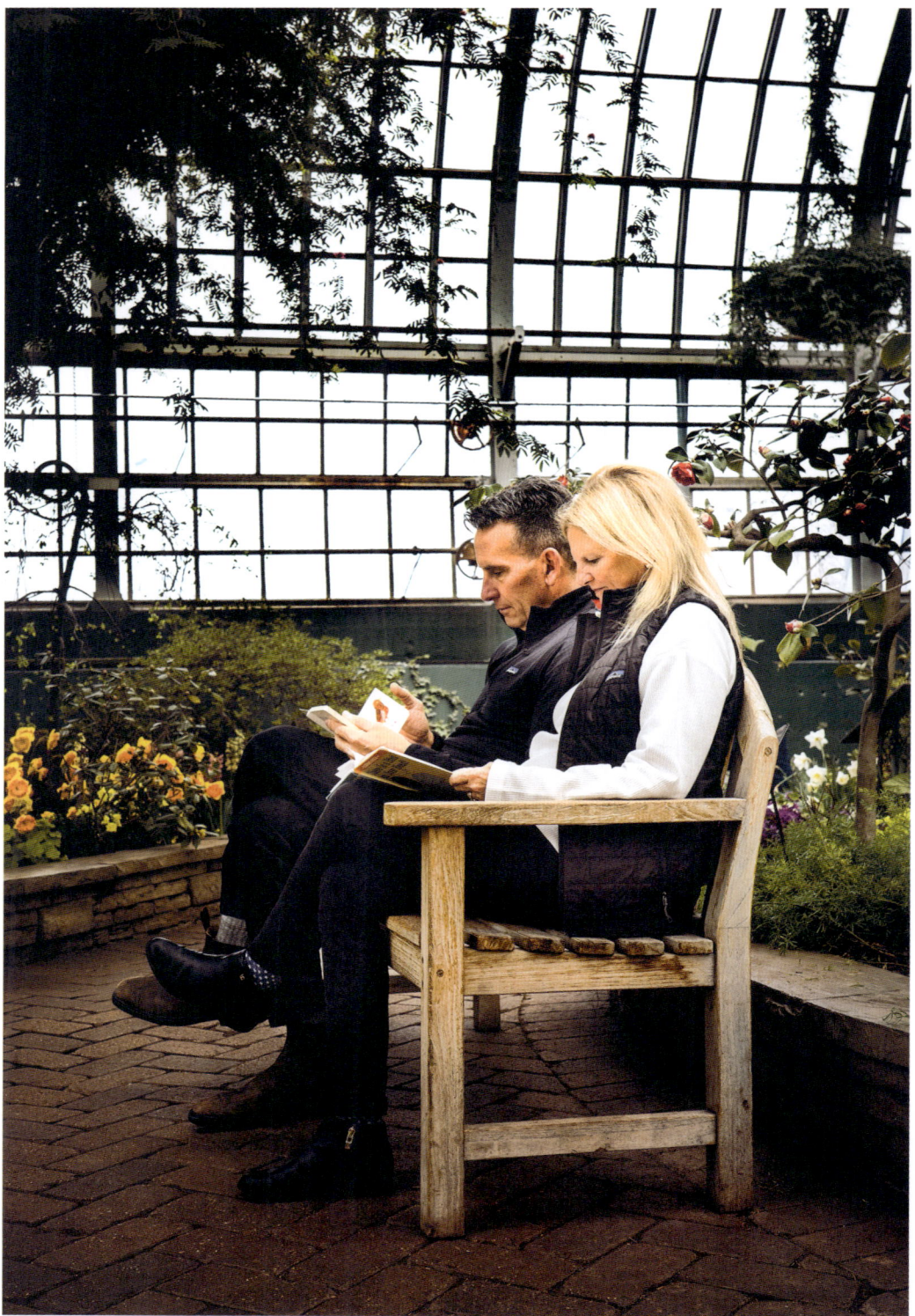

Chicago, Illinois → *United States*

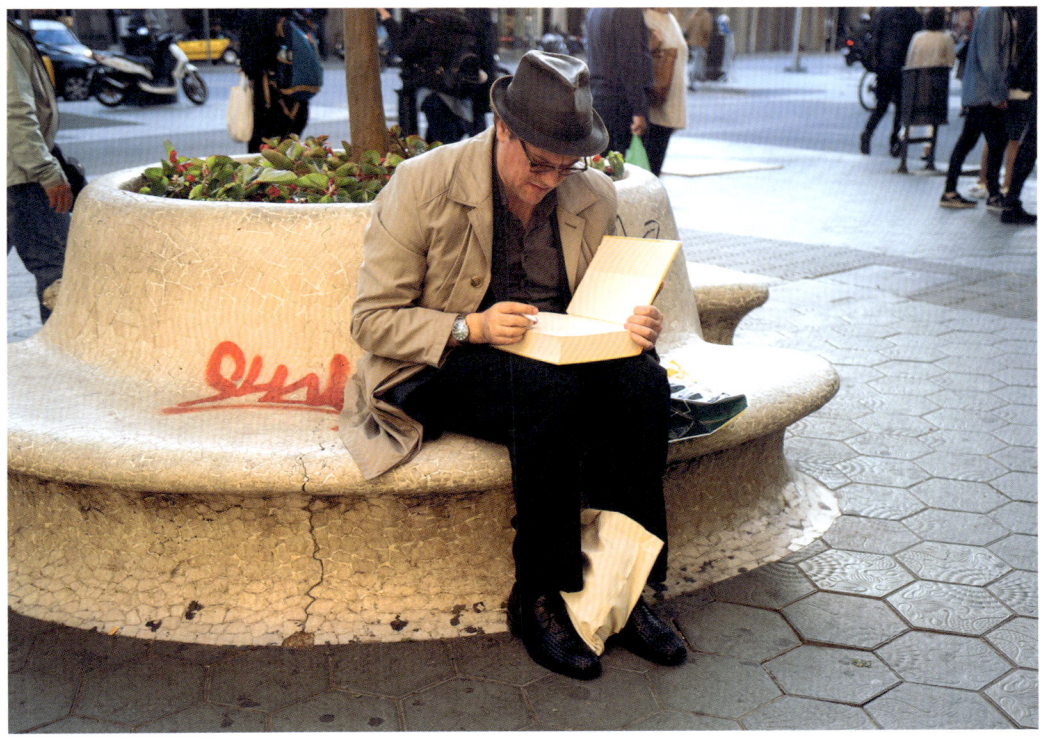

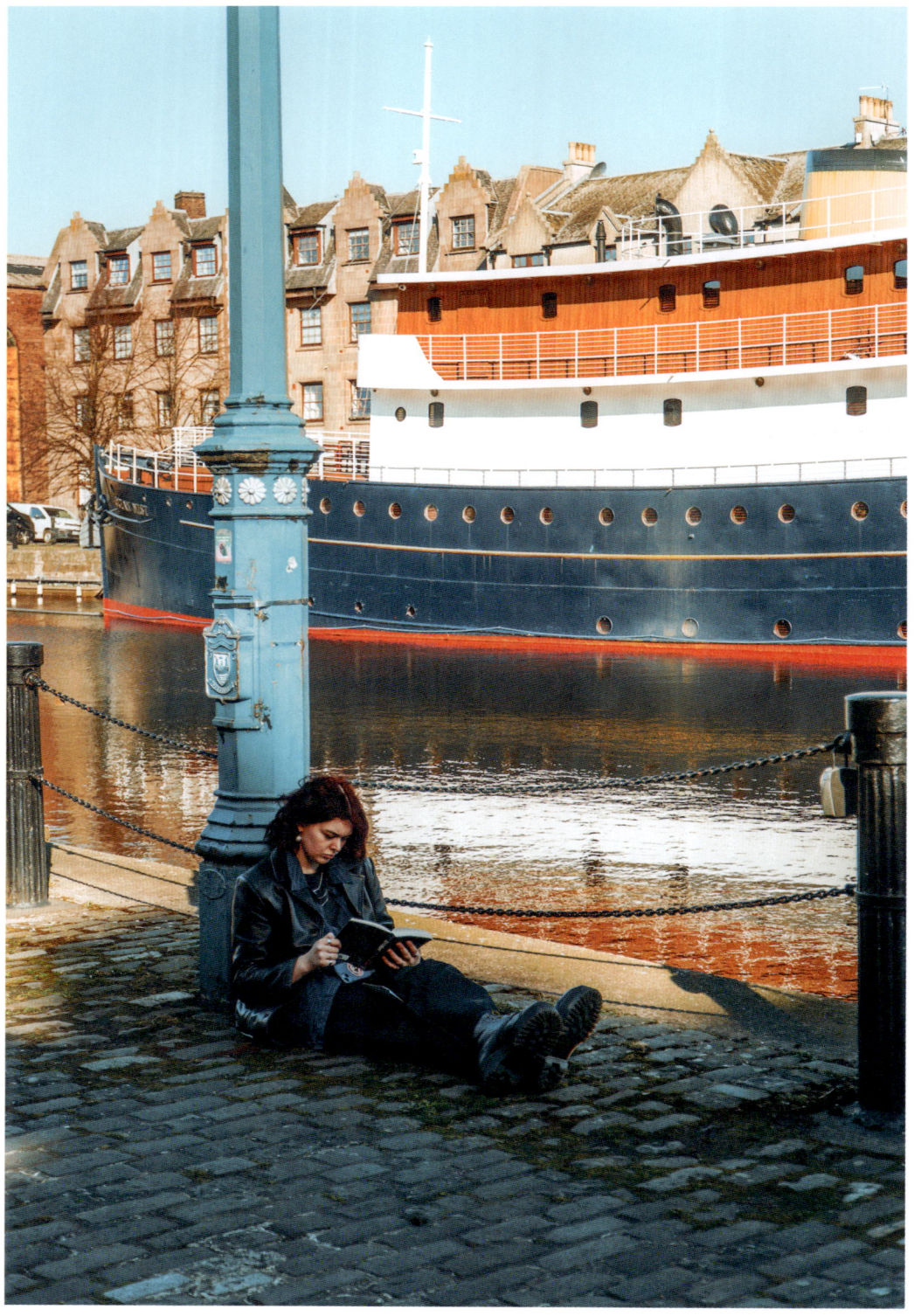

Edinburgh → *Scotland*

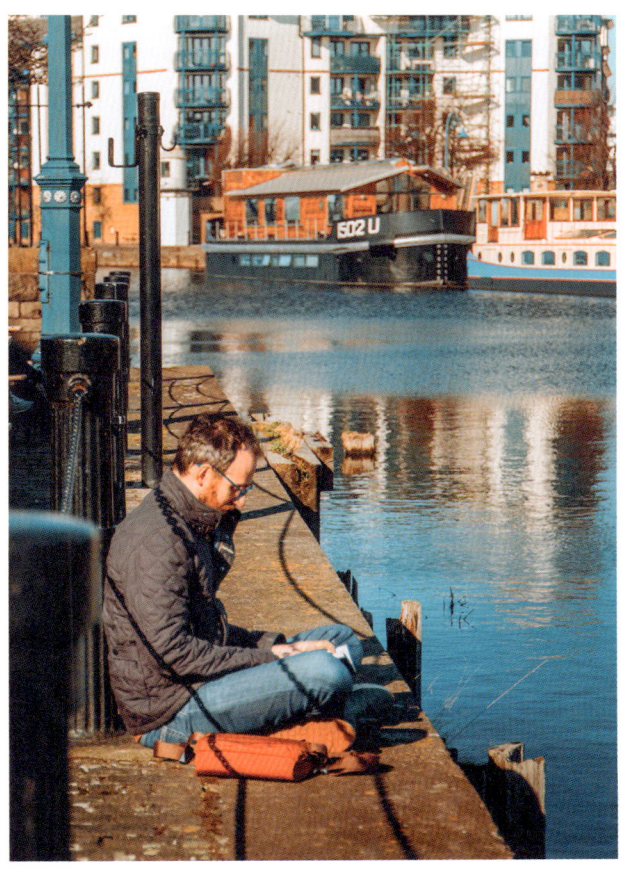

"It wasn't until I started reading and found books they wouldn't let us read in school that I discovered you could be insane and happy and have a good life without being like everybody else."

JOHN WATERS

Edinburgh → *Scotland*

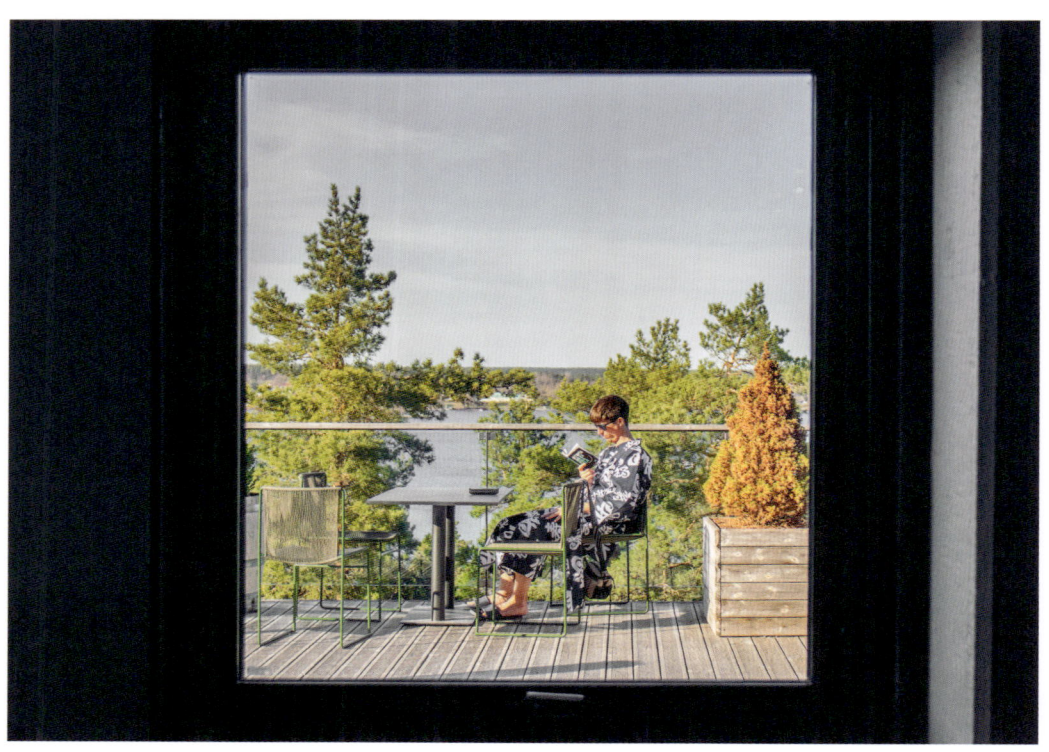

Stockholm → *Sweden*

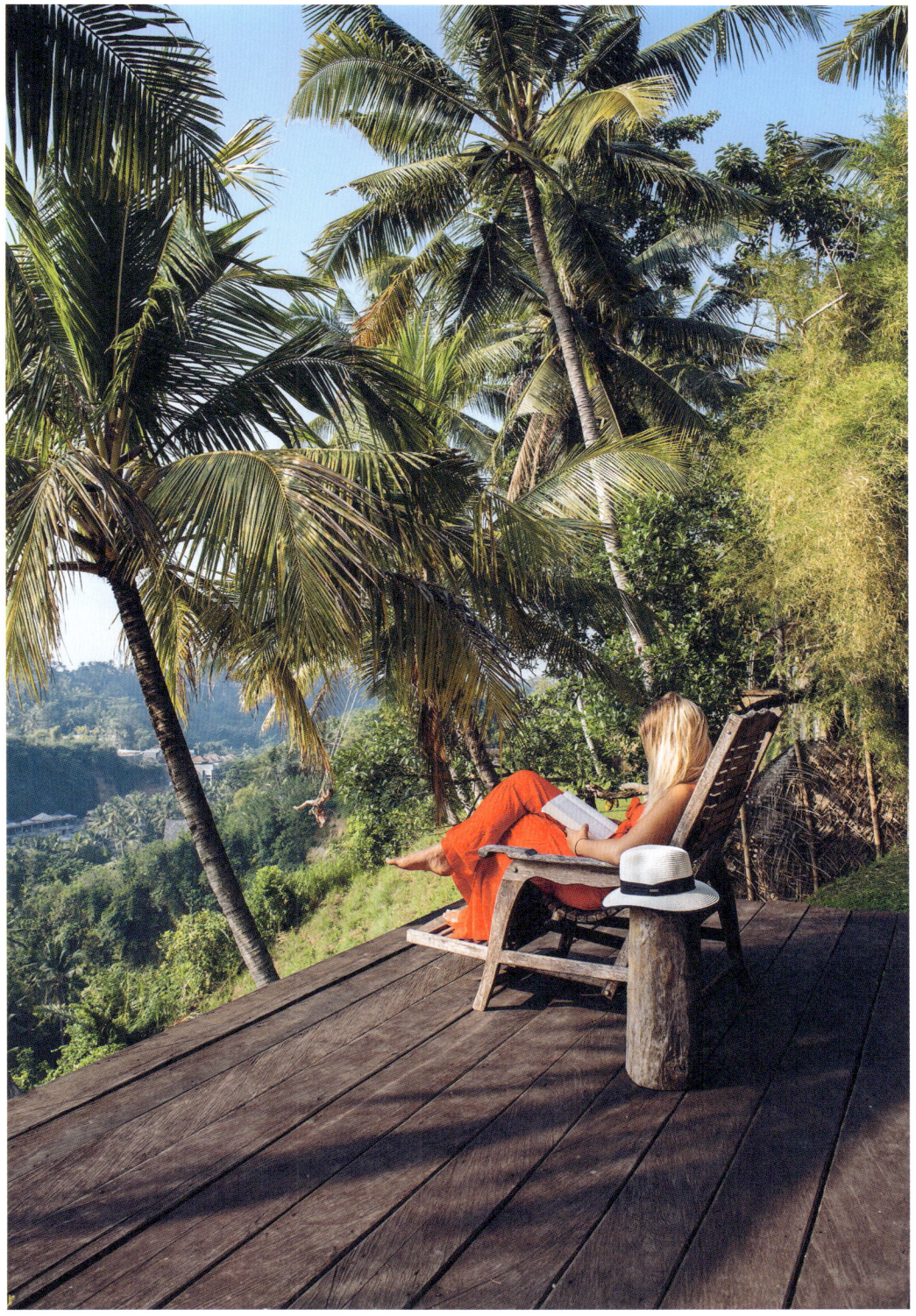

Bali → *Indonesia*

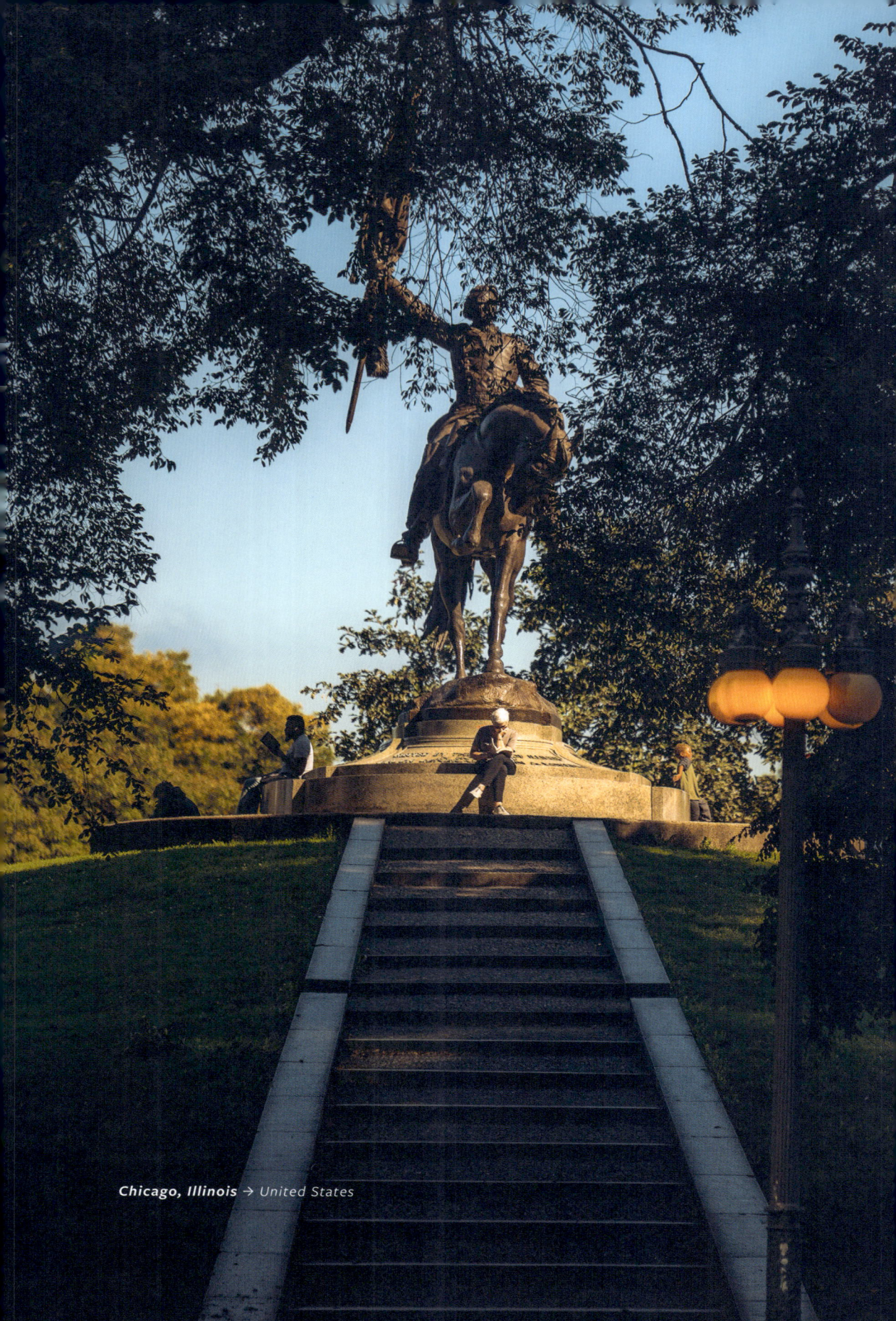

Chicago, Illinois → United States

JUNE WILCOX, *Owner*
M. Judson Booksellers → Greenville, South Carolina

Reading is a wildly efficient pastime.

It's not tide or temperature dependent, no equipment is needed, no group chat trying to find a time that works for everyone. All it takes is you and a book (and perhaps some reading glasses) and you're plunged into medieval Scotland, or tangled in a family drama, or learning something new.

Writing is equally solitary. Set a human with a beautiful imagination and a gift for weaving words in front of a blank page and whole new worlds are spun.

Two fully solitary activities whose alchemy creates community. Magic.

M. Judson Booksellers opened ten years ago in the heart of downtown Greenville, South Carolina. For a decade, two questions have opened nearly every customer conversation in the store and if we're honest, almost every conversation with each other as well: *What are you reading now?* and *What's the last thing you read that you loved?* Two surprisingly intimate questions. The answers help illuminate the path to your next favorite book, but they also say something about who you are, what you love, what you're drawn to. After all, as Frank Navasky reminded us, "You are what you read."

Storytelling is in our DNA. Whether on clay, papyrus, parchment, or paper, stories have been used for thousands of years to make sense of what it means to be human. Reading stories, we see the world through another's eyes, find meaning and a reminder that we all, actually, have a lot in common. A shared love of story is a hot-wired connection powered by a common understanding: stories matter, we are part of each other's stories, there's joy here.

The feeling is familiar: seeing someone reading a book you loved and the next thing you know, you're in conversation with a stranger; the family gathering where a heated debate breaks out about whether the book was better than the movie (of course it was); the certainty that you were alone until you joined a book club, and now it's five or twenty years later and you can't imagine a life without your people.

At the store, we have had a decade of witnessing thousands of examples of the love of reading as the connective tissue of community; watching people find their people, grow in empathy and understanding, and delight in the joy of talking to authors about the art of crafting stories into truths.

Five strangers from different cities randomly seated at the same table at an author lunch three years ago who now have returned to be together every month since.

A 16-year-old aspiring chef sitting around the community table talking with mothers and grandmothers about making Edna Lewis' pan-fried chicken recipe from *The Taste of Country Cooking*.

The eldest member of a book club, 83, discussing *A Tree Grows in Brooklyn* with the youngest member, 23.

A wedding in the foyer of one of our own, marrying a regular customer.

The local baker's excitement when asked to make a cake for Hernan Diaz, who found out hours before his appearance at the store that *Trust* had won the Pulitzer. The Sci-Fi Fantasy book club turned found family who is as quick to respond to a debate about the latest N. K. Jemisin as it is to a call to help another move, or gather donations for hurricane victims.

Building community and connection through shared experience: seeing and being seen. A spark ignited from two completely individual activities — a flame that gets passed from reader to reader to reader, growing the light without diminishing one's own.

So, what're you reading?

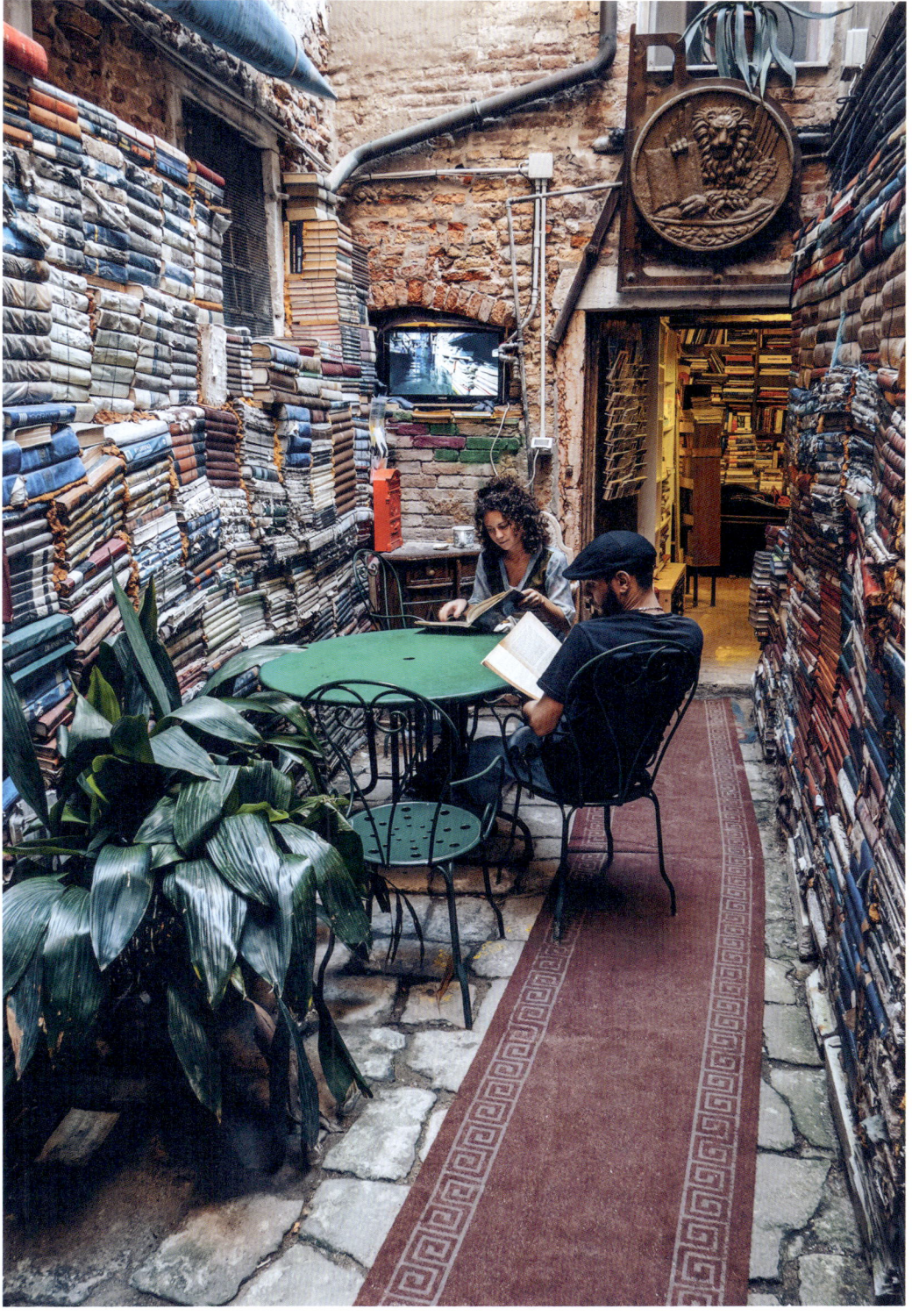

Venice → *Italy*

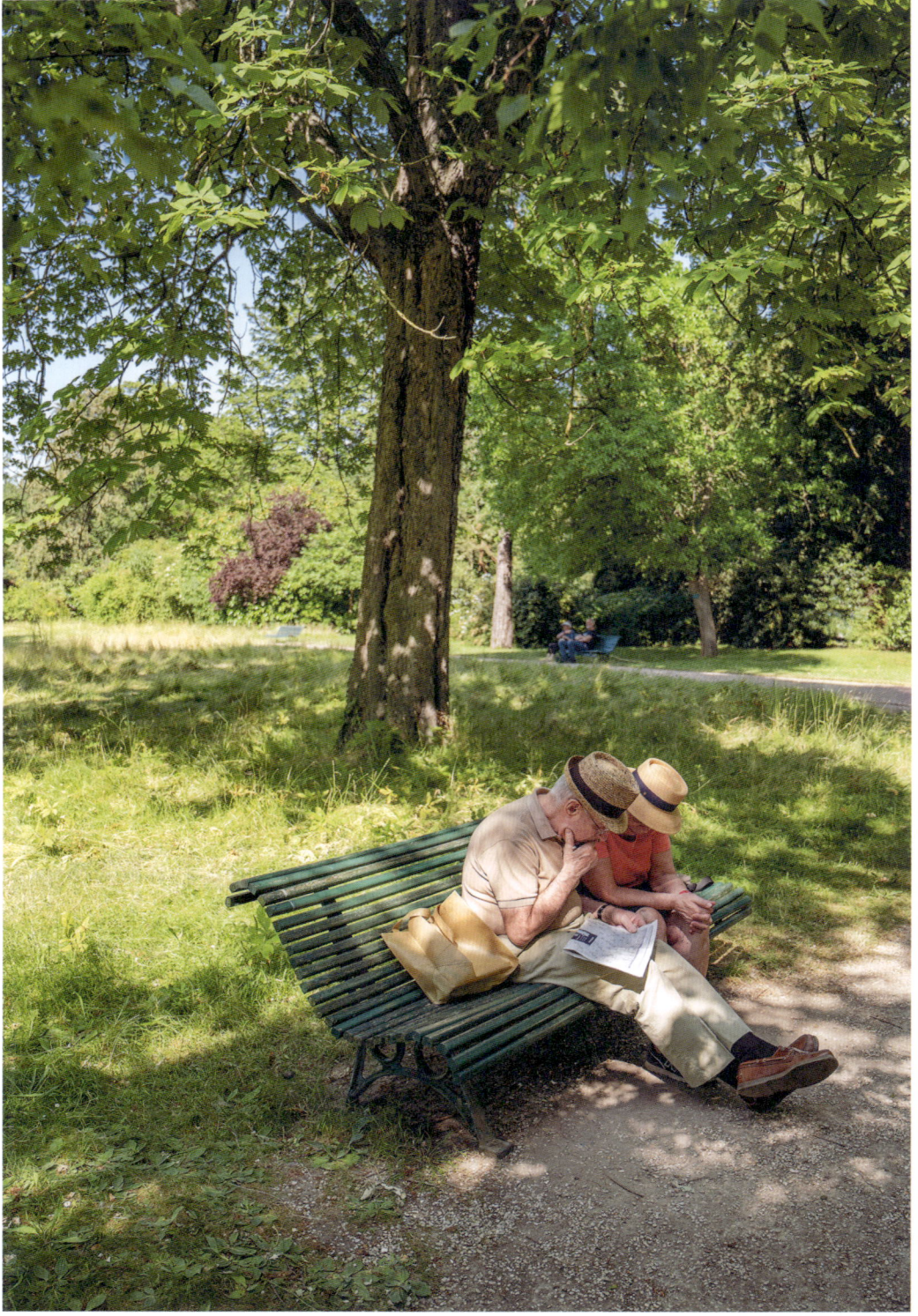

Paris → France

"A book is a gift you can open again and again."

GARRISON KEILLOR

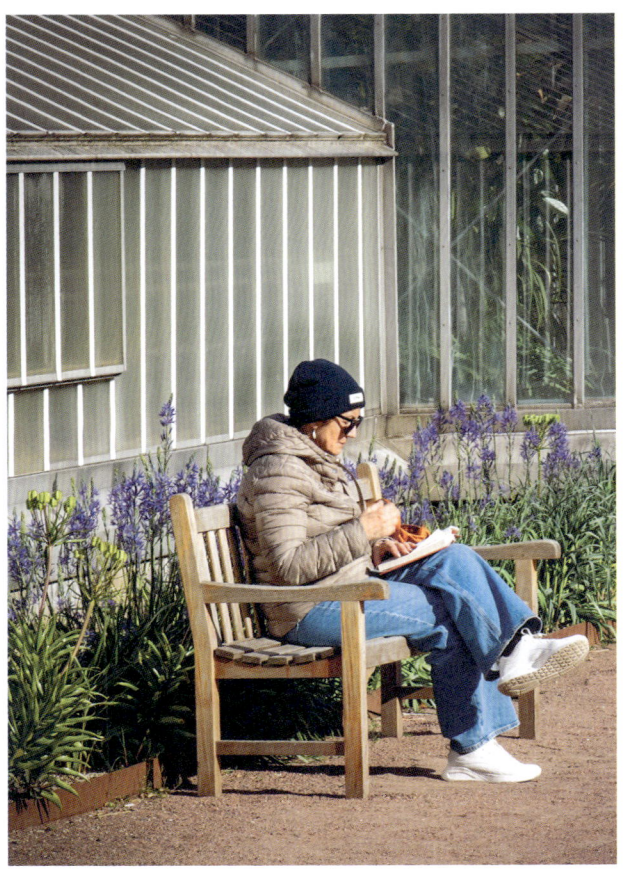

Gothenburg → *Sweden*

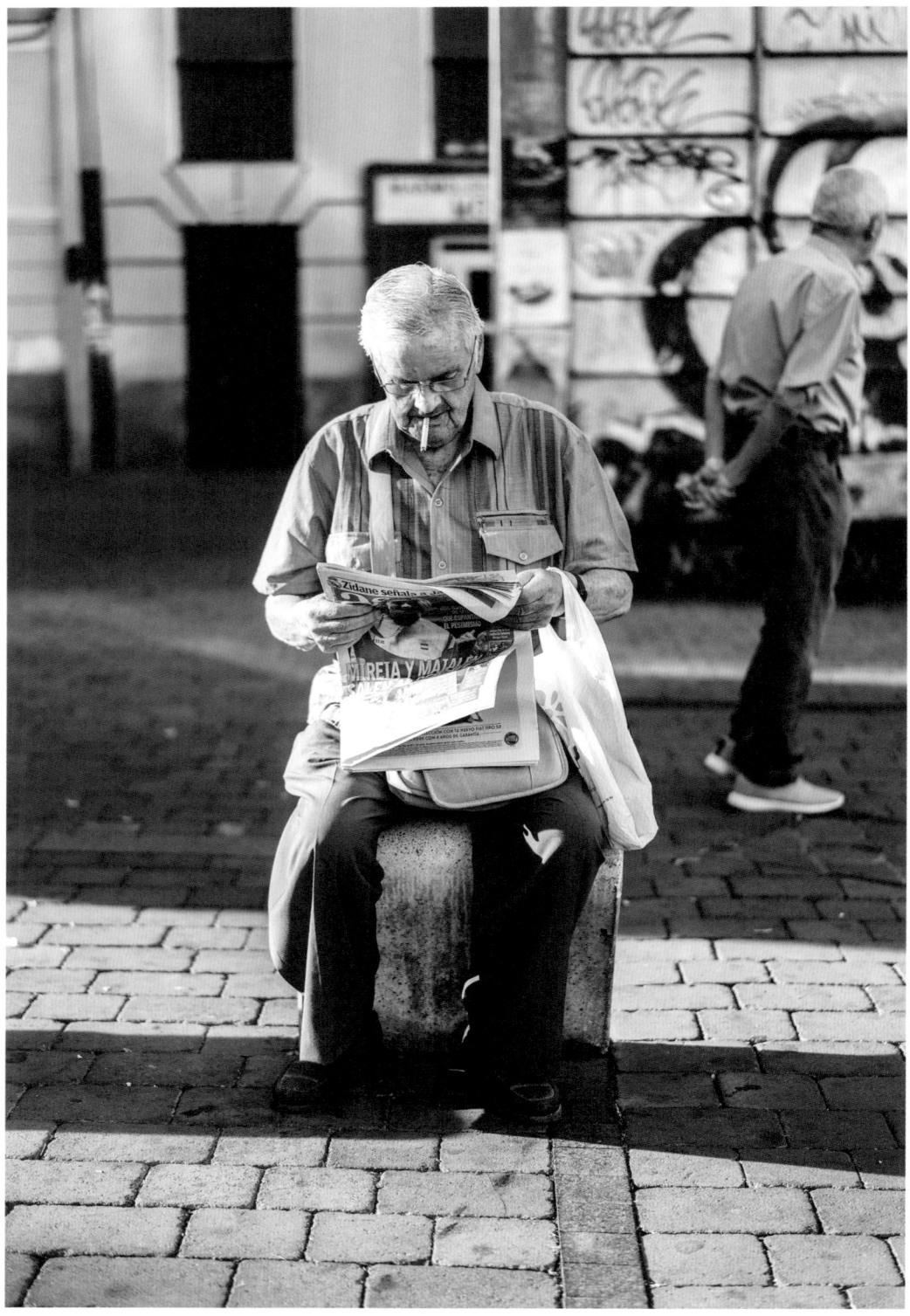

Madrid → *Spain*

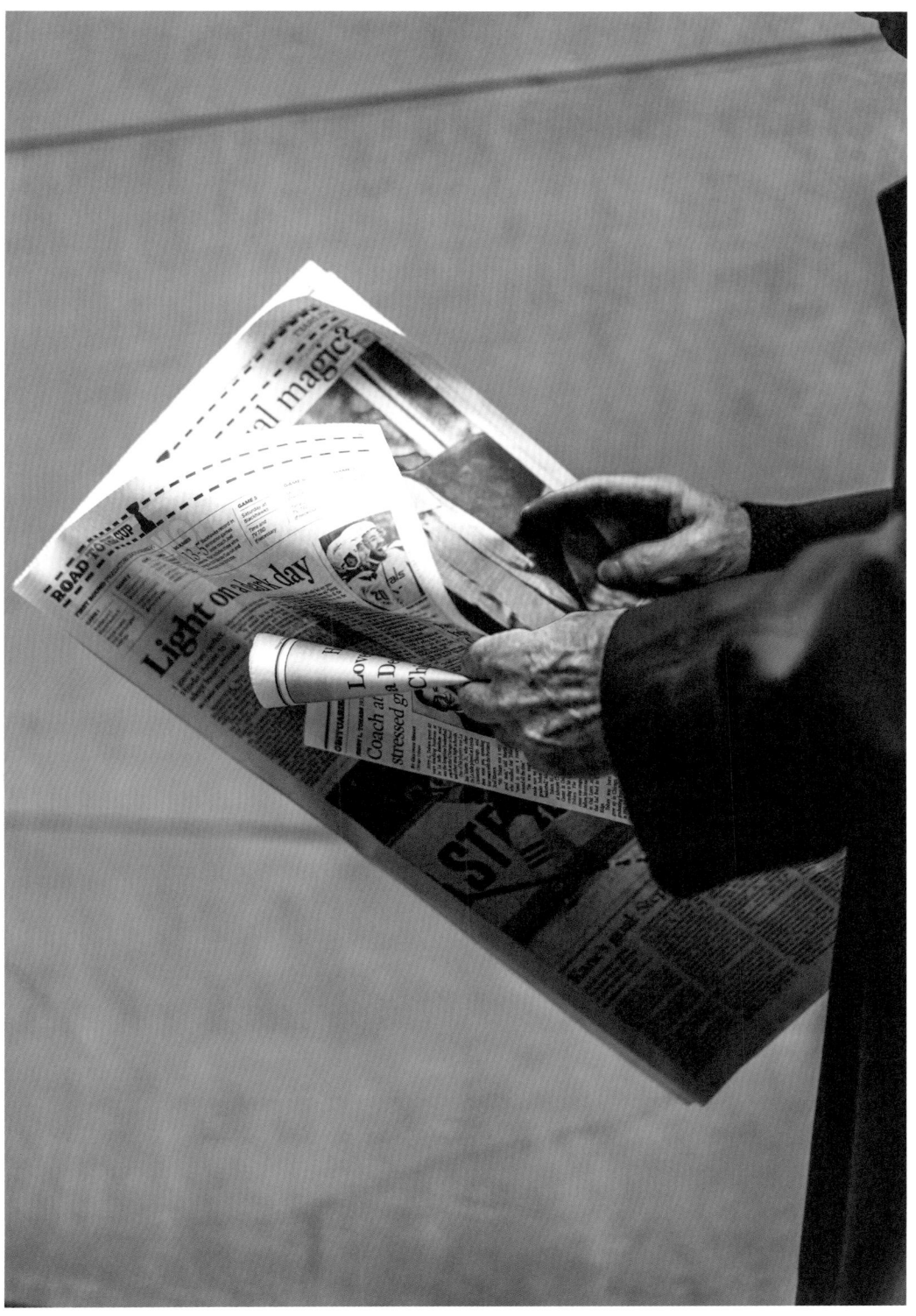

Chicago, Illinois → *United States*

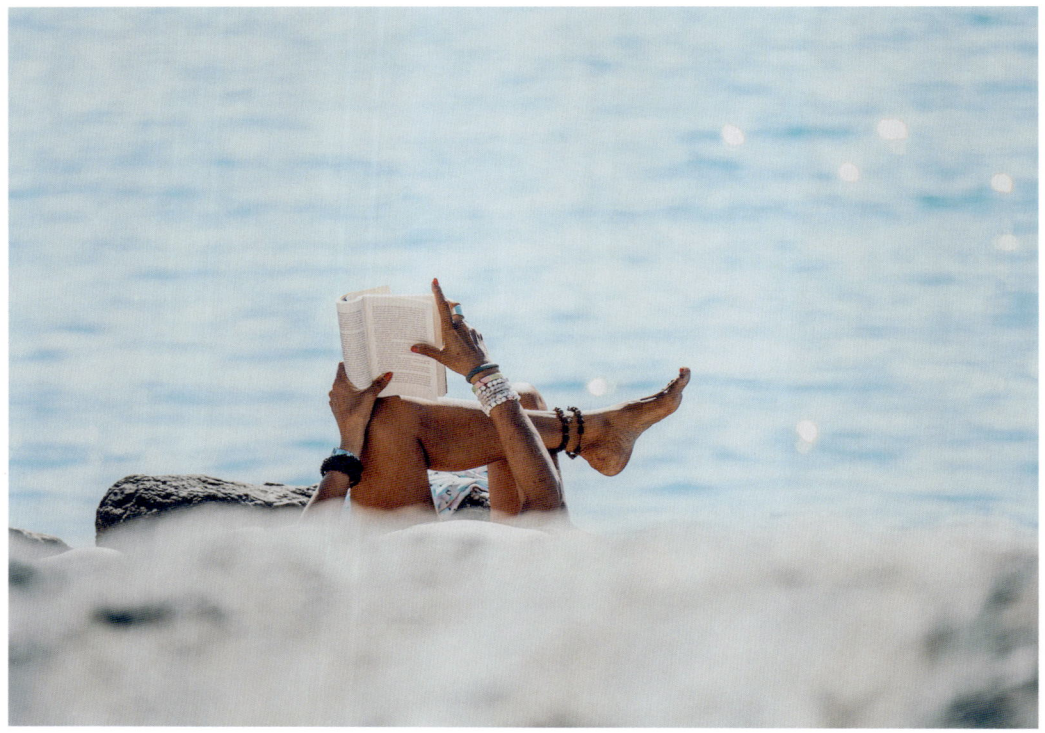

Genoa → Italy

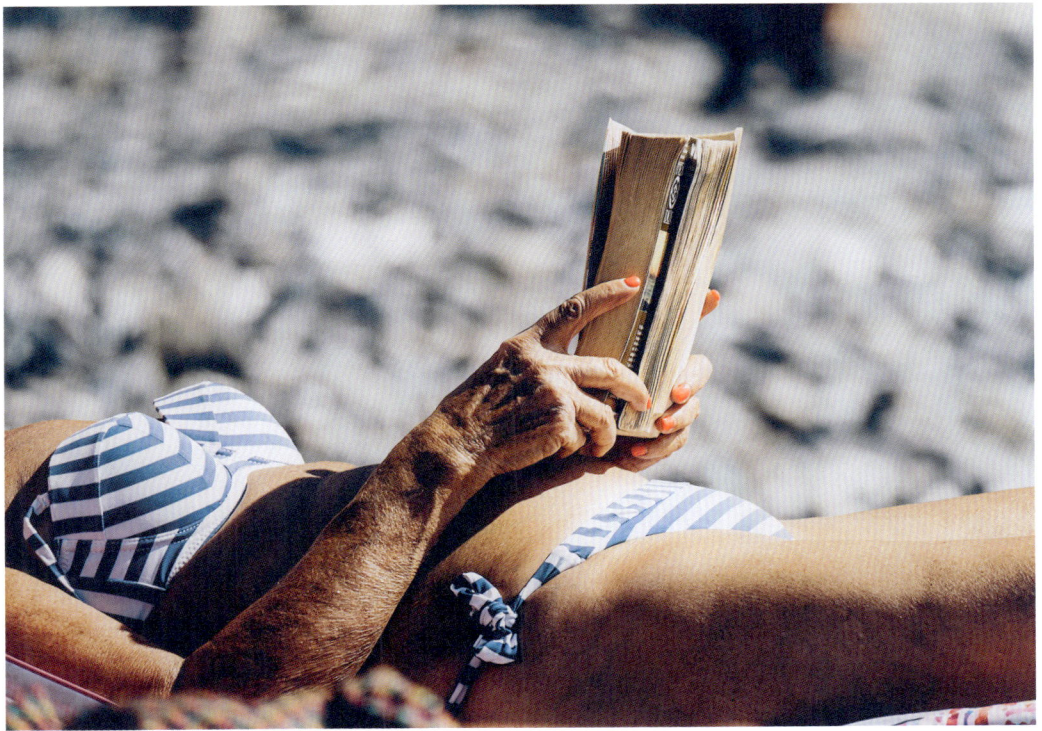

Genoa → Italy

"Some books leave us free and
some books make us free."

RALPH WALDO EMERSON

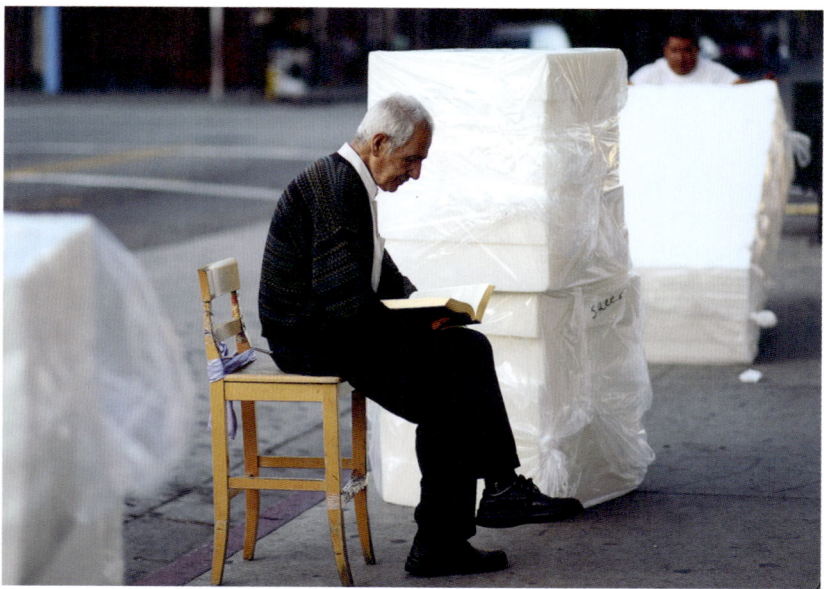

Los Angeles, California → *United States*

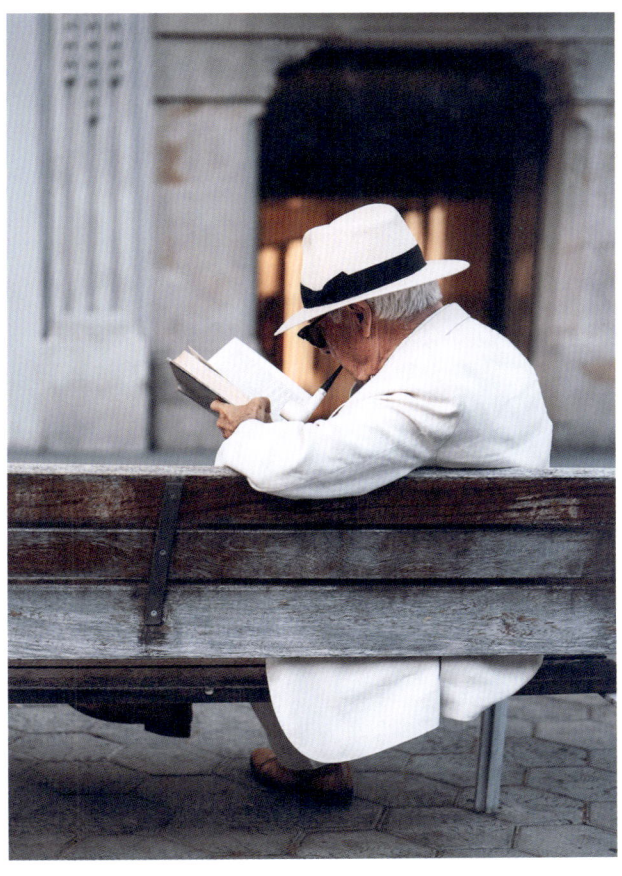

"One glance at a book and you hear the voice
of another person, perhaps someone dead for
1,000 years. To read is to voyage through time."

CARL SAGAN

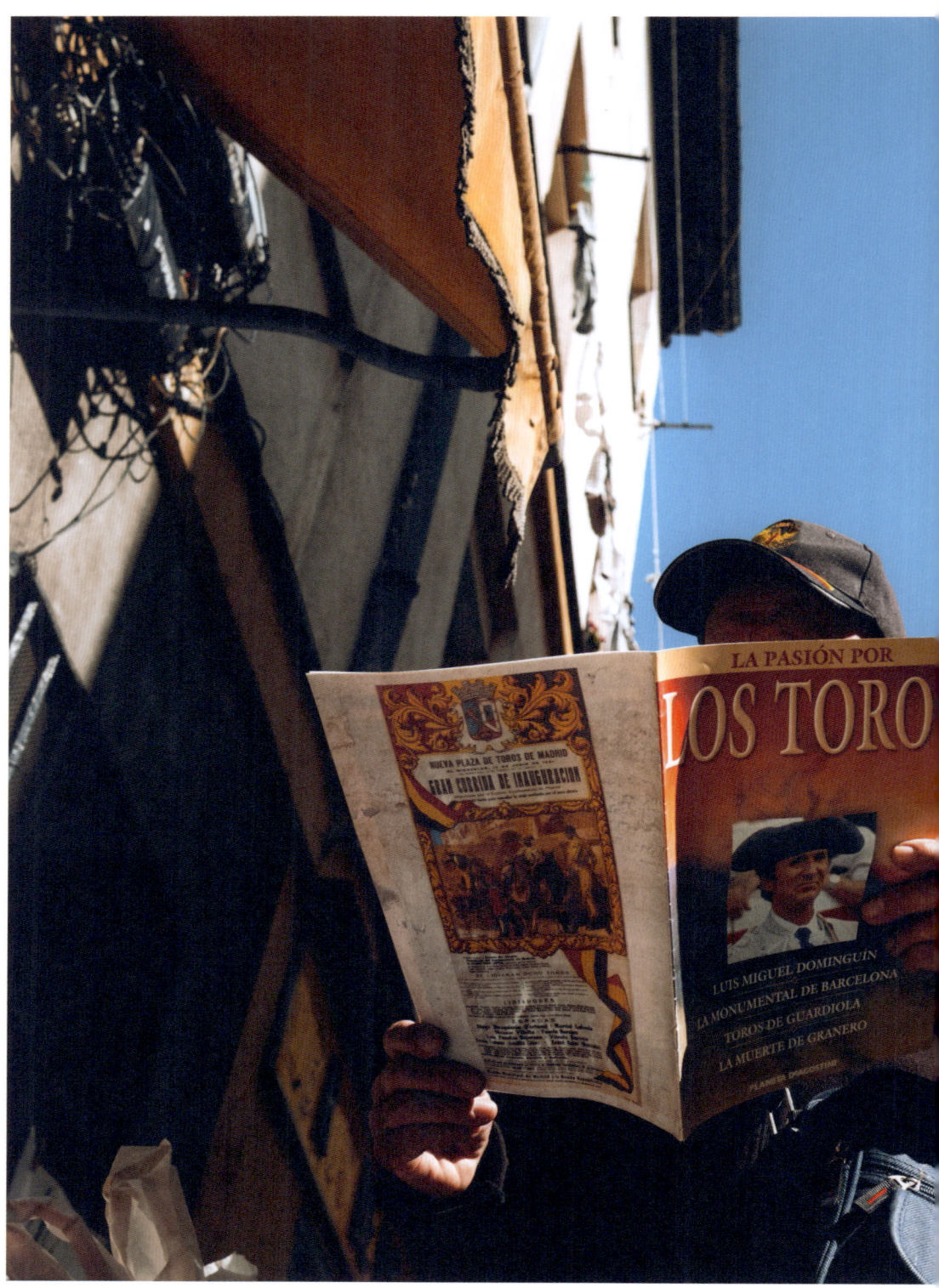

Madrid → *Spain*

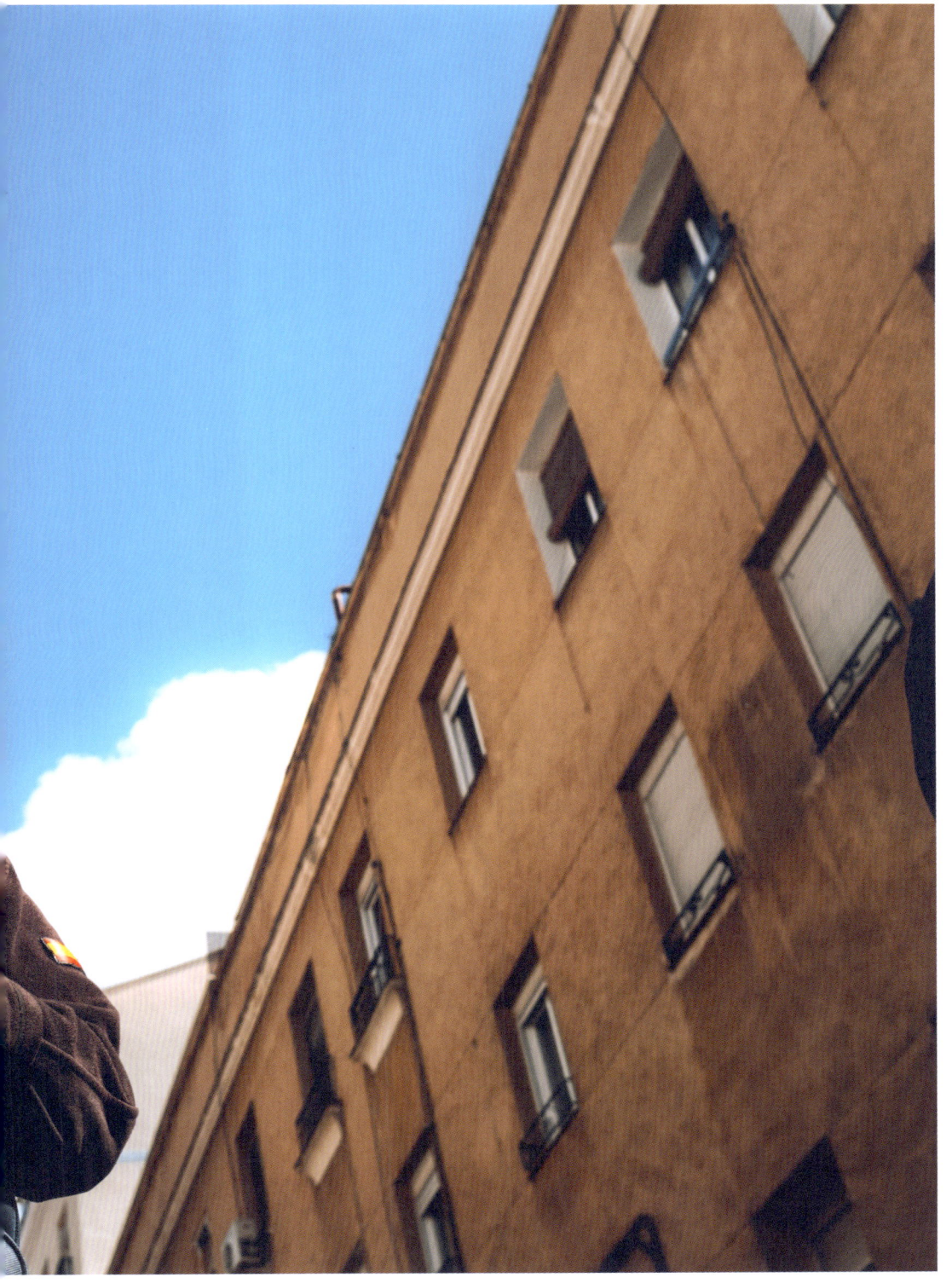

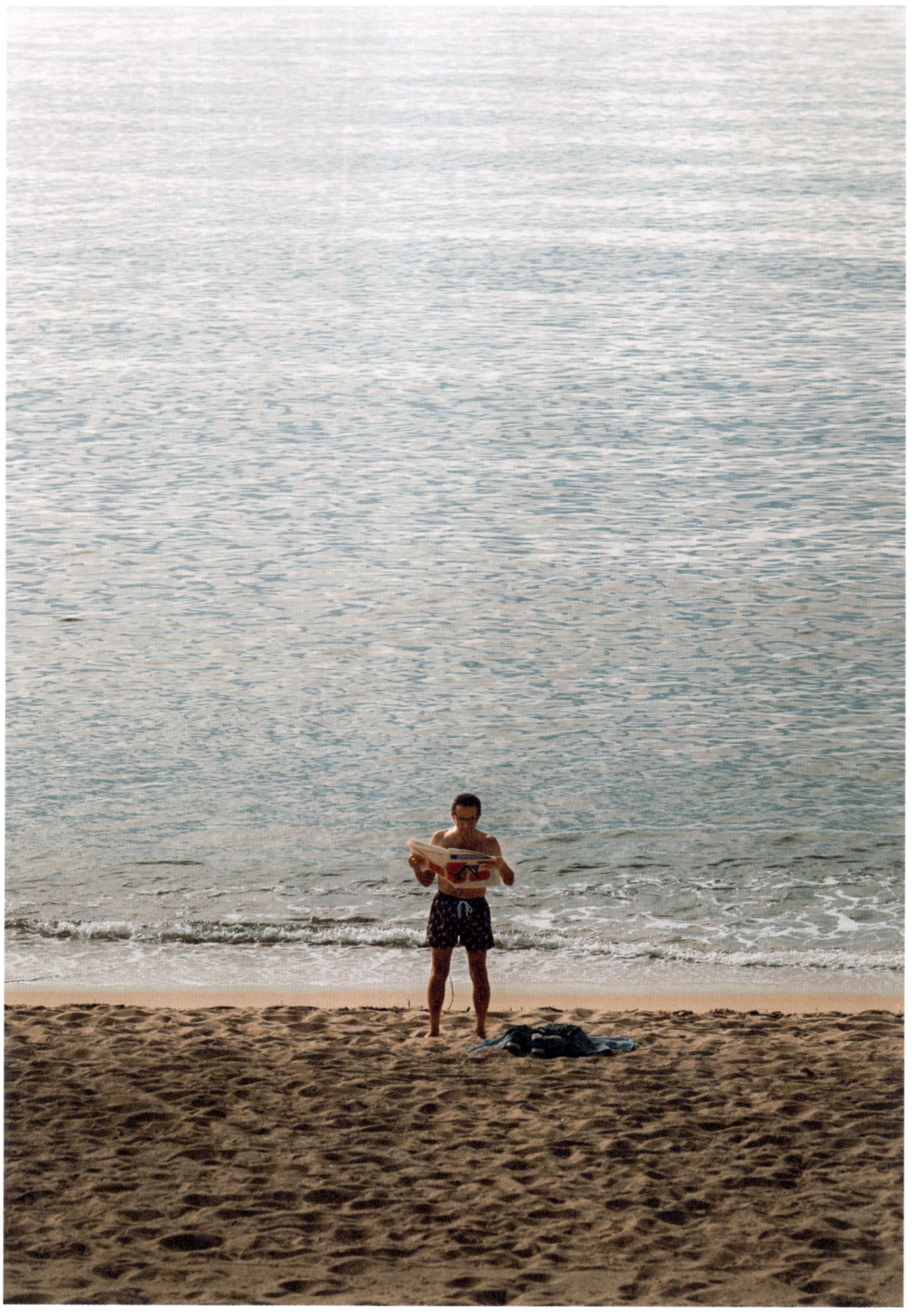

Barcelona → *Spain*

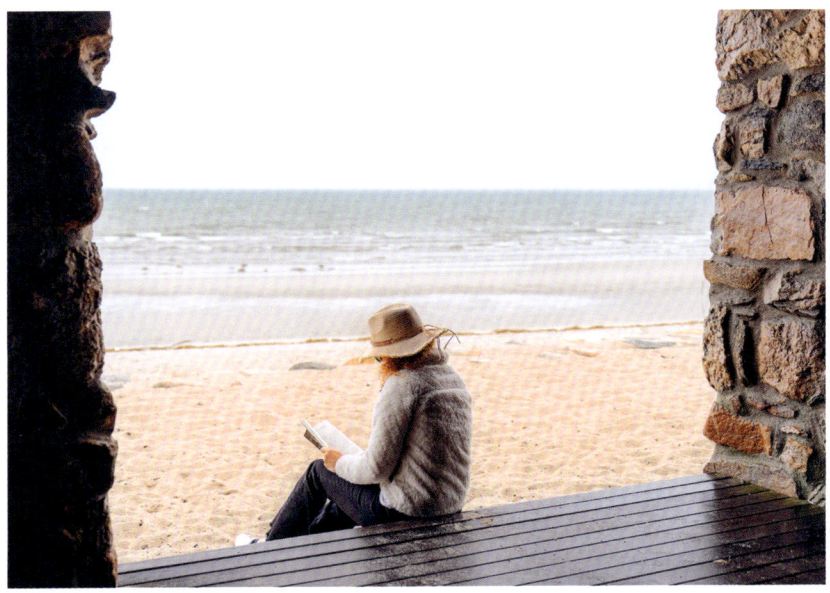

"Books have a unique way of stopping
time in a particular moment and saying:
Let's not forget this."

DAVE EGGERS

Old Greenwich, Connecticut → *United States*

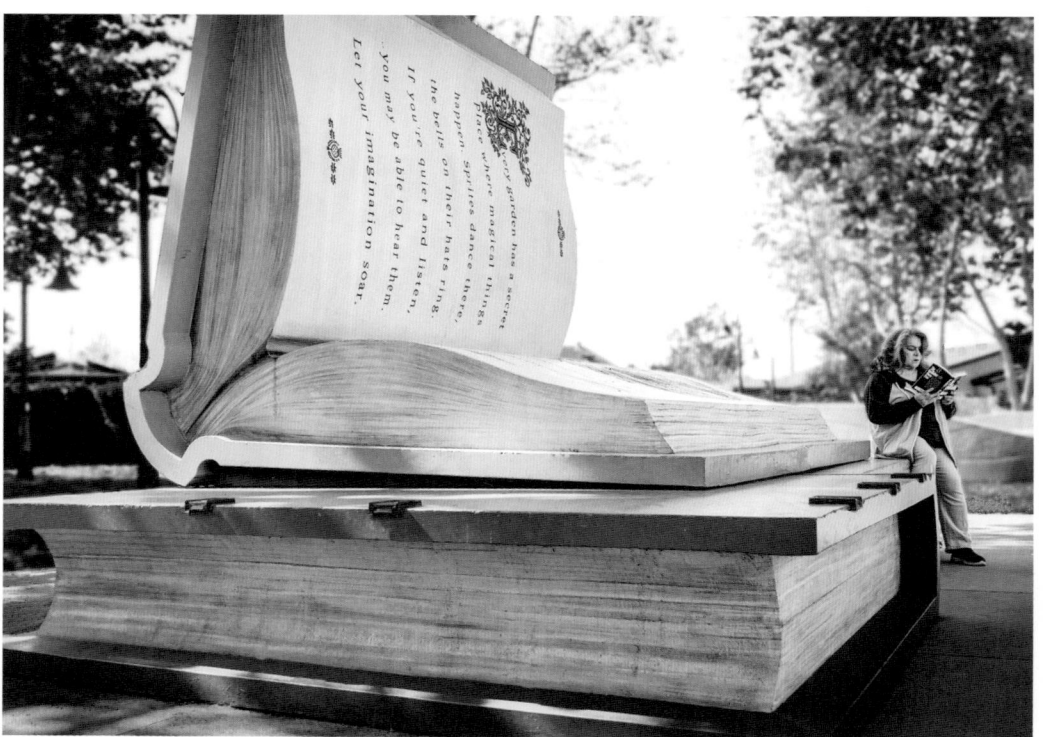

Bellflower, California → *United States*

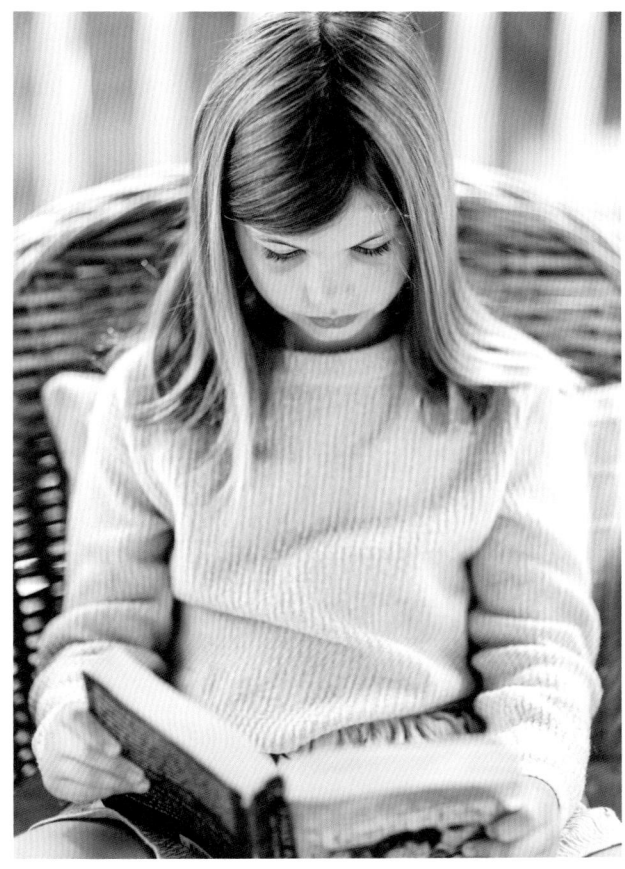

"I have a passion for teaching kids to become
readers, to become comfortable with a book,
not daunted. Books shouldn't be daunting, they
should be funny, exciting and wonderful; and
learning to be a reader gives a terrific advantage."

ROALD DAHL

Old Greenwich, Connecticut → *United States*

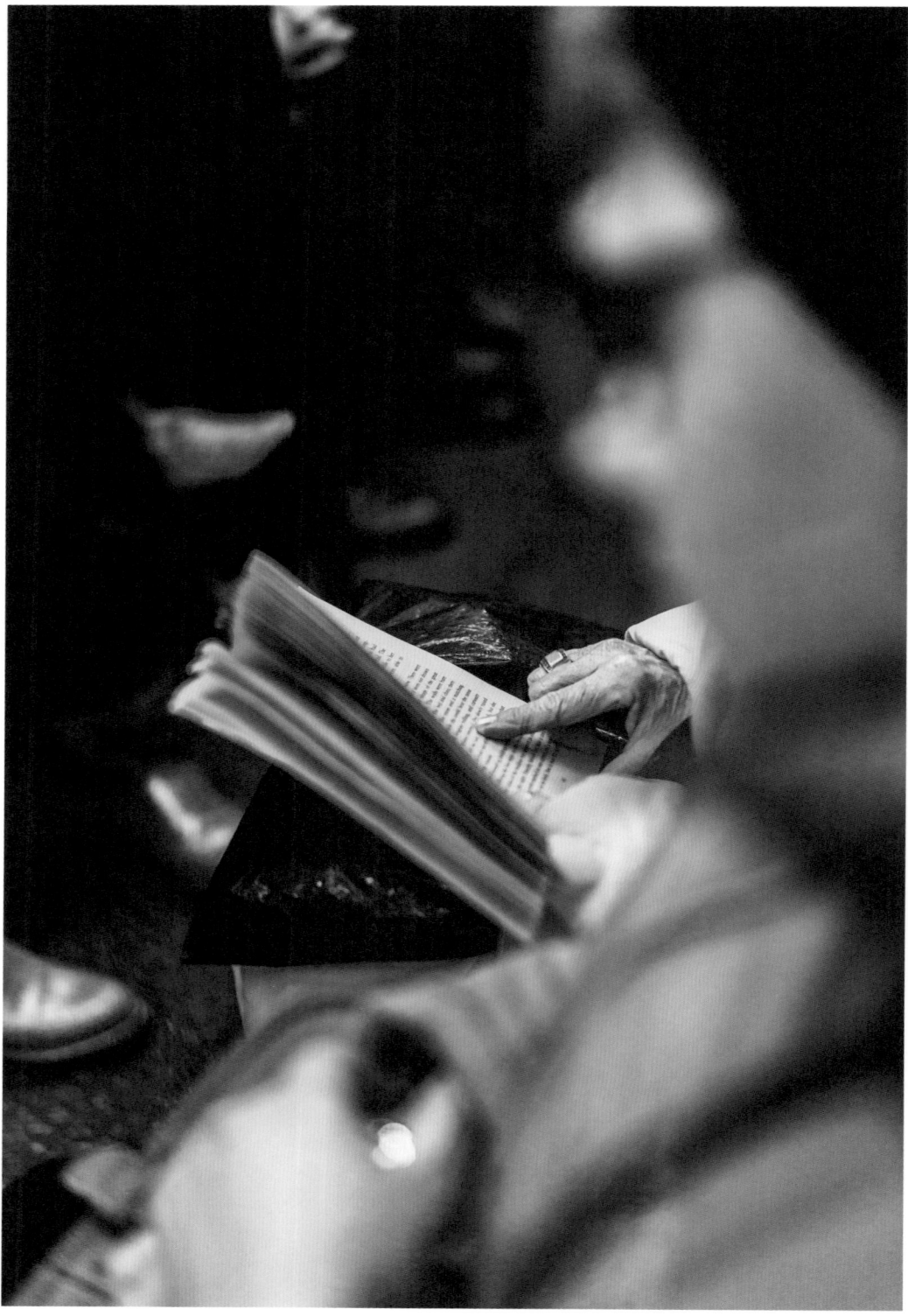

London → *England*

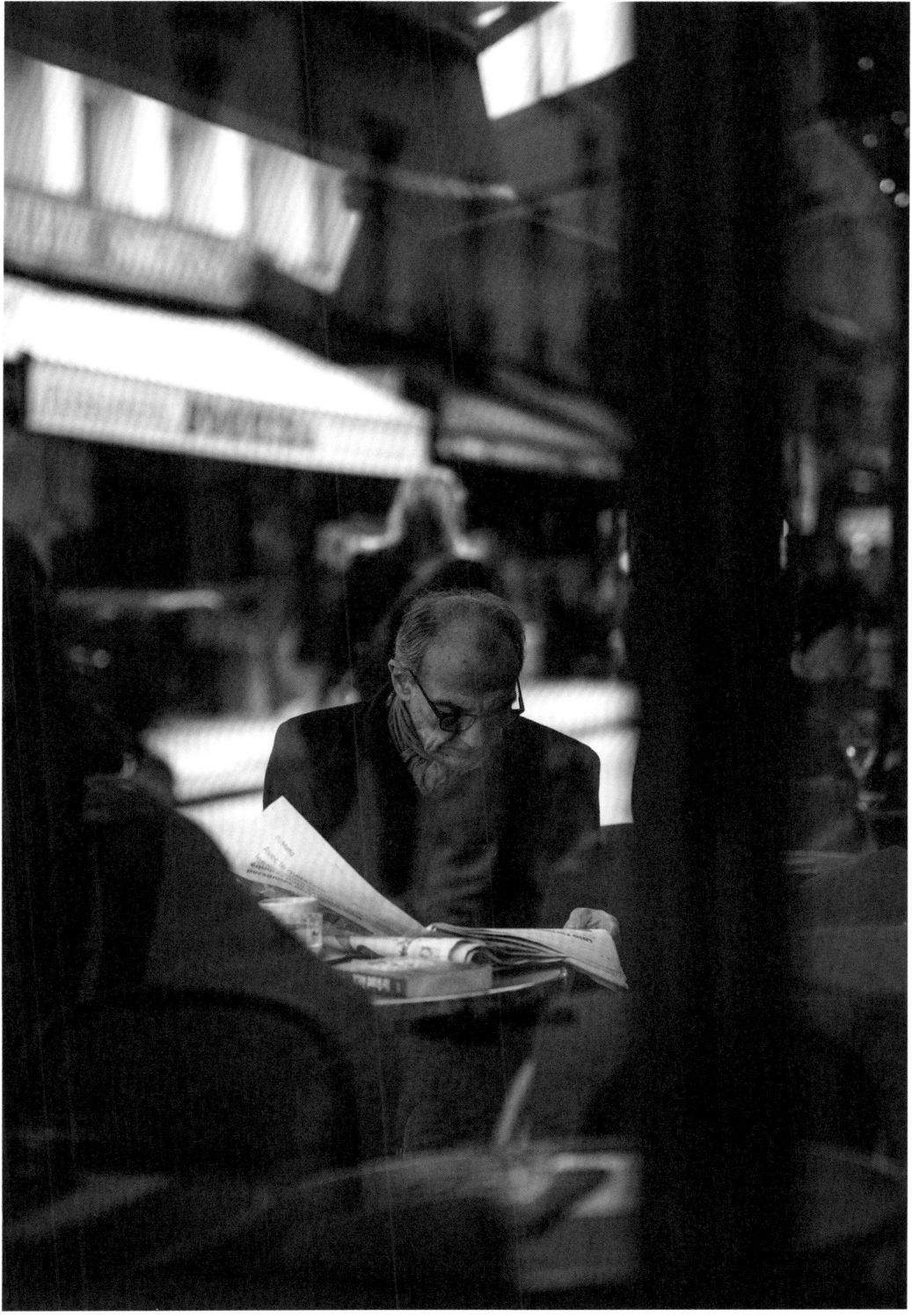

Paris → *France*

"Reading is important. If you know how to read,
then the whole world opens up to you."

BARACK OBAMA

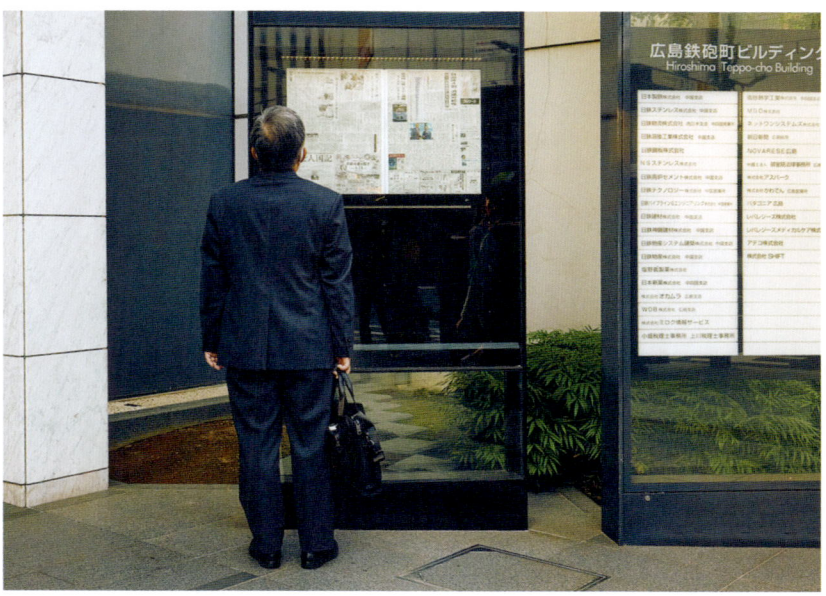

Hiroshima → *Japan*

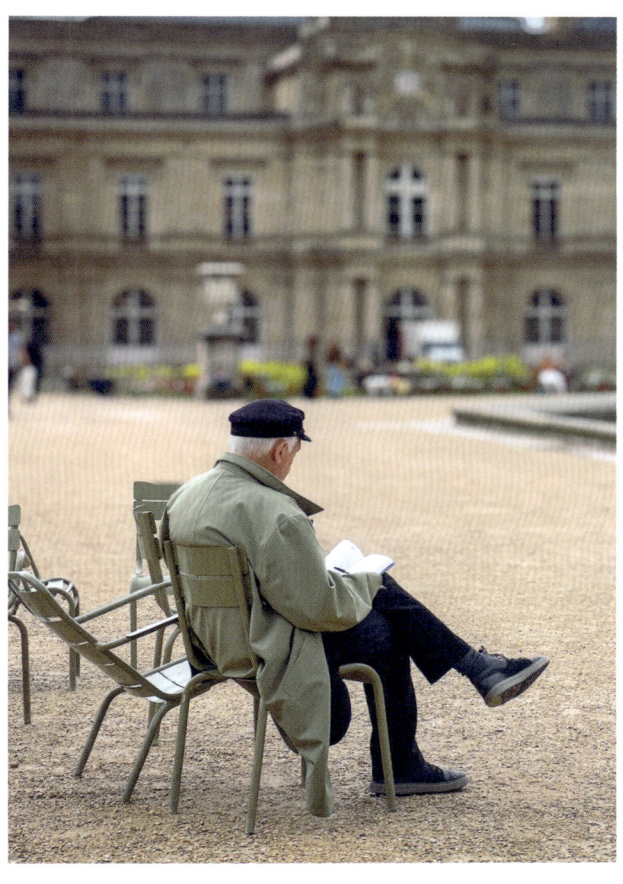

"Think before you speak. Read before you think."

FRAN LEBOWITZ

Paris → *France*

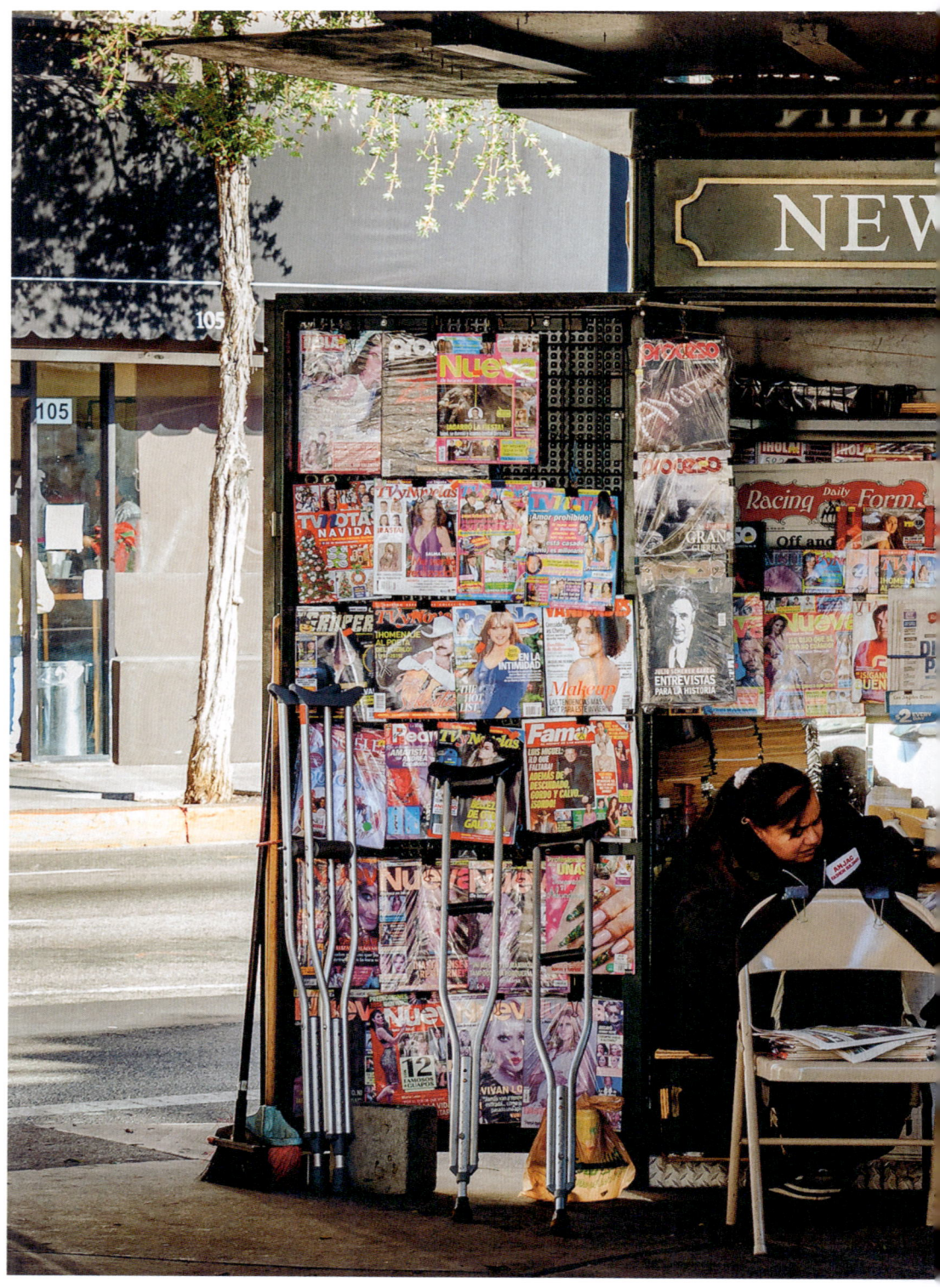

Los Angeles, California → *United States*

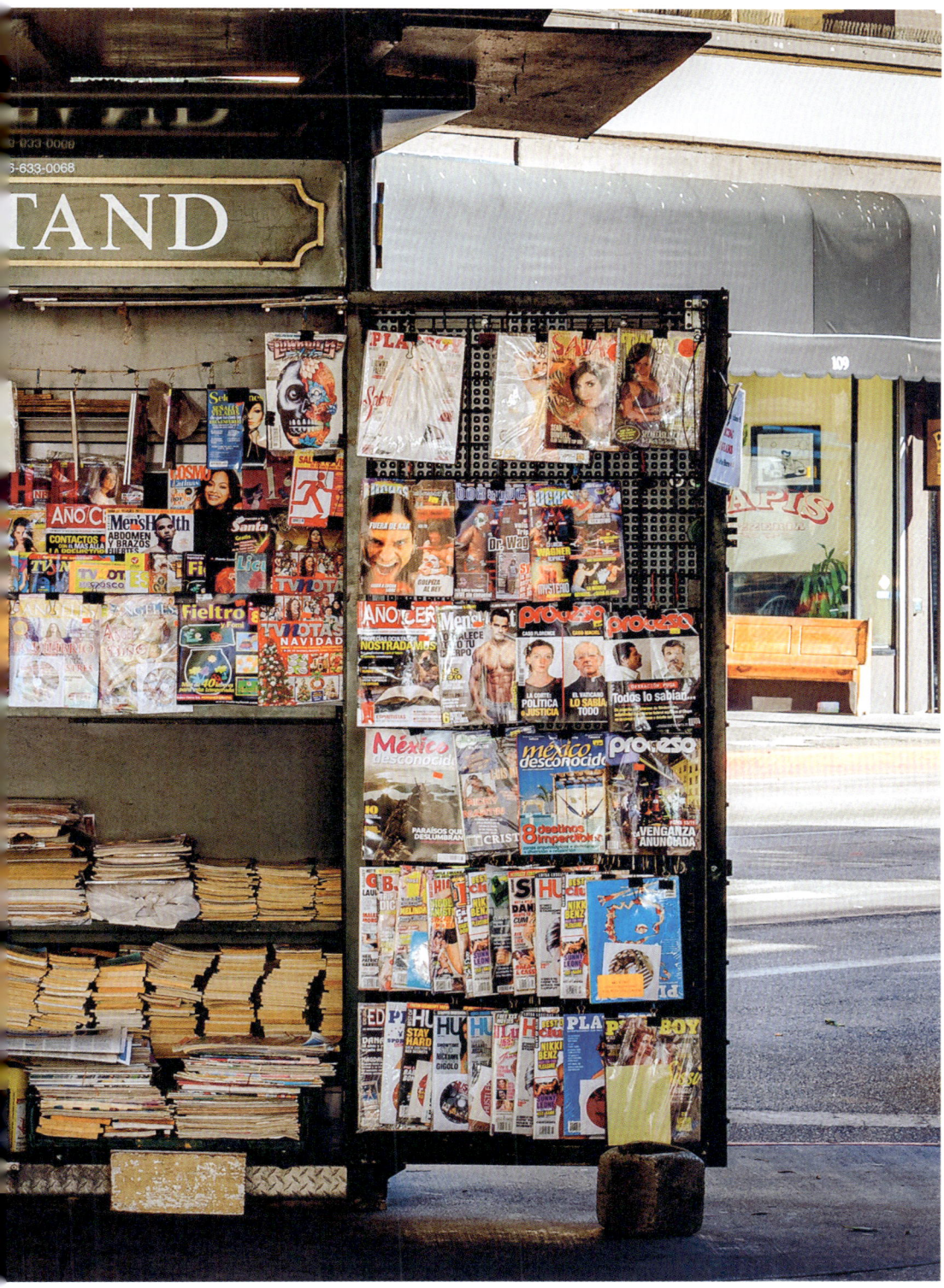

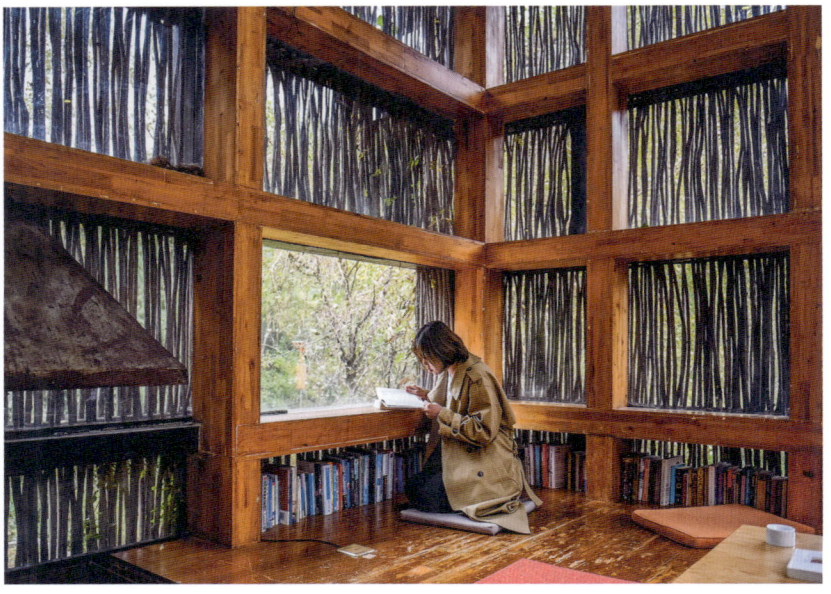

"Today a reader, tomorrow a leader."

MARGARET FULLER

Beijing → *China*

"My alma mater was books, a good library...
I could spend the rest of my life reading,
just satisfying my curiosity."

MALCOLM X

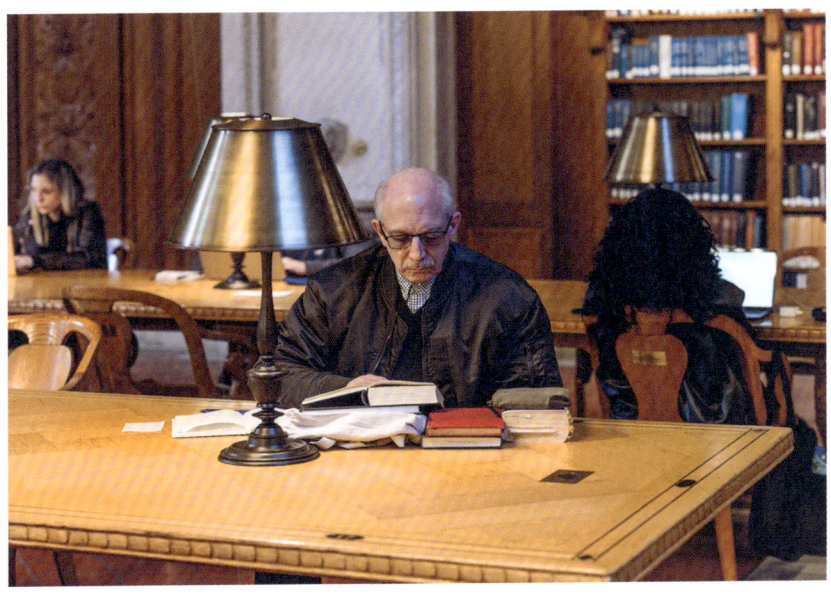

New York, New York → *United States*

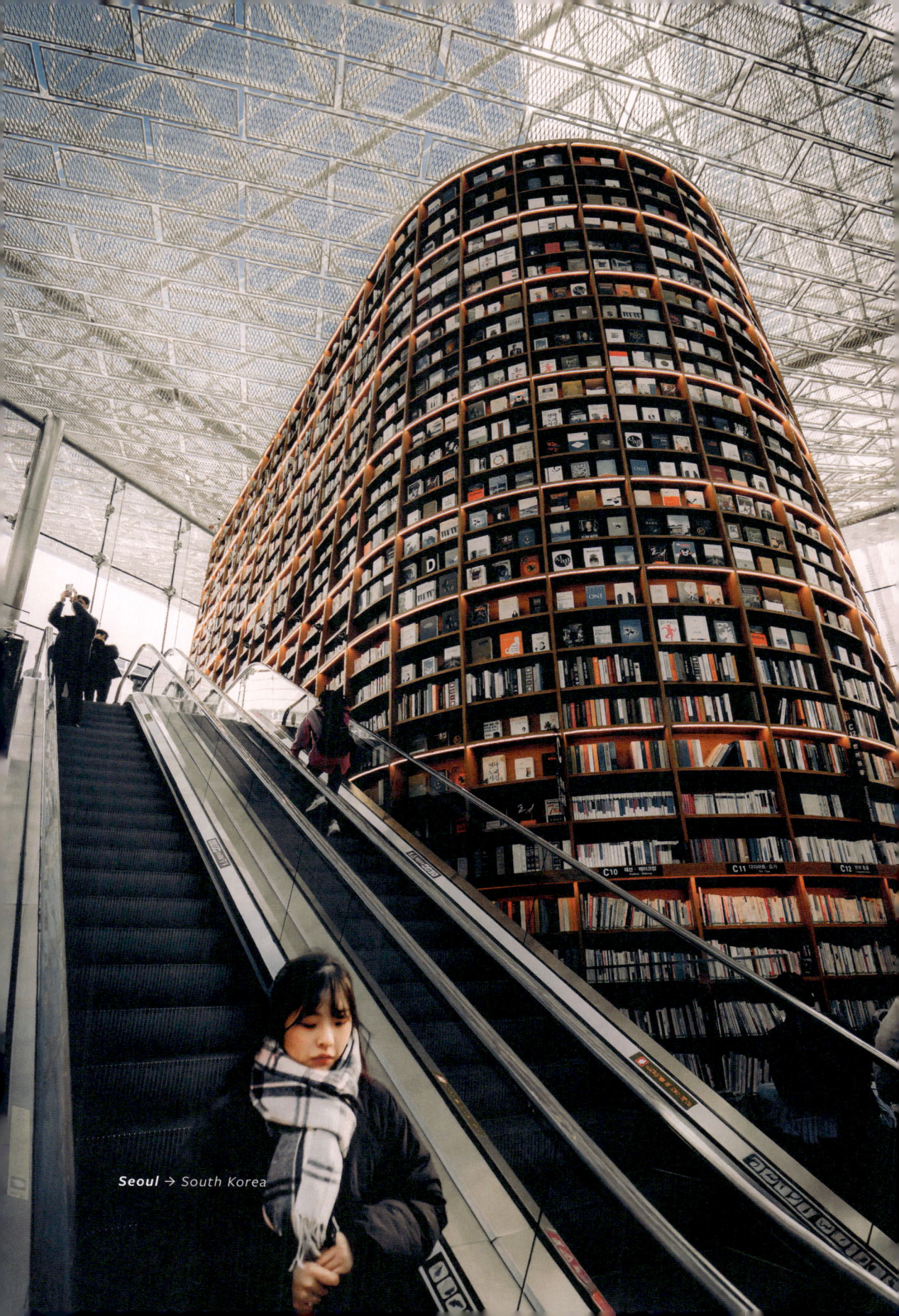

Seoul → South Korea

PETE MULVIHILL, *Co-Owner*

Green Apple Books → San Francisco, California

I was a library kid.

My parents brought me to our town's public library weekly, and it wasn't until I was in college, and a friend insisted I read Tom Robbins when I first actually bought a book. Why anyone would buy a book when you could read them for free was beyond me. But the single-wide trailer that served as the library in our small coastal Delaware town didn't have Tom Robbins, so off I went to spend $6 — two hours of ice cream scooping wages! — on a book I'd finish in a few days. But, you know, teenagers want to fit in.

I've now been working in a bookstore for more than 30 years, and while I mostly get my books for free, I understand the impulse to own them. Books matter!

For book lovers, beloved tomes are sacred talismans for the particular way they open our minds, or reveal our shared humanity, or entertain or educate us. All readers understand the power of a book, so I won't attempt to reiterate what's been said beautifully a thousand times before.

But I'll let you in on a few moments when my life was shaped, changed or redirected by a good book.

After my parents found me, at age 11 in the (very tame) sex section of our suburban public library, they checked out book after book on the subject (always very medical and poorly illustrated) for me. I'd accept them wordlessly and return them wordlessly. They never knew which, if any, I read, but it did save them from having to have "the talk."

At ten, *Bridge to Terabithia* was the first book that made me cry out loud.

When a condom broke in my early 20s, pre-internet, I let myself into the bookstore where I worked at 2am to borrow a copy of *Our Bodies, Ourselves* to, um, troubleshoot.

When I was 15, Zora Neale Hurston's *Their Eyes Were Watching God* felt like a window into experiences that had nothing in common with my own lived life but somehow resonated on a deeply human level.

I love to sleep, and it seems I need many more hours of sleep than most people. I'm also, alas, a slow reader. Whether it's a book or a cliff-hanger of a TV series, I always choose a reasonable bedtime and save the rest for another day. But when I read *Native Son* by Richard Wright, sleep no longer mattered. I stayed up all night, astonished.

The first sentences of *Lolita*, the playful structure of *Pale Fire*, the inventive spirit of *Ada, or Ardor* — when I first read Nabokov, I understood what it meant to play with language. And English was his third language!

Waterlog by Roger Deakin is a British classic that inspired the "wild swimming" movement. I helped bring it into print in America, and, inspired by its story and in search of some relief during Covid lockdowns, the publisher and I journeyed from Portland, OR, to San Francisco, CA, with swims, plunges, or dips in over 20 bodies of water along the way: waterfalls and bays and lakes and reservoirs and rivers, ending, of course, in the mighty Pacific just outside the Golden Gate.

My wife is a writer, and so many times over so many years she would come close to publishing a book only to be disappointed yet again. It took decades, but she persevered. And this year, *My Mother's Boyfriends*, her collection of short stories was published, and I couldn't be prouder. Complete strangers read it and love it, and somehow, that may give me even more pleasure than it gives her.

My son was a big reader as a kid — *Harry Potter*, of course, and Rick Riordan and Betty Smith and Douglas Adams. Then he got a smart phone and some pimples; Covid and high school arrived; and video games and rock climbing took over. He stopped reading books, and my wife and I wrung our hands and mourned.

This summer, he is home from his first year of college and working in one of my bookstores for a few weeks. His BFFs at school sent him home with, of all things, a mandate to read Tom Robbins, which he did. Now, after shifts at the store spent shelving, he comes home each evening with another book to read. Rebecca Solnit and Jessa Crispin have caught his attention, as have books on communication and psychology, and a dozen other subjects that intrigue him from the shelves.

His love of reading did not, indeed, disappear! It went dormant for a little while, waiting to be reawakened by the proximity to thousands of actual, physical books, each one of them just waiting to change his life in some way.

Which is exactly why bookstores matter.

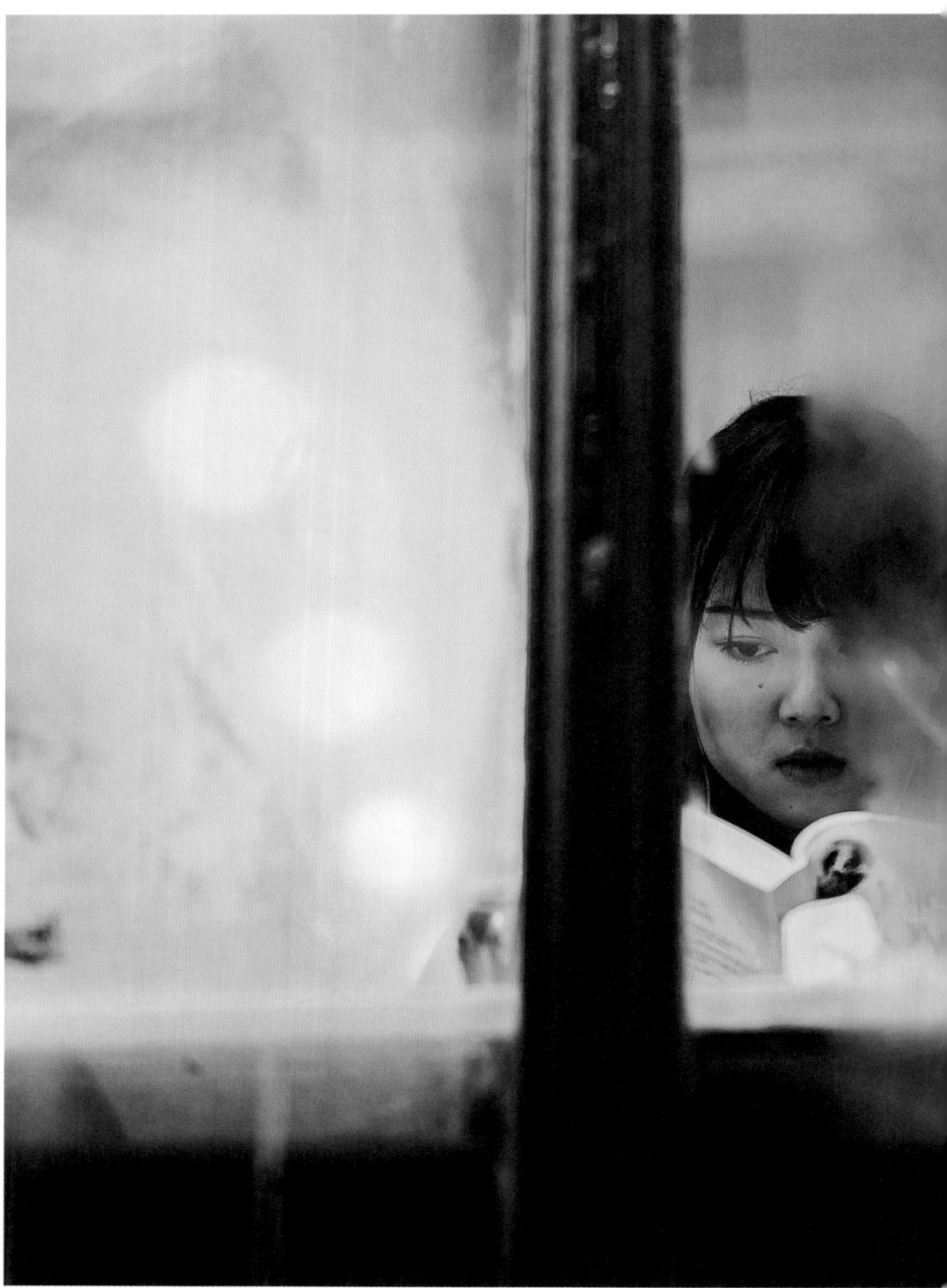

London → *England*

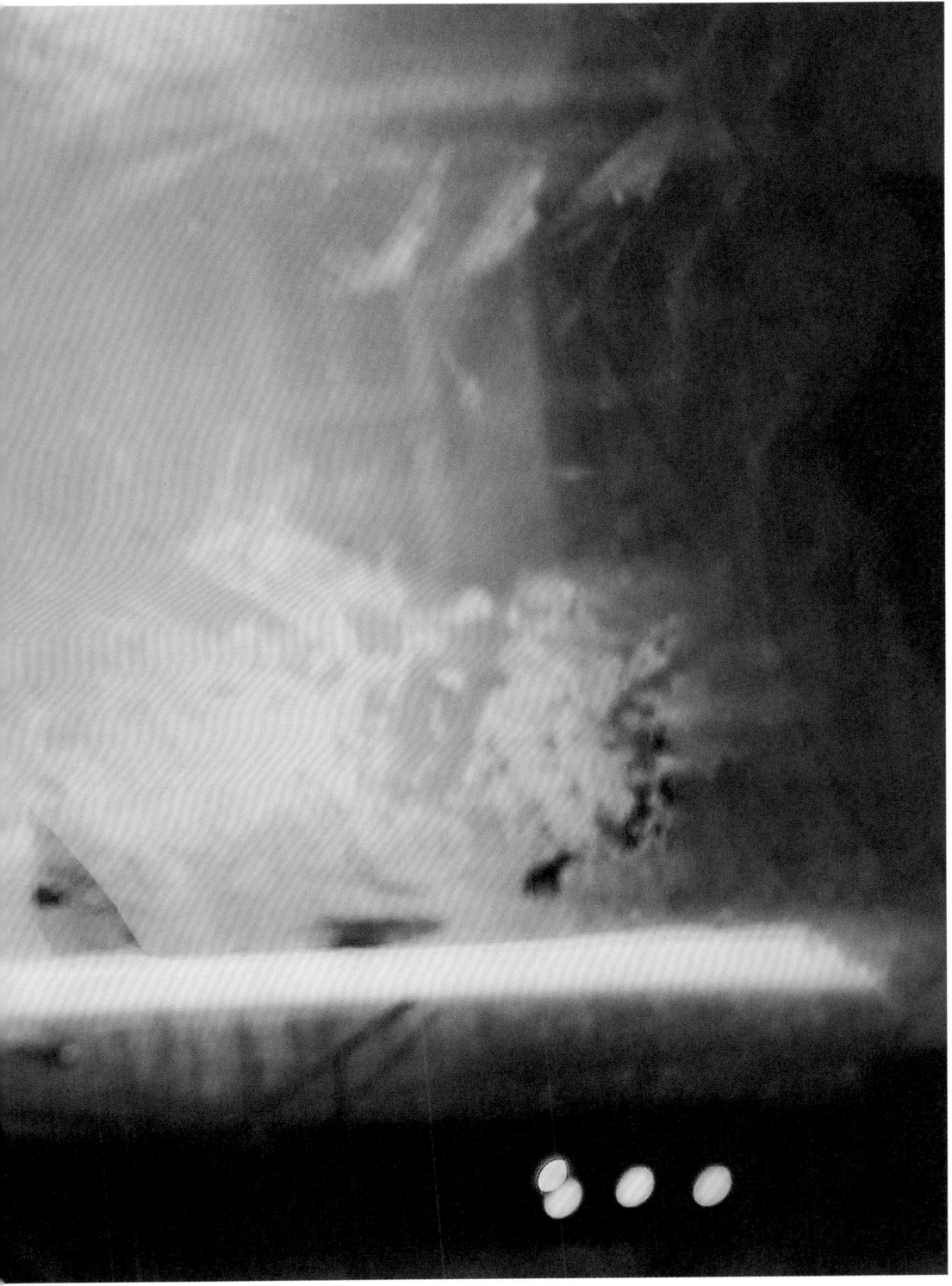

Photography Credits

COVER	Graham Chapman	037	Declan McWhinney	075	Oliver Bunica
002	Lucy Hamidzadeh	038	Christian Dumont	076	Andy Shigekawa
005	Lucy Hamidzadeh	039	Judit Prat Martí	077	Selene Sarı
006	Selene Sarı	040	Declan McWhinney	078	Lucy Hamidzadeh
008	Selene Sarı	042	Lucy Hamidzadeh	079	Greg Goyo Vargas
009	Selene Sarı	043	Judit Prat Martí	080	Lucy Hamidzadeh
010	Andy Shigekawa	044	Declan McWhinney	081	Lucy Hamidzadeh
011	Lucy Hamidzadeh	045	Peter Jonker	082	Selene Sarı
012	Judit Prat Martí	046	Andy Shigekawa	084	Selene Sarı
013	Elisabeth Argillier	047	Andy Shigekawa	085	Andy Shigekawa
015	Lucy Hamidzadeh	048	Selene Sarı	086	Sam Landers
016	Christian Dumont	050	Lucy Hamidzadeh	087	Selene Sarı
017	Lucy Hamidzadeh	051	Declan McWhinney	088	David Gonzalez
018	Declan McWhinney	052	Peter Jonker	089	Peter Jonker
019	Declan McWhinney	053	Declan McWhinney	090	Declan McWhinney
020	Tiffany Bell	054	Peter Jonker	091	Selene Sarı
021	Tiffany Bell	056	Declan McWhinney	092	Lucy Hamidzadeh
022	Declan McWhinney	057	John Michael Rivera	093	Declan McWhinney
023	Declan McWhinney	058	Declan McWhinney	094	Sam Landers
024	Peter Jonker	059	Lucy Hamidzadeh	095	Elisabeth Argillier
025	Tiffany Bell	060	Lucy Hamidzadeh	096	Sam Landers
026	Declan McWhinney	061	Lucy Hamidzadeh	097	Jeffery Xin
027	Lucy Hamidzadeh	062	Ian Kobylanski	098	Jeffery Xin
028	Sam Landers	064	Sam Landers	099	Selene Sari
029	John Michael Rivera	065	Selene Sarı	100	Declan McWhinney
030	Andy Shigekawa	066	Sam Landers	101	Lucy Hamidzadeh
031	Selene Sarı	067	Andy Shigekawa	102	Sam Landers
032	Peter Jonker	068	Christian Dumont	103	Sam Landers
033	Declan McWhinney	069	Lucy Hamidzadeh	104	John Michael Rivera
034	Selene Sarı	070	Sam Landers	105	John Michael Rivera
035	John Michael Rivera	071	Sam Landers	106	Judit Prat Martí
036	Declan McWhinney	073	Lucy Hamidzadeh	107	Bożena Budzyńska

108	Graham Chapman
111	Bożena Budzyńska
112	Elisabeth Argillier
113	Judit Prat Martí
114	Lucy Hamidzadeh
115	Lucy Hamidzadeh
116	Lucy Hamidzadeh
117	Lucy Hamidzadeh
118	Tiffany Bell
119	Peter Jonker
120	Peter Jonker
122	Peter Jonker
123	Meg Miller
124	Greg Goyo Vargas
125	Meg Miller
126	Lucy Hamidzadeh
127	Declan McWhinney
128	Ian Kobylanski
129	Elisabeth Argillier
130	Greg Goyo Vargas
132	Bożena Budzyńska
133	Jeffery Xin
134	Andy Shigekawa
138	Lucy Hamidzadeh
143	Selene Sarı
BACK COVER	Selene Sarı

Photographers

Elisabeth Argillier → *@elisabarg*
Parisian photographer in love with Paris and its incredible heritage who is particularly passionate about capturing its architecture and the enchanting Parisian rooftops.

Tiffany Bell → *@TiffanySBell*
Los Angeles photographer passionate about capturing unique perspectives and creating images that inspire and shows just how lucky we are to be alive.

Bożena Budzyńska → *@goralka102*
Photographer traveling the world in search of its wonders.

Oliver Bunica → *@olijbuni*
Pacific Northwest native, enthusiast of aviation, megacities, and good public transit.

Graham Chapman → *@gh_chapman*
Street photographer and video editor in and from Chicago.

Christian Dumont → *@dumontchristian8*
Parisian amateur photographer, passionate about black and white street photos.

David Gonzalez → *@davidgvisuals*
Landscape photographer with a passion for composition and creating captivating images, based out of Southern California.

Greg Goyo Vargas → *@goyocorvairphotography*
Los Angeles photographer who works on documenting Los Angeles in a stylistic convergence of the street, documentary, and fine art genres of photography.

Lucy Hamidzadeh → *@juicylucyham*
South East London native and writer with an undeniable passion for street photography.

Peter Jonker → *@peterjonkero*
Dutch photographer documenting daily life in the city.

Ian Kobylanski → *@kobyphotography*
London-based street photographer from Vancouver, Canada, known for capturing the vibrant energy and dynamic moments of urban life.

Sam Landers → *@sam_landers*
Chicago-based publisher, designer, and avid photographer with a passion for books and storytelling through photography.

Judit Prat Martí → *@chicagocolorsproject*
Minimalist photographer and astrophysicist with a passion for exploring Chicago, originally from the Barcelona region and living in Stockholm.

Declan McWhinney → *@declanrmc*
Street and conceptual photographer who is passionate about mental health and aims to portray the best of humanity through his work.

Meg Miller → *@megmillerphotography*
Connecticut and New York-based lifestyle photographer who loves finding the beauty in the everyday.

John Michael Rivera → *@kroeus.shots*
Travel, landscape, and car photographer from Rome with a passion for culture, perspective, and the stories hidden in every journey.

Selene Sarı → *@latmusphotography*
Aerodynamics engineer and entrepreneur with a passion for street photography. Capturing the concealed details of urban life, her photographs reveal the remarkable within the mundane.

Andy Shigekawa → *@andyshig*
Photographer, musician, and native Los Angeles resident who endeavors to create mood and elicit an emotional response in his photography.

Jeffery Xin → *@jeffery_bxin*
Interior designer and filmmaker with a passion for architectural and geometric elements, raised in Beijing and living in New York City.

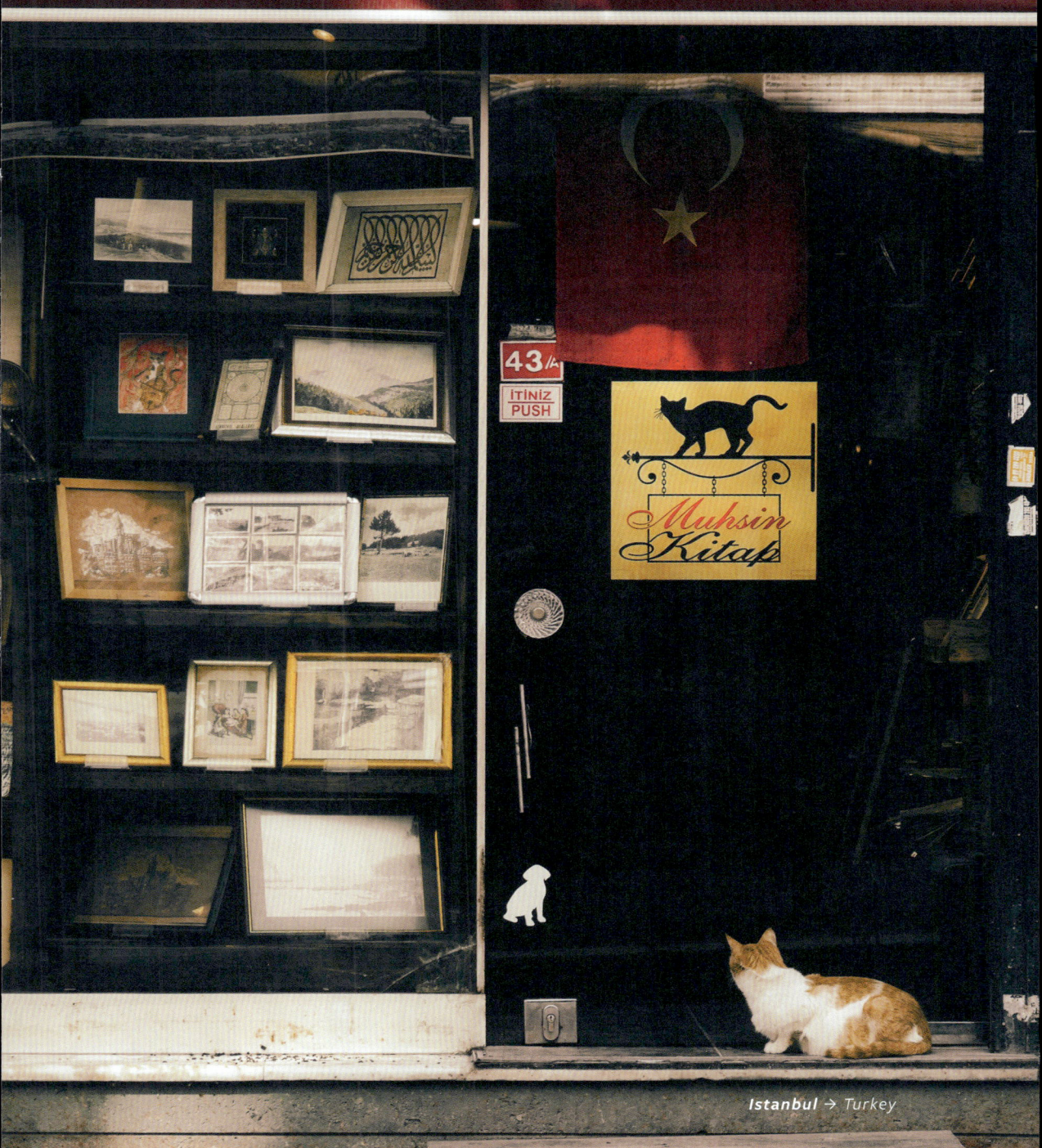

Istanbul → *Turkey*

LCCN: 2025943258
ISBN: 978-1-951963-48-4

Printed and bound in China
First printing, 2025

Trope Publishing Co.

+ INFORMATION:
For additional information
on our books and prints,
visit trope.com

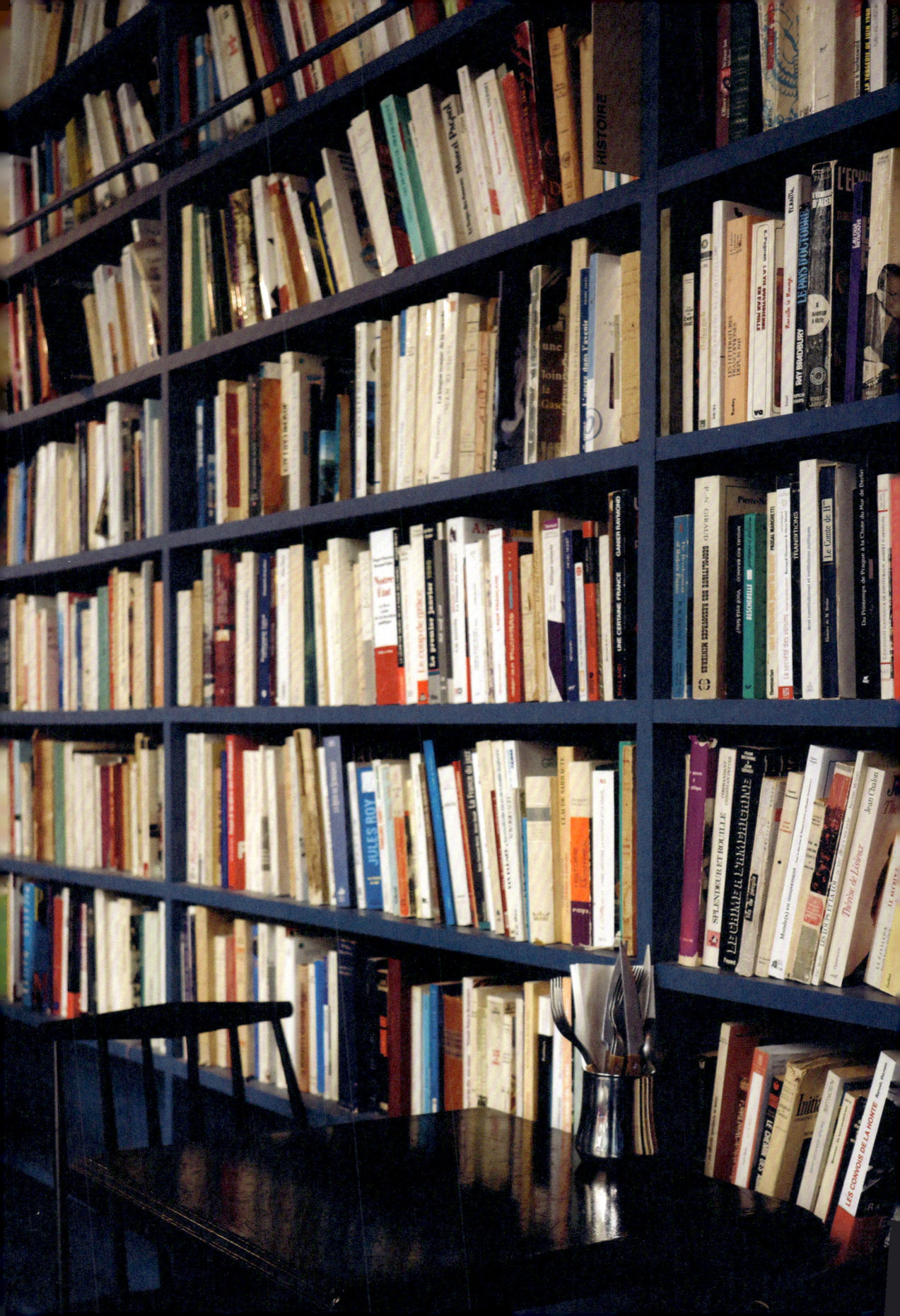